Gangs on Trial

In the series *Studies in Transgression,*
edited by David Brotherton

Series previously published by Columbia University Press

John M. Hagedorn

Gangs on Trial

Challenging Stereotypes and Demonization

in the Courts

FOREWORD BY CRAIG HANEY

TEMPLE UNIVERSITY PRESS

Philadelphia • Rome • Tokyo

TEMPLE UNIVERSITY PRESS
Philadelphia, Pennsylvania 19122
tupress.temple.edu

Library of Congress Cataloging-in-Publication Data

Names: Hagedorn, John, 1947– author. | Haney, Craig, writer of foreword.
Title: Gangs on trial : challenging stereotypes and demonization in the
    courts / John M. Hagedorn ; foreword by Craig Haney.
Description: Philadelphia : Temple University Press, 2022. | Series:
    Studies in transgression | Includes bibliographical references and
    index. | Summary: "The author recounts his experiences as an expert
    witness for defense teams working to dispel myths about gangs. He
    marshals findings from psychology to show how these myths bias court
    actors and lead to the dehumanization of those on trial, causing courts
    to overcharge and unjustly punish defendants"—Provided by publisher.
Identifiers: LCCN 2021023003 (print) | LCCN 2021023004 (ebook) | ISBN
    9781439922309 (cloth) | ISBN 9781439922316 (paperback) | ISBN
    9781439922323 (pdf)
Subjects: LCSH: Gang members—Legal status, laws, etc.—United States. |
    Defense (Criminal procedure)—United States. | Evidence, Expert—United
    States. | Stereotypes (Social psychology)—United States. | Forensic
    sociology—United States. | Hagedorn, John, 1947– |
    Criminologists—United States—Biography.
Classification: LCC KF9375 .H34 2022 (print) | LCC KF9375 (ebook) | DDC
    345.73/02—dc23
LC record available at https://lccn.loc.gov/2021023003
LC ebook record available at https://lccn.loc.gov/2021023004

♾ The paper used in this publication meets the requirements of the
American National Standard for Information Sciences—Permanence
of Paper for Printed Library Materials, ANSI Z39.48-1992

Printed in the United States of America

9 8 7 6 5 4 3 2 1

This book is dedicated to my mentor, Joan Moore, whose research stressed the humanity of gang members and variation within and between gangs.

Contents

PART II DEHUMANIZATION

PART III THE STRUGGLE FOR JUSTICE: REFRAMING
STEREOTYPES AND OVERCOMING DEMONIZATION

    Police, and Jail—A Personal Story   149

12 I Am Not a Hired Gun: Reframing and the Expert Witness Role   157

13 Humanizing Justice   183

    Epilogue to the Stories   205

    References   209

    Index   217

Foreword

In the era of mass incarceration, the social psychological processes of moral disengagement—especially dehumanization and demonization—became central components in the administration of what passed for "justice" in the United States. Depicting defendants in ways that robbed them of their human qualities facilitated punishing them with the utmost harshness. In the lexicon of crime-related media, people who committed serious acts of violence were "monsters," and legal decision makers treated them accordingly, often aided and abetted by jurors who were systemically and relentlessly miseducated about who commits crime and why. In this powerfully engaging book, John Hagedorn reminds us that we sent unprecedented numbers of people to live in shockingly harsh prisons for unheard-of amounts of time in the name of "incapacitating irredeemable animals, not rehabilitating human beings."

Hagedorn's book is an insider's account of many of the ways in which those morally disengaging tasks were attempted and too often achieved, and a chronicle of how one dedicated scholar activist fought valiantly and skillfully to debunk and deconstruct the demeaning stereotypes that were at the core of many of the horrific injustices that occurred. Hagedorn is right to argue that criminal courtrooms (in general) and capital trials (in particular) are places where stereotyping and dehumanization still too often rule. Indeed, his book conveys and explains, as well as any I have ever encountered, the nature of the disjuncture that I have repeatedly experienced in my own work inside the criminal justice system. At the outset of the capital cases on which I most often work, there is the sensationalized media image of a criminal defendant accused of a serious, violent crime, and an accompanying, ghastly account of his alleged behavior, one that is almost always shaded in ways that portray him as a monstrous being who is fundamentally different from the rest of the human community. And then there is the person I actually encounter. Human and flawed and damaged, in many of the same ways we all are, but always recognizably human. To the extent to which the person's behavior has deviated from some agreed-upon norm—and often the deviations are egregiously hurtful—they are nearly always the product of a mind- and heart-numbing accumulation of terrible trauma and deprivation rather than anything remotely resembling inherent evil or a monstrous essence.

Indeed, the overarching "crime master narrative" that our society has learned to employ and on which prosecutors invariably rely—that evil deeds are the simple products of evil choices made by evil people—is the basic stereotype that Hagedorn's work so skillfully challenges and thoughtfully rebuts. He confronts this and associated stereotypes in the most difficult kinds of criminal cases possible, ones where life as well as liberty are often at stake. When the alleged evil deeds are at the extreme end of the continuum of harm, then only the worst punishment will do in our system, and that very often means the punishment of death. If the deeds are done by juveniles—children under the age of eighteen—and the death penalty is therefore not a possibility, then the second worst possible punishment, life in prison, will have to do.

These are the kind of impossibly hard cases on which Hagedorn has worked, tirelessly and brilliantly, for many years. In his role, in fact, the challenges he has faced are even greater. That is because his specialty involves cases in which gang allegations are at the heart of the prosecutor's case that Hagedorn must confront and rebut. If the crime master narrative is heated to a fever pitch in cases where violent crime is at issue, it boils over in cases in which the defendant's actions are attributed to a "gang" to which he or she supposedly belongs. The power of the gang imagery and its capacity to inflame anger and instill fear comes at least in part from its connection to race. It has some primordial resonance with notions of insurrection, that groups of aggrieved minorities have banded together to take vengeance on their oppressors.

Of course, the ease with which racial and ethnic gangs have been demonized in our society facilitates the dehumanization of their members. In addition, the worst thing a fearsome and frightening "gang" has ever done—real or imagined—can be imputed to all of its members. The debunking of the crime master narrative in these kinds of cases, and the "reframing" of the true facts of the case, including who the defendant is and why he has done the things he has, into a compelling, humanizing counternarrative is a truly daunting task. The surplus meaning that the stereotype of gang membership carries for most jurors makes the demonization of the defendant so much easier, almost automatic, and extraordinarily difficult to dislodge. Not surprisingly, overcoming these prejudices and stereotypes can seem insurmountable.

Yet, as you will read, John Hagedorn has spent many years doing precisely that. He modestly describes himself as a social scientist, an activist, and a storyteller, and it is obvious from the pages that follow that he excels at all three roles. He is a consummate social psychologist whose insights about human nature are learned and subtle and seamlessly integrated into his engrossing narrative accounts. His activism is apparent in the courageous social justice roles he has engaged, repeatedly venturing far outside the comfortable confines of university life. But it is his storytelling prowess that is most in evidence here and where he is truly masterful. It is in the stories, the "social histories," as they are called in court, that we learn about the trauma his clients have experienced, the challenges and obstacles they struggled to confront and overcome, and the turning points in their lives when the forces aligned against them simply became too much and they succumbed. But it is also in these stories that we not only learn that everyone is more than the worst thing they have ever done, but also that they are more than the sum total of the traumas and impossible odds they have faced. No matter how hard the lives at the heart of his cases, Hagedorn shows us that a spark of humanity always survives, and that something uniquely human, precious, and irreplaceable is taken when someone dies before their time. Hagedorn has given us an extraordinary compilation of moving, powerful stories that only someone who has been on the front lines of these kinds of legal battles, and so deeply absorbed the details and meaning in the lives of his clients, could tell with such honesty and nuance.

Hagedorn is at once a deeply caring and compassionate narrator, but also a realist whose work is based on facts and framing. He relies on research to show, as he maintains, that although facts matter in trials, the frames into which those facts are fitted often matter more. Anyone who has appeared more than a few times as an expert witness presenting scientifically grounded facts that are designed to challenge the kind of stereotypes that dominate conventional legal and lay thinking about crime and punishment can sympathize with his characterization of the task as "pushing a research boulder up a Hades mountain of stereotypes." The tension and frustration of trying to live in the world of research and science, on the one hand, and performing in the sometimes irrational, emotion-driven adversarial world of legal maneuvering and courtroom drama, especially in high-stakes criminal cases, requires extraordinary resilience and commitment. Not surprisingly, perhaps, Hagedorn writes that his experiences in court have at times shaken his faith in the efficacy of reason and research. But he persists in the mission, and his clients and the larger criminal justice system are much better for it.

The courtroom is the perfect arena for jurors to be encouraged to indulge their prejudices and fears unless they are rebutted by skilled attorneys and their witnesses. A terrible event has victimized a typically innocent person with whom they can identify, who seems to represent their community. The person accused of committing the act differs in fundamental respects from them—in appearance and in terms of the life that person has lived. It is easy, under those circumstances, to activate the crime master narrative. Yet, as you will learn in the pages that follow, there are ways to respond and equally compelling counternarratives that can be advanced, whose persuasive power comes from the truths they convey.

Hagedorn has written an extremely courageous book, one in which he is willing to assert hard moral truths that cut against the grain of what passes for common knowledge about who commits crime and why. Yet he is also remarkably candid, willing to admit self-doubt about whether and how one can navigate in a legal world that involves deep and seemingly unbearable pain on both sides of the ledger. We have a system in which crime victims are taught that the only healing they should want or need is to see the maximum amount of punishment inflicted on the person who has harmed them. Hagedorn helps us understand why this is a hollow hope that encourages people to seek vengeance over compassion and understanding. It has distorted the very meaning of "justice" in a democratic society that values community and caring.

Nearly two decades ago I wrote a book that developed a simple but controversial proposition—that the continued operation of the system of death sentencing in the United States depended on the fact that those who administered it never quite told the truth about exactly what they were doing, why, and to whom. It was in some ways an attempt to show, with as much social psychological research as I could compile, what Albert Camus had said more eloquently many years before—that we surround the death penalty with "padded words" to prevent people from feeling the actual cruelty of it, and ensuring they never touch the "wood and steel" of whatever machinery or device the state uses to accomplish the gruesome task of "lawfully" taking a life. In a much different and extremely powerful way, Hagedorn has written another kind of truly compelling companion to Camus, bringing us face-to-face with the complex humanity against whom the death penalty is often directed and the callous, dehumanizing legal process by which capital defendants are turned into something less than persons so that the process of ending their life becomes tolerable, even palatable.

Hagedorn repeatedly warns readers that, despite his prowess as an expert witness, most of his gripping stories do not end well. But in a certain sense, his book surely does. Personal and professional experiences convinced him that we do not live in a just world, but he continues to fight for justice. Hagedorn wisely concedes that we cannot engage in this struggle solely for the promise of winning it—which, given the kinds of cases on which he works, he knows is often an elusive goal. Instead, it is the collective effort in the pursuit of justice that represents the only chance we have to bend the arc of history in the right direction. As this book demonstrates, Hagedorn is one of a small but growing group of criminal justice warriors dedicated to bending that arc. Like him, I believe we have gone through the dark ages of American criminal justice history. I also believe that, if we are ever going to experience a countervailing age of enlightenment that will bring about the end of these dark times, books like this one will play a crucial role. Hagedorn reminds us there are many places in the choir where people can sing the song of justice. When you finish this book, I am sure you will agree that his voice has been powerful and clear and resonant, and that we have been very fortunate to have had him in this choir. You may even be inspired, as he hopes you will, to take your place alongside him.

Craig Haney

Acknowledgments

Who should be acknowledged in a book like this? Perhaps first are the gang members you'll read about, including Ike Easley, Patrick Stout, and Jackie Montañez. Even though my involvement in their lives was often very brief, what they told me revealed a story behind the story that punctured gang stereotypes. And, more importantly, while many of them wore scary masks at arrest and were demonized at trial, behind their masks, I found flawed human beings—someone like you and me, not some monstrous "other." I challenge the reader to see herself or himself in these gang members who killed while not forgetting the forever-lost humanity of their victims. That contradiction is a central concern of this book.

You'll read about dozens of brilliant lawyers and mitigation specialists. What I admired most about Victoria Calvert, Peter Cannon, Herschella Conyers, Ali Flaum, Aviva Futorian, Bo King, Susan Lehmann, Andrea Lyon, Brad MacClean, Lee Sexton, Cyndy Short, Randolph Stone, Carrie Lynn Thompson, and Leigh Ann Webster, to name just a few, was not their brilliant legal or social work but their passionate commitment to the humanity of their clients. Some of my best tales were regretfully left out of the book, including Chris Foreman's truly fantastic case in Atlanta with Emily Gilbert of the Georgia Capital Defenders and the tragedy of Craigory Green in Chicago with Ruth McBeth of the Cook County Public Defender's Homicide Task Force. The reader might appreciate that this book does not run the one thousand pages I would have needed to tell all my stories.

The Georgia Appellate Practice and Educational Resource Center or Georgia Resource Center, to whom I'm donating the royalties from this book, represents what I most admire in the legal profession. The Georgia Resource Center does the incredibly difficult and thankless job of representing defendants on death row and prepares appeals from capital convictions. I am in awe of their work, often in the face of insuperable obstacles. In one of my earliest cases, the Georgia Resource Center's Brian Kammer bravely defended the humanity of Marion Wilson even as Marion and his codefendant Robert Butts were being literally demonized by police and prosecutors. I learned stereotypes can kill and witnessing Marion's and Robert's dehumanization in court compelled me to continue this work and write this book.

I need to acknowledge the emotional cost of doing this work that was borne by my life partner, Mary Devitt, and my children, Tracey, Katie, Marty, Zach, and Jess. Working eighty-three expert witness cases as well as commuting from Milwaukee to Chicago for twenty-two years to teach took its toll on our lives. Mary and I have been trusted intellectual and political colleagues for decades, and I can't overestimate her impact on my life. She also laboriously scrutinized the final manuscript and added clarity where needed. I also want to thank my good friends Doug Marvy, Paul Elitzik, and Matthew Lippman as well as former student, now professor Aubri McDonald for reading every page of earlier drafts of this book and giving me their powerful and unique insights. I want to thank Teresa Córdova at the University of Illinois–Chicago's Great Cities Institute for supporting my research on gang violence in Chicago.

My editor at Temple, Ryan Mulligan, has been an advocate for the book and improved it in small ways and large. David Brotherton, editor of Temple's Studies in Transgression, where this book has found a home, has done expert witness work himself and appreciates its importance. I want to thank Kristine Filip for her outreach for the book to the legal community. I owe an immense intellectual and personal debt to my mentor, Joan Moore, who died as this book was being written. Her early work on gangs and labeling theory (1985) inspired the approach of this book. I miss you, Joan.

Gangs on Trial weaves my own personal story with stories from the courtroom. Particularly, these pages summarize many of the lessons I've learned in a half century of participation in movements for social justice. As a white male growing up in a small town, I've had to confront my own racist upbringing as well as, over the years, find the courage to stand up to injustice. I also discovered that stereotyping and "them and us" thinking are not just a problem for "them." This book is a reminder that the struggle for justice is lifelong and must be fought on many fronts.

A Note on Names

Whenever possible, I have used the real names of defendants, prosecutors, lawyers, and places. I have sent copies of this manuscript to attorneys for accuracy as well as to assure them that the names of defendants and circumstances when used will do no harm. Most information cited in this book is public information, and I've used transcripts of trials and interrogations that are in the public domain. When possible, I've provided relevant portions of the manuscript to the defendants for review.

I have chosen to disguise the names and places of some of my cases either because I've deemed the information may be harmful to an inmate in prison or after release or the attorney or defendant has objected to the use of real names. When in doubt, I disguised the names and places.

After first introducing a new person, if I have gotten to know the person, I will refer to them afterward by just their first name. I use first names only of those I know.

Gangs on Trial

Introduction

The clock was the herald of death. Mary and I kept noting how our living room clock's minute hand seemed to tick louder as the day went on. As we heard the ticks, we kept looking up: 10:02 A.M. . . . 1:47 P.M. . . . 5:32 P.M. We tried to keep busy, but still the hours dragged by. I'm sure they were flying by for Robert Butts. Robert was on death row in Georgia and scheduled to be executed that very day, May 4, 2018. He was a convicted murderer who was alleged to be a gang member. I'd been working with him as an expert witness since 2005. A text came in the early evening that the U.S. Supreme Court had temporarily stayed his execution. We barely had time to feel a frisson of hope when, moments later, another text announced the court had declined to consider his case. At 9:58 P.M. (EST), Robert Butts was injected with a lethal dose of pentobarbital. Prison officials said that he twitched and said, "It burns, man." Then he took his last breath.

That night, I thought back over Robert's playful posts, under a pseudonym, on my Facebook page, daring me to figure out who he was. He wrote with another name because he was on death row at the time and used a smuggled-in "cell phone" to post. I was stumped trying to figure out who this mystery guy could be, and, finally, he had to call me to reveal his identity. I was astonished to receive a rogue phone call from Georgia's death row. His calls continued for several weeks until his phone was confiscated. I don't remember now all of what we talked about. I know it wasn't about his case. He was realistic about his situation and didn't want to get too hopeful. I told him I used some of his poems in a class I was teaching (Butts 2013), and we discussed his writing. We bantered as much as anything, just like two normal people. And now, he's dead.

However, like nearly all of the gang members on whose cases I've consulted as an expert witness, Robert wasn't innocent: he was actually guilty. He participated in a carjacking, and a completely innocent man, Donovan Parks, was shot and killed. Robert was one of eighty-three gang members, sixty of whom were charged with murder, on whose cases I consulted over the past twenty-five years. Seventeen were facing the death penalty. Only two or possibly three of those people were innocent. Most of the men and women whose courtroom tales I tell are not sympathetic. They belong to a stigmatized group: a gang. A former president of the United States and many Americans consider the people grouped under this label as "animals" or barely human. Why would I want to tell their stories?

I've discovered firsthand that what transpires in the trials of gang members is a far cry from what we would consider justice. The heart of this book is a set of stories revealing what actually goes on in a courtroom when the defendant is a gang member. This is not a dry legal text about due process or procedural justice. This book demonstrates, through real-life stories, how stereotypes, implicit bias, and demonization undermine any notion that a verdict or sentence could be based only on the facts as presented in court.

For example, consider the trials of Robert and his codefendant, Marion Wilson. They were said to be members of a gang in Georgia named "Folks." The court qualified a white police officer, Ricky Horn, as an "expert" on gangs, though, he admitted under oath, he learned most of what he knew of gangs from TV and the movies. Horn testified that "FOLKS," the name of the gang, was an acronym for Followers of Our Lord King Satan. Not only were the defendants young Black male gang members; prosecutor Fred Bright's coup de grâce was his assertion that they were devil worshippers to boot! In my postconviction testimony, I explained that "Folks" derived its name from a now-defunct coalition of Chicago gangs opposed to the rival "People" coalition. It's also a common slang term, as in "your people, my folks." It has nothing to do with the devil and his works and ways. Often, when we say a defendant has been demonized, we mean it figuratively. In this case, the term became literal.

Marion and Robert's trials were in Milledgeville, Georgia, a Bible Belt city whose main claim to fame was that it was Georgia's capital during the Confederacy. Milledgeville is also the principal city in Baldwin County, made infamous by Bryan Stevenson (2015) in *Just Mercy*. I'm sorry to report that injustice in that district didn't end with the railroading of Walter McMillian, the wrongfully convicted subject of Stevenson's stirring book.

At both Robert and Marion's initial trials, their literal "demonization" as followers of Satan went unrebutted by the defense. Do you think the prosecutor's declaration that these two young Black men were devil worshippers just might have influenced the juries to sentence them to death? We'll never know for sure. The jurors may have concluded that the crime warranted the death penalty based solely on the facts of what was a brutal murder. Don't forget, unlike Walter MacMillian, Robert and Marion were guilty as charged.

But we know from social psychology that dehumanizing someone, like calling them "servants of the devil," gives us moral permission to do violence against them—the undeniable violence of a death sentence. This psychological process is similar to how the initials written on Rodney King's police report, "NHI" or "No Humans Involved," justified his brutal beating (Wynter 1994). After all, if "they" are not really part of humankind then "we" are allowed to beat them, dispose of them, or even kill them. If "they" are animals, it's okay to put them in cages. As Donald Trump bellowed to a cheering crowd at a 2016 Nashville campaign rally, gang members "are not human beings! They are not human beings!"

I fundamentally disagree with the former president, and I think most Americans are neither so crude nor so barbaric. However, I'm mindful that many people are unconcerned with what happens in court to gang members and even less so with those who kill. Many think, "They are guilty anyway. Who cares *how* they are convicted?" There is considerable sympathy among Americans for the worldwide trend toward disregarding the rule of law and even nodding in approval at vigilante violence as long as it is against "them." Ionesco's (1960) satiric play, *Rhinoceros*, depicting how, in the 1930s, many Frenchmen turned into stampeding, Fascist beasts, has ominous and obvious contemporary parallels. It can happen here. In fact, it did on January 6, 2021.

The Awesome Power of Stereotypes

I've been doing gang research for nearly forty years. I've studied gangs firsthand in Milwaukee and Chicago. I have traveled around the globe for my research, to the point where one of my books is called *A World of Gangs* (2008). My books concentrated on understanding the conditions that give rise to gangs and what is often destructive rebellion. My slogan is "research not stereotypes." In this book, I use my research to dispel many of the most egregious stereotypes of gangs. But my experiences in court have shaken my faith in the efficacy of reason and research. I've discovered how the negative associations of the categories that people use to order the world, like gangs, persist even in the face of research, like my own. When I've attempted to educate juries, judges, lawyers, and the other participants in the court on how gangs operate and how people come to join gangs, they often are not convinced and continue to see gangs as some exotic "other." To understand what has been happening in courtrooms and minimize that divide, I realized I had to turn my critical gaze from "them" to "us."

I apply studies in social psychology to explain why guilt by association is, in fact, the default, metaphorical way all of our minds work—including jurors. Confronting stereotypes with research and reason doesn't always work either. I give some distressing examples from my own testimony of the "backfire effect"—juries turn off when they hear research or arguments that run counter to their firm beliefs. Studies have concluded that some people even dig in and become more resistant to persuasion when confronted with facts they don't like.

I use my courtroom stories to explain how our minds work subconsciously when primed by even the slightest mention that the defendant may be a gang member. I show how the image of a gang member, a type of persuasive construction called a prototype, is deeply embedded in our minds. This frightening image colors what we think about anyone in the category of "gang member."

For example, I asked my undergraduate classes, "Close your eyes and think of a gang member," and they overwhelmingly thought of an image of a dangerous-looking dark-skinned thug. Google an image search for "gang member," and several pictures like the one in Figure 0.1 appear. Walter Lippman (1922, 3) called stereotypes "pictures in our head" and some involuntarily come to mind as soon as the word "gang" is uttered. This is why prosecutors love to bring gang evidence into a case even when it isn't relevant to the crime. It is the definition of "pre-judice"—judging based on preexisting images and beliefs about gangs that color the evidence presented in court.

I let Patrick Stout tell you how he was forced to take off his shirt and reveal a tattoo on his arm that the prosecutor claimed was evidence of hardcore gang membership. These tattoos primed the jury to think Patrick was a dedicated, murderous gang member and were instrumental in persuading them to sentence him to death. Later, during an ineffective counsel hearing, I pointed out the tattoos, in fact, meant the opposite—that Patrick had little knowledge of the gang or its symbology. Fortunately, the appeals court overturned his death sentence, though it upheld his conviction.

Of course, race colors everything in a courtroom. A gang member is the "prototype" of the deep-seated fears white people cultivate of a "violent, criminal, and hostile" Black male: a fear of "the other." N. Winter (2008, 19) explains how we all hold in mind preexisting racial "schema," relatively stable patterns of racialized thoughts and beliefs that have developed culturally over centuries. He argues that racial schema (2008, 20) "can lead us to attribute stereotyped characteristics to people on the basis of only their

Figure 0.1 "Google Guy": This photo is typical of the results of a Google search for "gang member." (FBI Media Archive Photo, 9/1/2015.)

group membership" Jennifer Eberhardt (2019) and others write about this as "implicit bias." I describe how it automatically and universally affects a jury's decision-making.

I give multiple examples of how gang trials are about right and wrong but more ominously about them and us. The demonizing of gangs is an example of what psychology calls the fundamental attribution error, a widespread belief that crime is more the result of the offender's "evil" character than the circumstances of the criminal event. I show how stereotypes and demonization strip away an understanding of the context of a crime and the real-life biography of the offender.

I take you into the act of murder itself and debunk prosecutors' often-stated claim that murders by gang members are ipso facto cold blooded. For all but a handful of professional hitmen, the act of murder has horrific emotional consequences for the perpetrator. I let several gang members explain in their own words their shattering reactions to their own lethal acts of violence. I argue those reactions are evidence of humanity—monsters or animals aren't personally devastated by a kill.

But why does all this matter? After all, aren't stereotypes and demonization, as used by prosecutors, an effective way to get to a desired end—the punishment of violent criminals? Many believe evil constantly threatens us, whether in the guise of gangs, illegal immigrants, or terrorists. We are terrified and feel we are, therefore, justified to use any means necessary to exterminate the enemy, like pests or a virus, before it exterminates us. To this mindset, each trial is a battle of good against evil. But our courts place plaintiffs and defendants before their peers not to battle good and evil but to determine innocence or guilt of breaking the law.

I've found juries' exaggerated fears are often implanted and inflamed by prosecutors who make use of crude stereotypes of the "big bad wolf" to successfully frighten juries. This book reveals that the "us vs. them" demonizing of mainly nonwhite defendants has become routine for prosecutors. The prosecutor's job too often is not to discover the truth but to win cases. Successfully demonizing a defendant has the added benefit of being useful for prosecutorial career aspirations. My thesis is that the stereotyping and dehumanization of gangs and nonwhite others is the psychological rationale for our mass incarceration society.

The Myth of Sisyphus

This book is not a morality tale, like Stevenson's (2015) *Just Mercy*, where the injustice lies in the possibility that the innocent might be convicted. On the one hand, my forty years of experience with real live gang members strongly supports Stevenson's profound words: "Each of us is more than the worst thing we have ever done." However, most of the subjects in Stevenson's (2014, 17–18) book and movie are innocent, and we are outraged at their wrongful convictions and the lack of official compassion for their situations.

The stories in this book, on the other hand, are more complicated. They are about gang members who killed, sometimes over a gang rivalry or sometimes over a dispute in a drug transaction or robbery. Perhaps the subject of the story murdered someone in response to out-of-control feelings of humiliation or in retaliation for previous acts of violence. Some killings were fatal mistakes committed in confusion as a young man was high or furiously angry. You can understand some youthful killers, like Jacqueline Montañez, by understanding her childhood of abuse. Some, however, like Michael Cooks, were in the wrong place at the wrong time and their emotional reactions, along with the presence of a firearm, ended human lives.

While my testimony has resulted in acquittals and reductions of charges, typically the best I've accomplished is minimizing harm. In the last chapter, I tell you about Francisco, whose attorney congratulated me and said this sixteen-year-old's thirty-three-and-a-half-year sentence was a "victory." Without my testimony, the public defender said, it would have been much worse. Thirty-plus years didn't look like a victory to Francisco, to his mother, . . . or to me. My stories are filled with heartbreak.

The ancient Greek myth of King Sisyphus, who was doomed by the gods for eternity to keep rolling a boulder up a hill in Hades only to have it roll back down, is an apt metaphor for my stories. The writer Albert Camus famously declared that one must, ironically, imagine Sisyphus happy with his unending task, because it leaves him always striving toward the heights of his purpose. Like Sisyphus, my message is to carry on even if defeat is inevitable.

This book does not follow the standard narrative of heroes and villains or of an eternal battle of good versus evil. I'm in sympathy with the critiques of prosecutors by Paul Butler, David Medwed, Angela J. Davis, Babe Howell, and Emily Bazelon. However, I'm a social scientist, an activist, and a storyteller, not a lawyer or a journalist. My stories reveal verdicts and sentences that undoubtedly relied on harmful stereotypes outside the evidence. Most do not have happy endings. While I testify for the defense, I also don't believe anyone should get away with murder. In my world, right and justice do not always, or even eventually, prevail. So why would I want to do this work?

Why I Wrote This Book: Arthur Dent's Story

I don't think there was a single turning point in my decision to retreat from academia and use my research to combat stereotypes in court. I have more stories to tell about bizarre courtroom dramas than I can fit into these pages. Throughout the book, I add some personal anecdotes about changing stereotypes and my struggles with my own "them and us" mentality. Thinking back, a good example of why I have devoted the past few decades of my life to working as an expert witness is the ambiguous case of Arthur Dent.

Andrea Lyon, a clinical professor of law at DePaul University at the time and a lawyer so known for capital cases she earned the moniker "The Angel of Death Row," represented Arthur Dent and asked me to look at gang-related aspects of his murder charge. Like most homicide cases I've consulted on, at first, this case seemed open and shut. Multiple witnesses identified Dent, a thirty-four-year-old gang member, as "the old guy on a bike" riding through rival gang turf and shooting and killing Aaron Seay. Two eyewitnesses, Romelle Coleman and Alonzo Washington, gave video recorded statements identifying Dent as the shooter. The prosecutor is video recorded as asking whether their statements were coerced in any way and whether they were treated well by the police. All the defendants unsmilingly answered to the camera that they were treated well and their statements were voluntary.

I took the #60 CTA bus to Cook County Jail from my office at the University of Illinois–Chicago to interview Mr. Dent. The University of Illinois–Chicago is about a half-hour bus ride away from the forbidding cluster of buildings that housed at the time more than ten thousand prisoners and a similar number of staff. Cook County Jail is like an urban plantation with the incarcerated, mainly Black people and, over the past decade, an increasing number of Latino inmates, serving as its "slaves." The "overseers" become whiter and whiter as you move up the ranks from correctional officers to supervisors, court clerks, prosecutors, and judges. About 90 percent of those behind bars, like Arthur Dent, were being held awaiting trial, meaning they had not yet been convicted of any crime. What Nicole Gonzalez Van Cleve (2016) calls "Crook County Jail" symbolizes what Michelle Alexander (2010) calls the "New Jim Crow."

Getting through security into one of the eleven divisions of the jail is an exercise in the Kafkaesque. The rules change depending on who is at the division gate. Sometimes correctional officers briefly patted you down and sent you through. Other times, they found items that could not be permitted into the jail, like my medicine for diabetes or the wrong kind of notebook. One time, jail guards didn't allow me to put my meds in a locker, but they said I could hide them under the bush outside the gatehouse while I was in the jail. I could pick them up when I was finished, assuming they would still be there. Sometimes they let me in with my meds; sometimes they didn't. I just never knew when a rule would be enforced—or a new one made up.

Arthur was a tough-looking guy in his midthirties with a balding head. He was affiliated with the Mickey Cobra gang and had been shot and wounded a few months before by a member of the Gangster Disciples. The neighborhood where he had sometimes hung out, Ellis Towers, was a hot spot for violence between a host of gangs and factions of gangs. In 2005, when the homicide took place, violence within gang factions was as likely as violence between gangs. Andrea Lyon brought me into the case to explain that to the court. It was almost three years after the shooting and Arthur's case had not yet gone to trial. This is not an unusual time span for Cook County courts. In fact, one inmate was found to have been held without bail for more than ten years before his trial.

Arthur described to me the complex gang relationships in the area both between and within gangs and volatile interpersonal conflicts over drugs, other illicit businesses, and gang loyalties. The dominant gang in the area, the Black P Stones, was in turmoil due to the emergence of a new Emir, or street leader. The Emir, Arthur told me, was dangerous since he was always drunk.

Arthur listed a diverse set of male and female drug dealers and gang members with a variety of plausible motives to shoot at the victim, Aaron Seay. Arthur told me Seay had been a "stickup man" who robbed drug dealers and so, obviously, had many enemies. One of the main area drug dealers, Dora, bankrolled her business with an insurance settlement and had multiple relationships that had resulted in numerous personal jealousies that might also have led to violence. The Ellis Towers area was a tinderbox, and the shooting of Seay was one spark that everyone feared could set the area on fire.

When questioned by police, Romelle Coleman, a Black P Stone, at first suggested a fellow member named "Face Mob" as the shooter. Then, Arthur told me, Romelle realized admitting a P Stone did the shooting would bring on conflict between the Stones and the Gangster Disciples. So, during his interrogation, Coleman switched stories and put the blame on Arthur Dent. Arthur had a motive from having been shot a few months before, but he was neither a P Stone nor from the neighborhood. If he were named as the shooter, the local Black P Stone set wouldn't get the blame.

Arthur's alibi—that he was with his girlfriend a hundred miles away—didn't really hold up. All calls from jail are recorded, and I read a transcript of a call Arthur made telling his girlfriend to convince detectives he was with her and not in Chicago the day of the shooting. And to make things worse, this wasn't his first homicide charge. When he was eighteen, he was sentenced to thirty years for murder and was on parole at the time of this shooting. After hours of changing their stories, the two eyewitnesses gave a video recorded statement positively identifying Arthur as the shooter.

Leaving the cell where I interviewed Arthur, I was conflicted. He came off as "street," and his blunt and profane personality would grate on white police officers, prosecutors, and many jurors. His story had more than a few holes, and his prior homicide on his rap sheet wouldn't help. On the other hand, I liked him, particularly because his lively description of the Ellis Towers area blended gang history and clashes between flawed but larger-than-life personalities. The changing nature of violence on the streets that I'd been documenting for years was well illustrated by his complex tales of jealousy and factional conflicts. He had his own opinion about the perpetrator, but it was clear there were too many motives from too many possible culprits to easily figure this shooting out. I found credible his view that he was picked out by the police because of his record, who then coached the eyewitnesses to confirm the charge. In my eyes, however, even if police truly did coerce the accusation, it didn't mean he didn't do it.

A squinty-eyed chubby white deputy sheriff escorted me out of the cell, where I had interviewed Arthur, and led me to the front gate. He growled to me, "Why are you talking to a scumbag like Dent?" I answered stiffly, "I'm not certain he is guilty of the shooting he's charged with." The deputy, who was older and clearly believed he had seen it all, muttered, while looking straight ahead: "Well, if he ain't guilty of that, he's guilty of somethin'." Arthur Dent was an unemployed African American gang member, on parole, and had a violent past. As far as the veteran deputy was concerned, Arthur was deserving of prison because of who he was. The facts of this specific crime were less important. The deputy sheriff's belief in Arthur's guilt based on a judgment of his character and gang membership rather than on the evidence was like the movie *Groundhog Day* for me. I'd relive those sentiments over and over again in court.

The facts of this specific crime became a bit more problematic as I investigated the case. Years later, I would show my college classes the prosecutor's videotape of Coleman's eyewitness statement to police. I would ask my students what was wrong with this picture? No one really got it at first, but an "aha" moment arose when I asked them to look at the time stamp on the video. The video was taken in an interrogation room of a local police district in July 2005. Romelle was wearing a winter coat as he testified that Arthur Dent was the shooter. Yes, a winter coat in the heat of a Chicago summer.

In Lyon's videotaped deposition of Romelle Coleman, she asks him why he was wearing "a puffy coat" in July? He said police beat him up and the coat hid the bruises. He swears in his deposition for the defense that his testimony to police was coerced and that police told him to identify Arthur Dent as the shooter. They had decided Arthur was their man and coerced testimony to help nail their case shut. Was Andrea's videotape of Coleman renouncing his statement enough for acquittal? If you think so, you don't understand how justice works for gang members.

My expert witness statement centered on the deadly mix of possible motives in the area, due to the fracturing of gang sets. I had gone to the neighborhood and interviewed multiple local gang members who described a chaotic gang scene that did not in the least resemble the prosecutor's simplified tale of traditional gang rivalries and retaliation. I wrote in my statement to the court that gang members would often pin the blame for crime on someone who was innocent, mainly to protect people within their own gang. The eyewitness testimony, I argued, should not be uncritically accepted, citing Romelle's recantation of his testimony.

My statement did not say Arthur was innocent. Indeed, I had read all the evidence, and I couldn't decide in my own mind whether he was guilty or not. Getting him off was Andrea Lyon's job, not mine. My job was to point out the many factors that made this far from an easy-to-understand, "typical" gang shooting. I couldn't imagine how a jury could determine his guilt "beyond a reasonable doubt." But they did. Arthur was sentenced to natural life in prison. He sits today in Stateville, Illinois's infamous maximum security prison, living out his life, waiting to die behind bars.

Arthur Dent, a veteran gang member, was presumed guilty, and the considerable evidence to the contrary was disregarded by jurors. Prosecutors presented a "gang frame": in this case, a story of long-standing rivalries and retaliation. The prosecutor, like my deputy sheriff, told the jury Arthur was an evil man, a scary gang member with a violent past. I explore in detail, later in this book, the fundamental attribution error, which, as noted above, results in blaming a person's "evil" character for a crime while holding the circumstances as less important—if they count at all.

The jurors were likely afraid of Arthur, who, in their minds, exemplified the category of "gang member." They concluded that Arthur, and people like him, deserved to go to prison for life to keep their streets safe. Their hard stereotype of a gang member allowed them to discount any "discrepant information"—like Romelle Coleman's recantation or my testimony about possible multiple motives—that didn't fit the profile of a dangerous gang member who was violent by nature. Did Arthur actually commit the crime? The jurors may have thought, "Eh, give the prosecutor the benefit of the doubt. Isn't killing what gang members do?"

Even though Arthur may have been guilty, his trial had not been decided by a reasoned consideration of the evidence. He was sentenced to life in prison without parole. Stereotyping and demonization ruled, and my efforts to complicate an overly simple gang frame abjectly failed.

———

Arthur's tale exemplifies the ambiguity of my work. I've had to answer for myself the question of why I should care about what goes on in the trial of a man who may be actually guilty of murder? It comes down to some core beliefs. *I provide testimony in gang cases because I do not think prosecutors should be able to use stereotypes and lies to frighten juries to get a conviction or an overly punitive sentence.* The Constitution doesn't say only the *innocent* should get a fair trial. I believe in a justice system where the *accused* should be convicted based on what they did, on the evidence, not on inflammatory labels of who they are said to be or because they are members of a despised group.

More broadly, David Garland (2001, 136) writes, our punishment society targets "suitable enemies . . . for a conservative social politics that stresses the need for authority, family values, and the resurrection of traditional morality." This book draws a psychological link from stereotypes of gang members as the other to the deep recesses of America's racism and the ongoing justification for its mass incarceration society. I've concluded our harsh sentences are more of a displacement of popular fears, insecurity, and racism than a thirst for justice.

If you are offended by the existence of people like Arthur Dent and don't think it matters *how* he is convicted, you can stop reading this book right now. Unlike our former president, I believe another two words for "gang member" are "human being." I fear the growth of authoritarianism in our country and the disregard of the rule of law. Most of all, I've learned to reject the "us vs. them" mentality that justifies injustice and violence. While I'm hardly optimistic, I am not hopeless. Throughout the book, I sketch out some ways I've combated stereotyping, give some advice for defense attorneys, and offer support for the movement for progressive prosecutors. My stories reveal that context matters, and, while murder is an evil act, it is seldom committed by evil people.

I admit I'm torn by self-doubt. The victims of my sixty murder cases were human beings as well, and the anger and grief of their families and loved ones is heartfelt and justified, as Sister Helen Prejean (1993) painfully illustrates in her book, *Dead Man Walking*. I won't demonize those who channel their anger into calls for legal vengeance. However, I also think our correctional policy needs to reincorporate rehabilitation and our sentences, including for murder, are unnecessarily long, in prisons that are often inhumane. Most important, I show that the defendants in my cases are flawed human beings, not irredeemable monsters. I think we are more like them than we are willing to admit. In other words, I have met "the enemy" in person. And they are us.

I'm hoping the sum total of my stories and examples of stereotyping prompt the reader to question the fairness of the trials of members of stigmatized groups like gangs. The chapters that follow explain how our innate tendency to think in categories is exploited by prosecutors and feeds the ravenous appetite of our mass incarceration society for vengeance. The first part uses my courtroom stories to explain the awesome power of gang stereotypes and how they are stitched together into stories or frames that resonate with juries. Social psychology gives us various methods for how we might change people's stereotypes, and I explain how I applied them in the courtroom. The second part builds on the stereotyping mechanisms introduced in the first to show how prosecutors dehumanize gang members to get the most severe sentences. The final part looks at how I reframed gang stereotypes in court and tried to combat the demonization by humanizing defendants. I argue for persistence in this struggle, though my successes were few and their impact limited. I end by appealing for sentencing reform, advocating protest in the streets for more fundamental change, and demanding an end to the dehumanizing rhetoric of prosecutors.

My stories suggest we already may be living out a version of the dystopian *Handmaid's Tale* (Atwood 1986), where some people are reduced to categories and denied basic humanity. The reader is surely aware that this "us vs. them" mentality is not restricted to the courts but pervades public opinion and makes rational discourse difficult. I show through personal stories how I grew up immersed in racial stereotypes and tell of experiences that led me to political activism. I explain the events that challenged my own stereotypes and motivated me to use my research to combat prejudice and demonization in courts.

This book is a summary of my experiences aimed at encouraging others to resist our all-too-human tendency to dehumanize the "other."

CASE LAW

Brady v. Maryland, 373 U.S. 83, 87 n.2 (1963).

Rose v. Clark, 478 U.S. 570, 580 (1986).

United States of America, Appellee, v. William Clinton Roark, Appellant, No. 90-1334WM, U.S. App. (8th Cir., submitted December 13, 1990; decided January 30, 1991).

I

Stereotypes and Frames

1

The Nature of Gang Stereotypes

What Is a "Gang-Related" Crime?

E arly in 2002, I got a call from Brian Kammer of the Georgia Resource Center, a nonprofit law office providing high-quality representation to people on
death row. Kammer was looking for someone, anyone, who could counter the
state's argument that the 1996 murder of Donovan Parks was "gang related."
I was asked to give a deposition at a habeas corpus ineffective counsel hearing,
where Kammer would argue that had I testified in the original trial, I might have
persuaded at least one juror to have voted against the death penalty for Marion
Wilson. This was the case of Wilson and Robert Butts that opened the Introduction of this book. Kammer argued that Wilson's original attorney was "ineffective," in part, for not calling a gang expert to rebut numerous outrageous and
prejudicial claims by the prosecution about gangs.

Brian is an intense, totally dedicated attorney with much too much experience representing clients on Georgia's death row. He told me of the exonerations he had won and the rewards of his work, which included the many clients
whom he had befriended and worked for tirelessly. He said matter-of-factly his
unrelenting fear was that he would have to watch them die. Brian's caseload of
death penalty cases was visibly taking its toll on him. He became an avid cyclist
and runner to deal with the stress. I admired his dedication but was in awe of
his capacity to carry on when all of his clients were facing execution.

An actual line of cells makes up death row in the Jackson, Georgia,
prison where Marion Wilson was held. This was the same death row where,
a decade before, Walter McMillian waited before Bryan Stevenson (2015)

successfully argued for his freedom as recounted in *Just Mercy*. In a small common area, condemned prisoners would mingle during the day, passing the time during what could be a decades-long process of appeals. In a room just down the hall, the old electric chair had been removed to make room for a cot on which these men would be permanently "put to sleep" by lethal injection. The courtroom where the habeas hearing would be held was right next to it. In a small nearby room, in the shadow of the death chamber, I interviewed Marion as I prepared my testimony. In 1996, Marion Wilson and his codefendant, Robert Butts, had hitched a ride with Donovan Parks, a twenty-four-year-old correctional officer, stolen his car, and then killed him. In separate trials, they were both convicted and sentenced to die.

I was perplexed with why Fred Bright, the Baldwin County prosecutor, would even need to inject the specter of gangs into this case. It seemed like swatting a fly with a sledgehammer. The charge was "malice murder" or homicide in the course of committing an armed robbery. Malice murder by law made the defendants eligible for the death penalty, and there is no mention of gangs in that statute. In Bright's closing statement, however, he ranted that Marion Wilson—he called him by his street name, "Murdoch"—was a hardcore gang member and claimed the murder was "gang related."

I had consulted in a couple of gang court cases before this one. What was transpiring in these cases was much more than a rational sifting through evidence. For example, going over the transcripts of testimony in Marion's case, I found myself mixing up the original defense attorney and the prosecutor—they both trafficked in the same rhetoric and stereotypes. In more than one way, Marion was "defenseless" at his trial. Marion Wilson was, indeed, guilty, but his trial was much more than weighing evidence to prove his guilt beyond a reasonable doubt of the crimes for which he was charged. The trial transcripts were filled with inflammatory rhetoric on gangs, with a deluge of stereotypes and outright falsehoods assaulting a jury who could not help but be frightened to death. Marion's, not theirs.

I had read the social history of Marion Wilson's life. Wilson was the son of a white prostitute who had lived with serial partners, some abusive. Marion was pushed out onto the streets from the age of nine and had a long rap sheet of crimes. His biracial background caused him constant anxiety on the streets, as he struggled with his racial identity. With me, however, he was calm and thoughtful, in stark contrast to the portrait of a violent gangster painted by prosecutors. He talked insightfully about how racist and polarized Milledgeville was: how he had been harassed by police and all the trouble Black kids had in the local schools. Marion told me how African American neighborhoods had gangs long before the current Folks and Bloods. He said, sensibly, that drug sales were an everyday hustle in a small town with few jobs.

His descriptions sounded like a smaller Milwaukee, my hometown where I did my first gang research. As in Milwaukee, for Milledgeville's African American kids, the gang was a badge of resistance, though more temperamentally oppositional than political. He described a "gang" that was a loosely organized neighborhood peer group fascinated by the symbols and image of the nationwide Gangster Disciples. Affiliation to a powerful, Chicago-based gang allowed youths to feel part of something bigger. That fit with my research. I had written my first book, *People and Folks*, on that topic (Hagedorn 1988).

He told me he had joined the Folks gang and received his first rank as a teen in youth prison. When he got out, he shared his "knowledge," meaning gang lore and myths, with younger kids in the Manor, the isolated housing project in Milledgeville where he hung out with Robert Butts and others. "Knowledge" included facts like what each of the six points of the Gangster Disciple star stand for—"Love, Life, Loyalty, Wisdom, Knowledge, and Understanding"—as well as whimsical jailhouse quizzes: "Q. What kind of car does Queen Sheeva drive? A: 1986 Cadillac." Status could be earned, in part, on how well you memorized such gang "literature."

African American kids in the Manor hung out like any other informal, unsupervised peer group with little more than an age-graded structure. White law enforcement officials, however, had a different assumption that saw Black gangs as menacing, formally structured hierarchies. To police, the Folks gangs had military ranks descending from the Gangster Disciple's top commander Larry Hoover in Chicago down to soldiers, like Marion Wilson in Milledgeville. Sheriff Bill Massee and his deputy Howard Sills strained to apply their stereotyped view of gangs to Donovan Parks's murder. Here, in their interrogation, they are suggesting a motive while completely missing Marion's derisive sarcasm (Baldwin County 1996).

> BM: Let me tell you this. There's a lot of people in Milledgeville . . . think you all carjacked him, executed him, to raise your elevation in the gang . . .
>
> MW: I'm as high as I can be. I ain't got to go no higher. I ain't got to do nothing to go no higher . . .
>
> BM: How did get where you are?
>
> MW: I got it while I was at YDC [Youth Dept. of Corrections—jmh]
>
> BM: What's your rank?
>
> MW: I'm the goddam chief enforcer.
>
> BM: Do you all pay money to Chicago?
>
> MW: Nah. . . . See everybody think that I'm the leader . . . I don't got no bunch of people up under me.
>
> BM: Who's under you?

MW: This one person name of Kunta Kinte. That the only person up under me.
BM: What is Kunta Kinte's real name?
MW: That's his real name. Kunta Kinte.

I don't think the Milledgeville police ever found Mr. Kinte.

Where Do Gang Stereotypes Come From?

Sheriff Massee and Deputy Sills told the prosecutor, Fred Bright, that Wilson and Butts committed the carjacking and murder to get a higher rank in the Folks gang. Bright was a district attorney (DA) who bragged that he produced more death penalty sentences than any other prosecutor in Georgia. Indeed, in the next decade, he would seek the death penalty in twenty-one of thirty-one eligible murder cases. The police interrogation of Marion Wilson would give DA Fred Bright the "angle" to rack up two more death penalty notches in his lethal sentencing belt.

The Milledgeville police were operating on a common stereotype of gangs, that, if an offender is a gang member, any violent act must be somehow related "to advance or maintain status" in the gang. Rather than apply Occam's razor, that the simplest explanation is usually the best, Sills and Massee labored to jam the round peg of this crime into their square hole stereotype of how they thought gangs operated.

Gang members do commit crimes to "gain status," but not usually. Most crimes, and especially violent acts, have other, more mundane, motivations. For example, Marion told me he and Robert Butts set out to steal a car and sell it to a "chop shop" in Atlanta. Their motive was money, and the murder resulted when things went terribly wrong. While Marion had been a member of the prison-based Insane Gangster Disciples, it's not clear that Robert Butts was anything more than another kid hanging out in the Manor who needed money. Jurors were told, however, that this violent crime had more heinous, gang-related, motivations. And these, they assumed, made each of the defendants a fundamentally different sort of person than one motivated by the economic needs we all share.

Where did police get this idea in the first place? Milledgeville police "gang expert" Ricky Horn, incredibly, testified that he learned most of what he knew about gangs from "TV and movies," but these turned out not to be his only misleading source of information. After I was brought into the case, I asked Brian Kammer to subpoena the Baldwin County sheriff's training manual on gangs (LaRoque 1995). The manual was derived from training sessions by the Georgia Gang Investigators Association (GGIA). The GGIA is part of a national network of law enforcement "gang experts" whose function appears to be to demonize gangs and reinforce stereotypes for law enforcement and the public. You think I'm exaggerating? According to the Baldwin County manual, derived from GGIA training, "national statistics" prove the following demonstrably false statistics (LaRoque 1995, 16):

- Most gang members don't make it to their twenty-first birthday.
- Ninety percent are arrested by eighteen years of age.
- Ninety-five percent don't finish high school.
- Most gang members spend the majority of their life in prison or jail.

Among a host of other dubious "facts" the manual presents for police officers to teach the public was the assertion that "gang members usually dress alike." Apparently to make it easier for police officers to pick them out.

A second section of the manual is "Sheriff Bill Massee's Gang Awareness Guide," reprinted verbatim from the Chicago Police Department, naming Chicago's much more structured, decades-old gangs. How is a scary four-page-long list of Chicago gangs relevant to Milledgeville, Georgia: population eighteen thousand?

Here's how. The manual goes on to ignore the steadily declining crime rates of the time to claim: "Today brutal, senseless wanton acts of violence are becoming a daily occurrence" (LaRoque 1995, 9). The not-hidden-at-all message of the manual is that this is a dangerous world, and a police crackdown is our best bet to protect us and stamp out gangs. Directly to the issue in this case, the manual teaches officers that "many crimes are committed by gang members in an effort to glorify or raise the status of their gang. Individual gang members will commit acts of violence in order to gain prestige or rank with their respective street gangs."

That concept is what Massee and Sills were fishing for in their interrogation of Marion Wilson. While gang motivations are a legitimate issue for investigation, to ascribe the general idea of "gaining status in the gang" as the motive for a specific carjacking and murder might require more evidence than generalizations from a manual. To say that some crimes are committed to gain status in the gang is one thing. To say, therefore, *any* crime by a gang member is committed for the same motive is what is called the "ecological fallacy." For example, a common stereotype is that the Irish are heavy drinkers, so can we conclude Timmy Dolan is a drunk? Or since some think "Black people tend to be violent" must Marty King be a thug? His Eminence Timothy Dolan is, in fact, a Roman Catholic cardinal in New York City, and Dr. Martin Luther King Jr. was a noted pacifist. Generalizations or stereotypes cannot be applied to individual cases, but throughout this book I show that such generic statements by police experts are routinely admitted into evidence to prove a gang defendant's evil nature.

Both Marion Wilson and Robert Butts had confessed to the crime, and their conviction was inevitable. But rather than rely on the facts of the homicide and take into account the actual biographies of the defendants, the jury had swallowed whole the gang stereotypes and outright falsehoods of Fred Bright and his law enforcement experts. Butts and Wilson had separate trials. Bright, in a malicious and mendacious manner claimed at Wilson's hearing that he was "certain" Wilson had fired the shot that killed Donovan Parks. At Butts's later trial, in nearly identical language, Bright insisted it was Butts who had fired the lethal shot. Both juries quickly voted "death." My postconviction testimony had no impact on appellate judges. In this, one of my earliest cases, it dawned on me that, in the courts, reason and research had little effect in the face of powerful stereotypes, prejudice, and inflammatory lies. I wondered, "why?"

Police Expert Witness for the Prosecution

Stereotypes can be a prosecutor's best friend. Allegations of gang involvement, true or not, help prosecutors make a case and cement the harshest verdicts. Here is what the American Prosecutors Research Institute (APRI) manual for gang prosecution advises with a rhetorical flourish:

> Faced with the prospect of defending a case involving gang evidence, defense attorneys cower. Understanding the power of such evidence, the defense bar will try almost anything to prevent a prosecutor from admitting gang evidence against their client. The first and most clamorous cry is always the same: "Objection! Gang evidence is prejudicial." The prosecutor's response should be equally strident: "Of course it is! That's the point!" (Jackson 2004, 8)

Prosecutors are urged to use police officers as gang experts. "What is the proper subject matter for the expert?" the APRI manual asks. "The simple answer is, 'All the juicy stuff'" (25). Gang stereotypes are especially useful, the APRI manual states, in establishing motive:

> Gang experts can explain the inexplicable, define the indefinable and add rich color to an otherwise pale fact pattern. In other words, if the crime includes gang evidence, use it. (7)

Thus, police officers can establish, by their "expert" testimony alone, a sinister motive for a crime without needing any other evidence. They "explain the inexplicable." That is certainly what happened in the Wilson and Butts trials, where the juries were told the murder was committed to advance the defendants' status in the gang. The juries connect this story to the prosecution's claims of an imaginary wave of "brutal and senseless" gang crime in Milledgeville. For example, here is a transcription of a deposition by police "gang expert" Ricky Horn, as he described what he had said under oath at Wilson's trial. Horn is questioned by David Harth, Brian Kammer's hard-charging pro bono cocounsel. The clerk summarizes Harth's cross-examination:

> He [Ricky Horn, Baldwin County deputy and their gang expert] testified he suspects hundreds and thousands of crimes were committed in Baldwin County in furtherance of the gang. Harth returns Horn to his previous statement that he couldn't prove a single case of this. Horn replies that he thought he was testifying as an expert witness at that time. Harth asks what crimes in his opinion were in furtherance of the gang. . . . Horn concedes his answer at trial was rhetorical, not an exaggeration, but rhetorical. (Superior Court 2005, 58)

In fact, since the Folks gang had formed in Milledgeville a decade before, there had been no more than two dozen murders and less than a hundred assaults per year by *anyone* in all of Baldwin County: population more than forty thousand. Homicide, in fact, had declined in the 1990s, after the current wave of gangs had formed. It was the stereotype of gangs that lent credence to Horn's claim of increased violence, not the facts. I talked with Ricky informally during our depositions, and he was very pleasant and asked me some basic questions about my research. He seemed to me to be a "good old boy" deputy who was trying to do his job. We exchanged stories of growing up, with an uncertain future, in a small town surrounded by failing farms. I think he uncritically accepted his sensationalized training about gangs because it fit into what he had seen "on TV and in the movies."

For all his conviviality, on the witness stand, Ricky dutifully mouthed verbatim what he read in the gang manual with nary a critical thought and with devastating impact. Most important, he was asked by Bright to tell the jury what "FOLKS" stood for. He recited what he had read in the Baldwin County manual (LaRoque 1995, 6): "Note . . . Make sure you mention the FOLKS gang is the largest in Baldwin County, and that FLOKS stands for Followers Our Lord King Satan." I preserved the original typo, but the intention is no mistake.

I can't imagine where the label of "devil-worshipper" could be more damaging than in a Bible Belt town like Milledgeville. In legal terms, it seems this label was more of a "foul blow" than a hard one. I naively thought that exposing the utter falseness of this claim would reverse the death penalty almost by itself. I thought I should add supporting evidence to my testimony as an expert explaining the origin of terms "People and Folks" in Chicago. So, I went to Mickey Lombardo, a former Chicago gang squad officer who was then a high-ranking official in the Cook County Sheriff's Office. He said he had never heard something so ridiculous, and I asked him to inquire about it with current Chicago Police Department gang specialists. He told me all of the gang squad officers he talked to said they never heard any mention that Folks stood for "Followers of Our Lord King Satan." I testified to my findings on the stand.

The overall thrust of my testimony was that there was absolutely no evidence of any sort that the murder was related to gangs. In my deposition, I had noted that Howard Sills had said he couldn't find any evidence at the scene that the crime was gang related. While Ricky Horn was good natured and calm through the hearing, Howard Sills, who since the original trial had been elevated in status to sheriff in nearby Putnam County, became more and more agitated as the "gang-related" case unraveled. I watched him turn red as Kammer and Harth exposed the lack of evidence of any gang relationship to the crime. Sills repeatedly leaned over and whispered to the attorneys representing Wilson's ineffective initial lawyer and became animated almost to the point of disturbing the proceedings.

Once people internalize stereotypes, those stereotypes aren't easily dispelled. In this case, confronted with his admission that there was no actual evidence of the crime being "gang related," Sills doubled down. To my wide-eyed amazement, under direct examination by David Harth, Sills came up with a rather unusual and, if not for the stakes of the situation, laughable justification for calling the murder gang related. The clerk summarizes the exchange (Superior Court, 126).

> Harth: Any marks at the crime scene to identify it as gang shooting? Calling cards, bandana?
> Sills: Well, there was one thing I always thought it could have been.
> Harth: Must have thought of that since depo[sition].
> Sills: It was fact they used F shot. Sills never heard of F shot before crime. Very large shot, bigger than normal bird shot. The gun had been stolen out of a car, but that ammo hadn't been stolen with it. Always thought to himself that that F stood for FOLKS. It is not widely sold. Other grades are numbers, except BB shot. He recalls answering question about calling card at depo in the negative. More he thought of it, it has always stuck in his mind. Never investigated to learn if FOLKS ever use F shot. Just supposition.

Brian Kammer and I struggled to hold it in. To say that F shot meant that the shooting was a calling card for the Folks gang is as ludicrous as saying "BB shot" must mean a shooting was done by a basketball player.

When it was my turn to take the stand, Sills stared what must have been "S shot" daggers at me. I summed up my argument, paraphrased again by the transcriber (Superior Court 2005, 149).

> Hagedorn: There's no evidence F stands for FOLKS, but it is going to be seen that way. That's why Hagedorn does these cases. Cops jump to conclusions and need to be brought back to reality and use the social science lit and research to inform what they are talking about rather than speculating and seeing things that aren't there. When see graffiti it is sign that kids see the gang as solution to some problem. It is more useful to try to find out what is on those kids minds than to panic that Larry Hoover is marching on the town.

All fine and rational, but the jury had swallowed whoppers about gangs and delivered death penalties as demanded. The felony review court ruled:

> We find that the sentence of death in this case was not imposed under the influence of passion, prejudice, or any other arbitrary factor. (Wilson vs State, 1999 OCGA 17-10-35 [c] [1])

Really? I have not always been satisfied with my testimony, but, in Marion's case, I think I had presented a logical, research-based argument that gangs had nothing to do with this crime, and Bright had inflamed the jury with imaginary fears of gang violence. While there were several technical issues, the fact remains that I was not persuasive. Why? My experience in this case and others pushed me away from the literature on gangs and took me down a rabbit hole of studies in social psychology. I went from studying an unfamiliar but understandable world of gangs into a far less rational world of how and why we stereotype and demonize the other.

Why We Rely on Stereotypes

The literature on stereotyping is vast, and I don't intend to give you an academic treatise on social cognition, implicit association tests, idealized cognitive models, or the "brain bugs" of neuroscience. You can find ample references at the end of the book. Perhaps the best overview is Susan Fiske's (1978) contribution to the *Handbook of Social Psychology*, titled "Stereotyping, Prejudice, and Discrimination." My purpose here is to explain how the way we naturally think is manipulated by prosecutors and undermines the likelihood of a fair trial for stigmatized groups, like gangs.

The study of prejudice and stereotyping was profoundly influenced by the need to explain the WWII Fascist era: in other words, how average people could have turned into Ionesco's rhinoceroses. The origins of Nazi era *deplorables*, Frankfurt school philosophers decided, could be found in the strict parenting styles that developed an "authoritarian personality," which could be measured on what they called an "F scale." In this view, stereotypes are the products of prejudiced, bigoted minds.

However, in 1954, Gordon Allport's seminal study, *The Nature of Prejudice*, radically broke from this argument. Allport was very clear that thinking in categories—stereotyping—is normal, how the human mind actually works. Fiske says, "Humans inevitably categorize objects and people in their world, and that to prejudge is entirely normal" (1978, 360). Leyens et al. (1994, 1) claim on the very first page of their comprehensive review of the literature: "To think about others is to categorize them."

"Open mindedness is considered to be a virtue," Allport says with startling implications for criminal trials. "But strictly speaking it cannot occur. A new experience must be redacted into old categories. We cannot handle each event freshly in its own right" (1954, 20). Allport's work founded the modern discipline of social psychology. Jennifer Eberhardt (2019, 23), in her definitive book on implicit bias, sums up Allport's argument precisely:

> Categorization—grouping like things together—is not some abhorrent feature of the human brain, a process that some people engage in and others do not. Rather, it is a universal function of the brain that allows us to organize and manage the overload of stimuli that constantly bombard us. It's a system that brings coherence to a chaotic world; it helps our brains make judgments more quickly and efficiently by instinctively relying on patterns that seem predictable.

Allport explained why this habitual function is a problem when it comes to race: "A person with dark brown skin will activate whatever concept of Negro is dominant in our mind. If the dominant category is one composed of negative attitudes and beliefs, we will automatically avoid him, or adopt whichever habit of rejection is most available to us" (1954, 21). Think of how a "habit of rejection" applies to a juror's decision in a trial of a dark-skinned gang member.

I go into more disturbing, racialized aspects of stereotypes in Part II, but for now, let me point out that stereotyping is *not* a conscious process. "One of the most fundamental results in cognitive science, one that comes from the study of commonsense reasoning," George Lakoff (2008, 4) says, "is that most of our thought is unconscious—not unconscious in the Freudian sense of being repressed, but unconscious simply in that we are not aware of it." This view was popularized by Malcolm Gladwell's (2004) *Blink*. Stereotypes are a form of what are called "cognitive shortcuts." We see a person who is labeled a "gang member," and we automatically assume we know lots about him from our preexisting stereotypes despite a lack of specific information. S. Winter says, "*Categorization* is the very process of reasoning itself" (2001, 70). Perhaps, at this point, I ought to determine what is the stereotype of a "gang member?" If you "think of a gang member," a picture comes to mind—remember Walter Lippman said stereotypes are "pictures in our head"? Remember the "Google Guy" in the Introduction? We explore the power of "priming" and "prototypes" later in the book. For now, I simply present what *Roget's Thesaurus* (1995) tells us are synonyms of "gang member":

> bad person, evil person, no saint, sinner, hardened sinner, *limb of Satan*, *Antichrist*, evildoer, fallen angel, backslider, recidivist, lost sheep, lost soul . . . *one without morals*, immoralist reprobate, scapegrace, good-for-nothing, ne'er-do-well, black sheep, scallywag, scamp, rake . . . profligate, libertine, wanton, hussy, *loose woman* . . . , outcast, dregs, riffraff, trash, white trash, SCUM, object of scorn . . .

Eeek! Lock him up! This is our "implicit stereotype" of a gang member, and it unconsciously shapes how a jury views evidence about such, er, "limbs of Satan." In fact, Benferado (2015, 255) reports on a mock jury study asking potential jurors

> about whether they would be able to act impartially if the defendant turned out to be a gang member. Even when it was made explicit that the question was merely hypothetical, it had a powerful biasing effect: participants who were asked the question were significantly more likely to reach a guilty verdict than those who did not. According to the researchers, because gangs are associated with criminal behavior, exposure to the hypothetical question made that negative stereotype readily accessible and encouraged participants to find the defendant guilty.

One reason why these jurors were more inclined to find a gang member guilty lies in how we use stereotypes. Benaji and Greenwald (2013, 109) seem to be contributing directly to this book when they say in *Blindspot*:

> Stereotypes do not take special effort to acquire. Quite the opposite—they are acquired effortlessly, and take special effort to discount. . . . Yet if we were to think of our minds as court rooms in which trials are held to decide on guilt or innocence one of the downsides of stereotypes is that they compromise due process. By relying on them our minds indict before a prosecutor arrives on the scene.

Well, not quite. The prosecutor plays a starring role in encouraging stereotypical thinking. The cases of Robert Butts and Marion Wilson were not the only egregious examples in my work of how prosecutors marshal the lethal power of gang stereotypes, and I discuss various aspects of these cases throughout the book. In my early cases, I was shocked by how persuasive stereotypes could be and how juries responded to fearmongering and outright lies. What I've learned over the years is that, unlike real people like Robert Butts, stereotypes do not die.

The next chapter concludes this basic introduction to how prosecutors use stereotypes. Twenty years later, in another Georgia courtroom, I had to confront the same erroneous assumption that a crime by a gang member must necessarily be committed in the interests of the gang. In the case of Chester Niven, the DA used gang statutes to vastly overcharge the defendant and transform a tragic death into a premeditated homicide to "elevate Chester's status in the gang." In the case of Johnnie Norman, a bogus gang-related label prompted the prosecution to seek the death penalty. Neither story has a happy ending but, in each, catastrophe was averted. Still, both are further examples of how our inclination to think in stereotypes allows prosecutors to seek the most punitive sentences.

CASE LAW

Berger v. United States, 295 U.S. 78, 88 (1935).

Wilson v. The State, 99P0651 (271 Ga. 811(525 SE2d 339) (1999). Chief Justice Benham, Murder, Baldwin Superior Court, Before Judge Prior (decided November 1, 1999; reconsideration denied December 20, 1999).

2

"Increasing Status in the Gang"

Fast Thinking and Overcharging
in Gang-Related Crimes

About twenty years after the Butts and Wilson case, I served as expert witness on another "gang-related" murder in a rural Georgia town not far from Milledgeville. The facts of this case made it impossible to ignore. The attorney, Lee Sexton, was shocked that the DA had used a Georgia gang-related statute to charge his client with multiple counts of murder and assault in what seemed to him to be a case of self-defense or, at most, manslaughter.

At the time of his crime, Chester Niven was a twenty-three-year-old man living with his parents and working in rural Georgia. He loved rap music and was the sole white boy in a group that hung out together listening to and performing hip-hop. Like many youths of any race, he was fascinated by media images of gang life. Seeking to emulate the belongingness and masculinity he saw in these images, he began to dress in red. He began to claim, dubiously, that he was "initiated" into the Bloods in an adjacent county, since his county had no Blood sets or chapters. He told me he had never been to any meetings and knew nothing about Blood organization or leaders. I quizzed him about the Bloods, including the particular way Bloods fold their flags, or handkerchiefs, and he didn't appear to have a clue. He seemed to be a lot like Baldwin County deputy Ricky Horn: he got most of his knowledge from the mass media—in Chester's case, rap music. I asked him what being a Blood meant to him, and he quickly said, "Red bandanas." He was one of many youths for whom the gang is more of a media-driven identity than an organizational affiliation. His red bandana, however, would get him in deep trouble, lead him to a confrontation that cost the life of a human being, and send him to prison.

The incident was captured on surveillance video, so Chester's actions were not in dispute. He strolled into a local gas station to buy some beef jerky. He had a handgun concealed under his shirt and a red bandana hanging out of his back pocket. William Sims, an African American man who had admitted a year before to police he was a Blood, came in at about the same time. He asked Chester, "Who you claim?" a common question gang members might ask those presenting symbols of membership about what gang "set" they belong to. There was a short and testy exchange of words.

Sims was apparently offended that Chester was claiming Bloods when he appeared to be no more than a wannabe. To Sims, or any actual gang member, Chester was "false flagging." Sims ripped the bandana out of Chester's pocket. I watched the surveillance tape as Chester whirled around and pulled out his pistol and pointed it at Sims—who wasn't intimidated in the least. Sims grabbed the gun from Chester and beat the tar out of him for about a minute. Sims then turned and walked out of the gas station into the parking lot, keeping Chester's gun.

Chester was humiliated but his emotions found an immediate outlet. He had a second gun hidden in his pants leg and angrily went outside after Sims, who glared at him while holding Chester's original gun. In a split second, Chester shot Sims dead. Then, in behavior I've never seen in any of my homicide cases, Chester patiently waited for police to arrive, handed over the murder weapon, and submitted to arrest. As I noted in my report, these are not exactly the actions of a hard-core gang member.

As I watched the police interrogation video, I observed Chester's emotional responses to police questions. He admitted what happened and said he was frightened for his life. He had been flying on adrenaline during the fight and broke down completely at the police station. He cried on several occasions and called his mother and girlfriend. I think this may have been the only gang-related conflict Chester had ever been in, and he panicked after the initial confrontation. I thought Chester's self-defense claim would be a stretch, though Chester claimed Sims was raising his gun before Chester shot him. The surveillance video did not capture the fatal interaction that took place outside the store.

The local police were sympathetic, I suspect in part because both they and Chester were white and the dead man, William Sims, was Black. The DA who brought the first indictment was in his last few days before taking an appointment as a judge. He had little incentive for controversy and indicted Chester on voluntary manslaughter, a crime that recognized the emotional spur-of-the-moment nature of the shooting—a reasonable assessment.

But a different, rawer politics came into play quickly. A new DA came into office having campaigned as a "gang buster." As with the Wilson and Butts case twenty years before, gangs were still Georgia's number one bogeyman and the new DA thought he could make his bones by getting tough. And did he get tough. He went back to the grand jury who had indicted Chester for manslaughter and brought a superseding indictment for thirty-three counts of violations of the Georgia Street Gang Terrorist Prevention Act. Included in those thirty-three counts were twelve counts of murder done with "the intent to obtain or earn membership or maintain or increase his or her status or position in a criminal street gang."

I have never figured out how one dead person could merit twelve counts of murder. While the initial charge would yield a twenty-year sentence, the new charges meant at least natural life, and the DA theoretically could seek the death penalty. Overcharging is a standard practice for prosecutors, but this was way over the top.

I met Chester and his family in the lawyer's offices. I was a bit embarrassed when I saw his family. Chester's dad was wearing all red, and with Bloods on my mind, I assumed he was Chester. Nope, Chester's dad was a University of Georgia Bulldogs fan and wearing his college team's colors, not "Blood red." He also was in his fifties and his son, Chester, a skinny kid standing by his side, was in his twenties. I was guilty of jumping to the conclusion and stereotyping based on the simple color of Chester's dad's shirt. I felt like a fool.

Chester was out on bail, which had not been revoked after the change in charges. He was quiet and more than a little freaked out. He couldn't answer any of my questions about the Bloods. It was all about rap music for him. His Facebook pages were filled with lyrics with violent imagery from rap songs. I asked him why he was carrying guns. He said he had been around guns since he was little and was both a marksman and a hunter. Carrying pistols was also part of his self-image, the same that informed his intrigue with the idea of gang membership. I told him walking around with a concealed weapon while making false claims of gang membership was one of the dumbest things he could have done. He agreed, but it was too late. The Bloods were already threatening his family, and he would surely have a tough time in prison.

While my interview with Chester assured me that the prosecutor had no basis for any story about violence as a means of gang advancement, I'd learned, however, that just introducing the gang frame was persuasive in court, so merely presenting my expert opinion might not be enough to sway the court. For the DA, since Chester claimed to be a Blood, obviously the "motive" for his action must be to "maintain or increase his status in the gang." The DA didn't even need to think about it because the narrative that confirmed his angle was readily available culturally to him and to the jury alike.

The words of the statute itself and stereotypes prompted him to assume Chester's actions were done "to increase his status" in the gang. My advice to Lee Sexton, the attorney, was to make a preemptive strike and introduce a different way of thinking about gangs in general, one that showed how little knowledge the DA's assumption was based on. If the DA thought he might get embarrassed at trial, maybe he'd reconsider the charge. He likely thought such a high-profile sensational charge would support his career ambitions.

I could hardly dispute that the shooting was gang related. It was. But the indictment went further than could be proven, saying the shooting and battery were done to elevate Chester's status in the gang. As in the Wilson and Butts cases, two decades before, there was no evidence whatsoever that any "elevation" of Chester's status was on his mind at all. Further, I suspected Chester's Blood set hung out more in rap lyrics than on any street corner.

I knew that just asserting these realities might not be enough to counter the knee-jerk resonance of the prosecutor's assumptions with the Hollywood-infused fears of a jury. So, more than asserting that his story was wrong and leaving the jury to decide if his account or mine resonated more, I would have to change the conversation toward a different kind of thinking, one that encouraged the court to approach the stories looking for logic and new information rather than a "bad guy" or a narrative they recognized. I pulled out all the stops in my written statement by arguing: one of the earliest findings of gang research is "no two gangs are alike." The idea that violence is a means for elevation in a gang is not universal and needs evidence to support it in a given case. I wrote:

> In some gangs, high status is determined by business sense, how much money you can bring in on drug sales or other entrepreneurial ventures. For others, violence is discouraged as dangerous to business operations. In some gangs, violent acts are a sign of low status by "expendable" members following orders that allow leaders to escape culpability. Some more structured gangs require memorization of "laws and prayers" or other literature for advancement. Other hierarchical gangs, like the Gangster Disciples in Chicago in the 1990s, awarded promotion to those who went on to college.

As we see later, one common way to break people out of stereotypes is "subtyping." You admit the validity of the assumption in some cases, but just not in this one. If the prosecution wants to affirm the "violence as a means to elevate status" stereotype in this case, it requires proof. But unlike Milledgeville's grandstanding Fred Bright, this DA was new and eager to advance his status in his own gang, that of Georgia's gang of DAs. I reasoned, since the freshly minted DA wanted approval and prestige, he couldn't really afford to fail to get a conviction and would not risk putting his stereotype through the logical steps required to prove whether it applied in a particular case.

Sexton would argue that the DA had brought the wrong charge. The DA read not only the report but the writing on the wall as well. He was sharp enough to see the logic in my argument and worried that the judge might toss the case. He may yet have got his conviction under the Georgia Street Gang Terrorist Prevention Act, but I think he concluded the risk to his career was too high if he failed or the conviction was reversed on appeal. Surely, race was also an important consideration in how the DA evaluated the potential success of his gang frame. If the races were reversed and had Chester been Black and Sims white, one wonders if mercy would have been shown. The new DA dropped the gang-related and first-degree murder charges back to the original voluntary manslaughter. Chester pleaded guilty. The DA got a conviction. Chester got twenty years.

Sexton felt victorious, but I worried about Chester's security in prison. The short time he was held in jail before trial he was in protective custody due to threats on his life. Prison would be worse, and I asked Sexton to speak to the judge about influencing Chester's prison placement. If it became known in a Georgia prison that this white kid had killed a Black Blood gang member, Chester's life wouldn't be worth diddly-squat.

I took three lessons away from Chester Niven's case and the Wilson and Butts cases. First, how hard it is for stereotypes to die. In two shootings twenty years apart, prosecutors either assumed or asserted, with no evidence, that a crime by a gang member *must* have been committed for gang-related purposes. If anything, matters had gotten worse as Georgia law, like many other states, now linked gangs and terrorists. Wording in the current law suggested to prosecutors that they could get an enhanced sentence by simply claiming a gang member's crime was done to advance their status in the gang. Both prosecutors assumed they did not need any evidence to make this case.

The second lesson was that not all crimes that are alleged to be gang related actually are. I realized how useful stereotypes are for prosecutors' occupational self-interest. Stereotypes are useful to prosecutors' ambitions because they are so easily accepted by jurors: they play on existing fears that have the veneer of common sense and are more readily brought to mind than the counterarguments, however informed. Fred Bright just had to say "gang related" and let the stereotype do the work as the jury first voted "guilty," then "death." Chester's DA convinced a grand jury to wildly overcharge with no evidence to back him up.

But I'd also learned a third lesson from comparing the outcomes of the two cases and how my own approach had adapted. When I'd explained at the habeas hearing in Milledgeville that Wilson and Butts's crime were not gang related, judges didn't find my informed opinion persuasive. When I'd challenged Chester Niven's prosecutor to prove that Chester's gang was the sort that rewarded violence, he backed off the charge. Why? Part of the explanation may be the different incentives for the different prosecutors at different moments in their careers, but part of it might have been how I'd invited the court to think about the information I was giving them. I turned my attention to Daniel Kahneman's (2011) *Thinking Fast and Slow* to make some sense of all this.

Fast Thinking = Stereotypes

Daniel Kahneman is a Princeton psychologist who holds a Nobel Prize for his research on common biases and errors of thinking. We have two modes of thinking, Kahneman found. Fast thinking or System 1 is the norm. We make quick judgments based on our stereotypes or reliable categories that allow us to make a new situation or person familiar. Studies have regularly found that 80–90 percent of our thinking is unconscious, automatic responses, called cognitive shortcuts. Chester's second prosecutor quickly assumed that the shooting must be related to Chester's claimed gang status because that is consistent with an existing association he held. He assumed, reasonably, that a jury would swallow this, having their own associations, as the Butts and Wilson juries did. Gang narratives, such as prosecutors relay in the courtroom, are persuasive to juries because of the easy links they make that jurors recognize.

Slow thinking, or System 2, is for reasoned, deliberative judgment. The two systems work in different ways and engage different parts of the brain. Whereas the first system uses patterns the brain has already established to sort incoming information into a preexisting path, System 2 forges a new path. This system is more taxing and difficult but less likely to be swayed off course. A jury, judge, and even a prosecutor, it should be assumed, uses System 2 because it is more likely to be correct and fair. Given the stakes of the court—life and death, freedom and confinement—they should be presumed to use reason, put emotions to the side, weigh all the factors, critically assess testimony, and make a considered judgment. But do they?

Kahneman and other cognitive scientists have found that prompting the brain to use System 2 is hard. Social psychologist and author Susan Fiske says, "People normally engage in cognitive shortcuts unless motivated to go beyond them." (1978, 363). Our minds expend effort to concentrate, let go of the shortcuts they have previously established, and make the subtle but critical distinctions that are the building blocks of reason. In a courtroom, jurors and judges need to concentrate fully on all the evidence and filter out what is true from what is merely easy to associate. There are physical limits to our power to concentrate. Kahneman reports on a study of German judges making parole decisions. As they poured over the documents, using System 2 concentration, their blood sugar dropped. Their physical state had a profound effect on their decisions. In the hours directly before a meal, when the judges were tired and hungry, almost all the parole applications were rejected. After a meal, nearly two-thirds were granted.

Now this doesn't mean we should set up buffets in the jury box. As I show later, there have been even more extreme suggestions on how to address stereotyping in courts. At this point we might conclude that faced with hours, days, or weeks of evidence, jurors tend to satisfice, or settle on the sufficient solution instead of working for the optimal one. The term "satisfice" was first used by Herbert Simon (1956) to describe how in any organization, decision-making is typically based on the first easy answer that fits, not the one that takes the most thought.

Prosecutors satisfice as well, making the solutions they propose easy for judges and juries to adopt. Like Chester's new DA, they find gang-related charges a "no-brainer" in tacking on additional counts to get enhanced penalties or frighten a defendant into accepting a plea. Realistically, if Chester had gone to trial on all thirty-three counts, the jurors would have been likely to think, as Angela J. Davis says in her study of prosecutors, "With all those charges, he must be guilty of something" (2007, 51). By invoking the Georgia Street Gang Terrorist Prevention Act, the prosecutor puts the stereotype of a violent gang member (and of a terrorist!) directly in the minds of the jurors, no matter what the judge might tell jurors to disregard. We discuss the startling power of priming in a later chapter.

System 1 encourages the kind of no-brainer thinking that, beyond pattern recognition and analogy, also traffics in prejudice and stereotypes by associating something new with something familiar, what is sometimes called "illusory correlation." When juries see a gang member, a kind of "halo effect" takes over, our stereotype associates the defendant with our image or concept of a gang member, however limited that may be. The human brain decides guilt psychologically by association. And it happens in less than an eyeblink. Kahneman goes on to say System 1 is a kind of confirmation bias, which is to say that it looks for evidence to support its initial beliefs (2011, 81) rather than make careful decisions based on accumulated evidence. Antonio Damasio goes so far as to say implicit stereotypes are laced with emotion and can be called "somatic markers" or feelings deep within us. Damasio (1994, 174) says of a stereotype: "Think of it as a biasing device."

Kahneman points out "System 1 is highly adaptive in one form of think-ing—it automatically and effortlessly identifies causal connections between events, sometimes even when the connection is spurious" (2011, 11). "Caus-al connections" in court are exactly what is at stake in determining who is guilty. Robert J. MacCoun's authoritative review of jury studies points out how jurors make decisions. He states, "One of the earliest findings in mock jury research was that, despite judges' instructions to the contrary, many jurors form tentative verdict preferences early in the trial" (1989, 14). In another study of jury deliberation, Maynard and Manzo (1993, 174) explain:

> Jurors often enter the jury room with a more or less firm position regarding the defendant's guilt. As the deliberation proceeds, some of them may find, in and through their own and others' talk, pre-cisely that argument which articulates the position to which they hold.

In an article examining why gang evidence is so prejudicial, Eisen et al. (2009, 8) agree that juries are driven, at least in part, by this confirmation bias. They explain how confirmation bias works when gangs are involved in a trial (my italics):

> Once a negative stereotype is activated, people often seek informa-tion that is consistent with that stereotype. *Simply notifying the jury that the defendant is a member of a criminal street gang involved in violent crime suggests to the jurors that the defendant is a danger to society, independent of the evidence offered.* According to this model, once this bias is instilled, the jurors may then filter the evidence presented through the negative stereotype that has been activated, attending most closely to information that confirms the established bias activated by the label "gang member."

This is why Chester's prosecutor felt he could succeed with such irre-sponsible overcharging despite the fact, as Daniel S. Medwed states, that "ethics codes forbid prosecutors from 'overcharging' solely in the hopes of gaining leverage" (2012, 141). I think that there was a great likelihood that a jury would have found Chester guilty of at least some of the charges the DA eventually retracted, and he would have been sentenced to life in prison. A prosecutor doesn't have to think deeply to know that, by invoking the gang stereotype, it will haunt juror's minds throughout the trial. Gang ste-reotyping turns tragic events, like Chester's macho shooting of William Sims, into a case with much more severe penalties as well as potential ad-vance in status for the "tough on gangs" prosecutor.

Sometimes, as with Butts and Wilson, the gang charges add logs to the fire of a prosecutor's calls for a death penalty. As the APRI manual (Jackson 2004, 7) said, "If the crime includes gang evidence, use it." It doesn't matter if that evidence is misleading or even outrageously false. To say a homicide has a gang-related motive in capital murder cases is a near guarantee that prosecutors will ask for the death penalty. And, in addition to the incentives to pile up convictions and harsh sentences in a political context that rewards "tough-on-crime prosecutors," sometimes the stereotype seems to provide the quickest and easiest story. Sometimes the reality of sorting out how a tragedy came to pass is difficult and complex to arrive at. In such a case, it is much less demanding—cognitively or even emotionally—to jump to the story suggested by fast thinking, and much more painful to undertake the learning and nonjudgment demanded by slow thinking to arrive at the full weighty story. Too see how this works, let's travel from rural Georgia across state lines to rural Alabama and examine how gang charges in an emotionally disturbing homicide led to young Johnnie Norman facing the death penalty. Was he a confused teenage kid or a revenge-seeking Crip hit man? You surely can guess which label the prosecutors chose.

Susan Lehmann, a private investigator with whom I'd worked before, told me about a death penalty case in Camptown, a rural Alabama town where prosecutors were alleging a local chapter of the Crips had ordered a hit on a rival gang member. Her client, a nineteen-year-old African American man, Johnnie Norman, had clammed up after his arrest and refused to talk to his lawyer or make any statements. The other teenagers, his fellow "Crips" who were charged in the murder, had all cut deals and decided Johnnie was going to take the fall. The only narrative explaining the crime, in the absence of a statement from Johnnie, was the prosecution's story that it was gang-related retaliation. The prosecutor announced he would put this cold-blooded gang "hit man" to death.

As the white wannabe gangster Chester Niven and Deputy Ricky Horn did, young Black kids also often have a stereotyped image of the gangster, drawn more from mass media, hip-hop, kinfolk, and acquaintances than from any personal experience or affiliation. While this stereotype provokes macho behavior in many people looking for a taste of control in a context where they have very little, it also leads many to idolize a lifestyle of alcohol, drugs, guns, and volatile group dynamics. This lethal combo can turn teenage anger and immaturity into murder. The Alabama Bureau of Investigation officers who arrested Johnnie and his three other companions determined that the murder of Don Macelroy was "gang related." In an earlier shooting incident, Macelroy had identified the shooter to police. Now that Macelroy was the victim, and Johnnie's friends claimed Crip affiliation, investigators assumed that Johnnie was ordered by higher up Crips to kill the snitch, Don Macelroy, who also happened to be one of Johnnie's best friends. Susan believed Johnnie was no kind of hit man. You can judge for yourself.

I traveled to Camptown, population of about one thousand, and met with Johnnie's attorney, Bud Smith. Bud didn't like Johnnie and was frustrated that Johnnie obviously didn't trust him. Johnnie refused to talk with him at all and give him any kind of story that would contradict the gang-related narrative spun by police. Typically, in cases that haven't come to trial, I'm cautioned by attorneys, "Don't let him confess to you" since that would make it dangerous for me to testify at trial if the prosecutor were to cross-examine me about the substance of my interview with the client. In this case, a jury trial in rural Alabama would be as disastrous as the one in Milledgeville that ended up with death sentences for Butts and Wilson. My standard policy in gang-related cases is to do whatever I can to keep a case from going to trial and instead introduce enough new information that the prosecutor and defense settle rather than risk outright loss at trial. I'd seen it before: stereotypes can kill.

I decided to try to persuade Johnnie to tell me what happened, from his childhood, to his joining the gang, to the murder itself. Unless Johnnie could provide me with an alternative explanation, the gang-related narrative of prosecutors was going to control the trial. Interviews for my work are high stakes: I only have a short time to make a connection with the defendant and get a story that he often has not shared even with his attorney. It doesn't always work. The barriers of race and age are sometimes insuperable. In this case, I needed Johnnie to tell me what actually happened; that meant him confessing. It was more important that Johnnie's lawyer have a counternarrative than it was that I be able to testify. I was reasonably certain he had, in fact, shot Don, his friend, since he had admitted as much in a recorded tearful call from the jail to his grandmother. I thought his only hope to avoid the death penalty was for his attorney to arrange a plea deal buttressed by a counternarrative to the gang-related story of the prosecutor.

Susan introduced me to Johnnie in the jail where he was being held awaiting trial. She had "built me up" as someone Johnnie could trust. He needed someone to be on his side. His closest friends had all turned on him, and the guy who he looked up to most in his "gang," Damon Reed, had put all the blame on Johnnie and got off with only a short sentence while Johnnie faced the death penalty. I didn't blame him for not risking anything by keeping quiet. He had been betrayed and was scared.

Susan left, and Johnnie eyed me up nervously. He was a short young Black man, now twenty-two years old, with medium-toned skin. He had been in county jails for three years since the shooting. At first, he didn't smile at all and had sad, wary eyes. His social history said he had a very low IQ, and he came from a home where his aunt had been abusive to him and his older brother. After he told me about how miserable small-town Alabama jails were, with no regular access to recreation or other distractions, I asked him about the Crips gang. It was as I suspected. The "gang" was actually only Johnnie and his two friends, all of whom were in the car where the homicide occurred. Police said they were always seen wearing white and blue, allegedly Crip colors. I learned those also happened to be the colors of their local high school. Johnnie really knew nothing about the Crips that he hadn't heard in rap lyrics or seen in movies.

I discovered their "Crips" gang was merely a scary-sounding label for a wild group of close friends who liked to smoke dope and act tough. And, in all-American fashion, they all carried guns. As they had been for Chester, for Johnnie and his friends, guns were a way to appear macho and impress girls. The victim, Don Macelroy, did not claim to be a Crip, but said he was a Folks gang leader, kin to the Folks gangs of Marion Wilson. Authorities noted Macelroy usually wore black, which they mistakenly called Folks colors. The uncontested leader of Johnnie's self-styled "Crips gang" was Damon Reed, a guy whom teachers and others called an "alpha male" with whom Johnnie would "tag along." A school counselor Susan and I interviewed who knew them both said crudely that Damon viewed Johnnie as a "disposable diaper," who could be ordered to do "the dirty work and could be thrown away."

As our interview went on into a second and third hour, Johnnie became animated as he described the events in the car leading up to the murder. Folks gang member Don had been insulting Damon, saying he really wasn't a "high ranking Crip" because he "wasn't going to do shit." They were all high from drinking and smoking, and things were getting more and more tense. They were heading to a nearby mall to "pick up girls," but Don Macelroy wanted to go pick up his pistol first, bragging that there were going to be a lot of "dead n----s" from some previous slight. Everyone else in the car already had pistols on them.

As juvenile insults between Don and Damon heated up, Johnnie told me, the young men threatened to kill each other. As things got out of control, Don Macelroy yelled out: "Bitch a-- m-----------s! I'll kill one of you m-----------s!" At that point in his story to me, Johnnie began to shake as he described what happened. He told me Damon began to scream, "Shoot him! Shoot him." Don was Johnnie's good friend, but Johnnie idolized Damon. Johnnie was also high on something and was nervously fumbling with his pistol as they rode. Damon had a gun on him too, but, instead of getting his out, he yelled to Johnnie: "Shoot him!" Johnnie wondered what would happen to him if he didn't shoot? Later on, Damon would brag to a friend: "I ain't killed nobody but my mouth can get someone killed."

In the heat of the moment, Johnnie didn't know what to do. Everyone was shouting. He loved Don Macelroy, but Damon kept telling him to shoot. He was confused and distraught but finally just pulled the trigger and shot his good friend Don twice in the back of his head. After the shooting, one of his friends in the car with him told police Johnnie stood outside the door shaking and asking, "What happened?"

We had talked past lunch, lost in time, and Susan had come to pick me up. I told Johnnie I'd be back later in the day to talk about how to deal with his lawyer. Susan later wrote in her report that when I came out of the jail I was "in shock," and it took me a while to calm down. It wasn't the only time a young man had confessed and vividly described a murder to me. TV or movies do not prepare you to understand what it means to someone to kill, much less kill one of your best friends. Killing violates the deepest moral prohibitions internalized in our soul, and it shatters something human within us. One thing was clear: Johnnie was no "cold-blooded" killer, and this crime was no premeditated ordered hit from any organization. Like most violence, it was the product of anger, immaturity, humiliation, and fear combined with substances and firearms. Though Don lay dead, there was more than one victim.

When I returned to the jail, I asked Johnnie to tell the attorney the story he told me. The best way to get rid of the death penalty, I told him, was to tell his lawyer the truth and let him try to plea bargain the case. He agreed. We were both exhausted.

My letter to the attorney, Bud Smith, dismissed the gang angle as totally irrelevant to what had happened. There was no structured gang, only three friends who dubbed themselves "Crips." The murder can be explained most clearly by interpersonal dynamics. Further, I wrote:

> There is a tendency for police and prosecutors to see gang processes behind what can often be explained by more mundane motivations. Research tells us that stereotypes, unless challenged by research or "discrepant information" can be the basis of mistaken action. Often stereotypes replace evidence and guide the reconstructing of crime scenes to match mistaken ideas about gangs.

I argued explicitly that the charge was wrong. Like with Chester Niven, many years later, this crime was gang related only in the sense that three of the boys in the car considered themselves members of a self-identified "gang." Nor was the shooting intentional. I cited verbatim the Alabama statute that manslaughter means a crime was committed in the "sudden heat of passion under provocation," a startlingly apt description of Johnnie's shooting.

However, unlike Chester, Johnnie wasn't white. Damon Reed, his fast-talking "leader of the pack" had parlayed his plea deal into a scarcely believable two-year sentence. He would be back out on the streets before Johnnie's sentencing took place. In Johnnie's plea negotiations, the challenge to the gang-related nature of the crime and Johnnie's mental deficiencies, well documented by Susan, persuaded the prosecutor to drop the death penalty but not the first-degree murder charge. Johnnie was sentenced to life in prison. But, given Johnnie's low IQ, life circumstances, and the prosecutor's agreement that this wasn't really a gang-related case, Bud Smith managed to get the prosecutor to agree to a sentence of life *with* parole. This meant Johnnie could have a parole hearing in June 2023. This was no guarantee of release from an Alabama prison, but a reason for hope.

———

This is just one of many cases, in which I've testified, where prosecutors immediately concluded that a crime was gang related, on the basis of little but their own expectations, and used that stereotype to increase the penalty for a crime. In this case, the person I thought was most responsible for the murder, Damon Reed, got the lightest sentence. It was also in Damon's interest to downplay the gang angle, and, when Johnnie confessed to being the shooter, the gang connection faded to background noise, where it belonged. Confronted with the complex reality of Johnnie's story and the inadequacy of what had seemed a simple explanation and nudged by the very definition of manslaughter, perhaps the prosecutor applied System 2 reasoning in his decision to drop the death penalty. While I still don't agree with the charge, the possibility of parole in fourteen years was not unreasonable. In a more just world, Johnnie would have gotten treatment not incarceration.

But the point is that prosecutors, like jurors, don't typically rely on reasoned judgment or System 2 thinking when they can charge a murder as gang related. Such charges help get convictions, bring the most severe penalties, including a death sentence, and almost always give the prosecutor a conviction. Prosecutors know stereotypes have a powerful effect on jurors who are easily frightened into System 1 "stereotype-congruent" fast thinking. Slow thinking often gets left behind.

Throughout twenty-five years of expert witness testimony, I've tried many tactics to combat System 1 stereotypical thinking. In the Butts and Wilson cases, simply asserting facts and reason was useless. In both Chester's and Johnnie's cases, all out assaults on a gang frame and a shift toward more complex explanations were successful in getting prosecutors to reduce charges before trial. In the chapters that follow, I summarize my normally frustrating experience in getting juries, judges, and prosecutors to go beyond stereotypes and System 1 fast thinking.

An underlying psychological problem in our capacity to challenge stereotypes is a deep-seated belief that our assumptions and associations describe and order a just world. Simplistic stories of evil men doing harm to innocents and being brought to justice by white-horse-riding heroes wielding the sword of justice are part of the lore we valued and applied to what we saw as we grew up. Think The Three Little Pigs and the Big Bad Wolf. In the bedtime stories we were told, justice inevitably comes to the evil, hungry wolf in a pot of boiling water. And didn't we as children laugh and feel relief when the evil wolf boiled to death?

Breaking from the myth of a just world often requires the most extreme method of stereotype changing—conversion. This method also has its downsides. The next chapter explains my conversion, which sent me on my journey into the courtroom.

3

Is This a Just World?

How Stereotypes and Beliefs Change—
A Personal Story

Stereotypes rooted in deeply engrained stories of good and evil are altered only with great difficulty. One reason they are so difficult to think about critically, according to Michael Lerner (1980), is that we have an underlying belief in or "cognitive bias" toward a just world. This means we expect people's outcomes to follow from their choices, with good choices leading to good outcomes and bad choices leading to bad outcomes. This baseline expectation is important to our brains because, when we make a choice or take an action that we understand to be good, we believe we'll be rewarded or we choose not to do something that would socially be understood as bad, we'd be punished. We teach children to expect these outcomes so that they will behave, and we ourselves depend on the world operating on this logic to give meaning to our choices and actions. Such beliefs are reflected in religion as well as in the Enlightenment idea of progress. Voltaire's *Candide* expresses his belief in a just world despite a life of disaster. The Bible's Book of Job concludes with the same idea, that Job's suffering for his faith showed his merit. Poet Alexander Pope defined a just world with a conservative slant, thundering, "Whatever is, is right." Karl Marx expected the dialectic dynamic he saw in history to end in an inevitable utopian world free of exploitation. History, he says, is on the side of the working class. Fundamentally, Lerner argues, all people want to believe that there is order in the world and that good things happen to good people, and bad people, like the Big Bad Wolf, eventually get what they deserve.

We expect criminal trials to bear out our expectation of a just world; prosecutors are the voice of law and order, and juries are the instruments of punishing those who violate the sacred laws of justice. A defendant walks into a trial at a disadvantage when jurors assume that he must be responsible somehow for his being on trial. Stereotypes of gangs fit into this logic since they classify a gang member as outside the moral order. Stereotypes filter out all the "discrepant" information that might paint a more nuanced picture of a gang defendant. They also inhibit any questioning of the accuracy, motives, or even legitimacy of those enforcing the law, like police and prosecutors. Within the logic that we are naturally drawn to, the representatives of the law are more like natural forces of order than they are fallible humans like the rest of us. For jurors with a firm belief in a just world, stereotypes reinforce the belief that the trial is a battle of good versus evil. Boiled down to essentials, the prosecutor is the people's protector, who in effect tells the jury the defendant is an "evil" wolf trying to eat them up. In the psychology of the courtroom, as Benjamin Fleury-Steiner (2004) says, the jury and prosecutor represent "us" and the defendant "them."

But it isn't really all that simple. For many of us, the logic of a just world holds true to our experiences and our sense of the world. This was the case for me throughout the early years of my life. However, as we gain new experiences it sometimes becomes impossible to believe in a just world. The Black Lives Matter movement has exposed persistent and lethal racism within police departments across the country, as I write with the horrifying images of the murder of George Floyd fresh in our nation's collective eyes. The New York Times reports that since 2015, five Black people have been killed by police each week. In 2019, police killed 1,004 people, and police have killed at least a thousand people a year for the past decade. According to Paul Butler (2017a), young Black males were twenty-one times more likely to be killed by police than their white counterparts. Of Black men born in 2001, Butler reports, one in three will serve time. For decades, more than a hundred young Black men were tortured by Chicago Police Department lieutenant commander Jon Burge, who would later be convicted of covering up for the torture but was never prosecuted for the torture itself. Few police officers are successfully prosecuted for shooting unarmed Black men. Since 2005, American police have killed more than 15,000 people but fewer than 150 officers have been charged with murder.

While more than 2.2 million people are behind bars today and 4.5 million under some sort of supervision, disproportionate arrests and incarceration continue to plague the justice system, While African Americans make up about 10 percent of the U.S. population, they are more than half of those serving time in state prison, according to Craig Haney (2006) in his comprehensive history of the pain of incarceration. Innocence projects, like

Bryan Stevenson's Equal Justice Initiative and Steve Drizin's and Rob Warden's Northwestern Universitys Center on Wrongful Conviction have uncovered horrid injustices and won exonerations for the wrongfully convicted. According to the National Registry of Exonerations, nearly half of more than nineteen hundred defendants wrongfully convicted and later exonerated are African American.

While none of the cases in which I served as an expert witness were eligible for exoneration, that doesn't mean racism was not at work. In most of my cases, a gang member faced either the death penalty or a sentence of natural life or its equivalent, even for crimes for which another person may have received a much lighter sentence. These young men will be locked up until they are elderly or die in prison no matter how much they have reformed. Even I was shocked to learn that in the United States, according to the Sentencing Project, one out of every five incarcerated African Americans are serving the equivalent of life sentences. Nearly half of all those in prison serving life sentences are Black. Clearly, the justice system is not treating Black defendants with the same consequences as white defendants.

Reading statistics like these, as evidence piles up piece by piece to support a simple-to-understand but difficult-to-confront story, may gradually erode your belief in the basic fairness of our justice system. They may push you to rethink stereotypes of gang members as "animals," or worse, who deserve to be caged. Mary K. Rothbart (1981) calls this slow evidence-based method of how we can gradually change our stereotypes, "the bookkeeping method." Much of the focus on people's radicalization through YouTube and social media works in this way: an accumulation of posted facts, images, and videos gradually causes someone to "tilt" his or her beliefs from conventional ones to a new belief system. It is the implicit method of this book, to pile up one case after another pointing out the outrageous use of stereotypes and sensational lies by prosecutors to convince you that dehumanizing rhetoric needs to be restrained in court. It is how lawyers work in criminal trials, where the "weight" of the evidence persuades jurors "beyond a reasonable doubt." Or not.

My testimony in court cases often follows the bookkeeping method, using research to dispel specific stereotypes, as with Milledgeville's bogus "gang-related" murder. In Chester Niven's case, I subtyped, a second method of persuasion cited by Rothbart. The subtype method concedes the stereotype might be true for some but doesn't apply in this case. Both methods aim to get the jury to "reframe" the story told by prosecutors to a narrative that doesn't have an evil gangster big bad wolf at its center. Neither method is very effective in homicide trials with the deceased's family looking on and the prosecutor demonizing the defendant, drowning out reason and new information with emotional pleas that match a preexisting logic or story.

I realize when I speak of how a juror's mind might be resistant to new information or trapped by stereotypes, I may sound like I'm drawing a line between them and myself. This is not true; human minds follow the same strategies for taking in or resisting new information, and American culture inundates us all with the same biases. I think back to how I was brought up immersed in racial and bigoted stereotypes. I can understand white racism well since I recognize it in my own upbringing. Some of these racial stereotypes and my own belief in a just world were shattered by a police billy club on a church parking lot long ago. These events literally propelled me to my lifelong commitment to social justice. My change was an example of Rothbart's final technique, conversion, what Fiske and Taylor (1980, 152) describe as "resisting small changes but can change massively and suddenly, given sufficient disconfirmation." Our nation may be experiencing such a "conversion" now on race after George Floyd's murder provided a glimpse for white people into the trauma wreaked on devalued Black lives. I trace my commitment to my work in court back to my decision to attend my first civil rights march in August 1967.

While I was growing up, racism was pervasive and unconscious. I learned casually racist and anti-Semitic rhymes, homophobia, and traditional masculinity as part of white adolescent culture. But please note: I didn't run with some extremist group or white supremacist subculture. These attitudes were "normal" as I grew up. It's how I was socialized to see the other.

In Clintonville, population forty-seven hundred, my white peers did not acknowledge Black people and especially Native Americans from the nearby Menominee Reservation as sharing the same respectable standards as "us" white people. For the record, Clintonville at the time had no Black residents. I wasn't aware of any Native American residents in my hometown, and I believe Clintonville had only one Jewish family. Into my teenage years, I had no idea of what it meant to be gay. My friends and I accepted stereotypes and spread them. I don't remember anyone, from our schools or churches, who had ever taught us otherwise or expressed disapproval.

Rather than go to University of Wisconsin–Madison after I graduated high school like other "brains" in our class, I wanted to go back "home" to the city of my birth and enrolled in the University of Wisconsin–Milwaukee. For small-town kids going to college, especially baby boomers like me, the cosmopolitan atmosphere on campus eroded many of our narrow-minded stereotypes. Like most students, when I began college in 1965, my process of change resembled the bookkeeping method, where continued exposure to new information over time caused me to recalibrate my idea of normal. I read about the civil rights movement and the war in Vietnam and had heated discussions with fellow students. My attitudes were slowly changing. Lerner (1980, 50) says faced with injustice, some will side with the oppressed, and that is where I was incrementally headed. My underlying faith that the world operated the way it should and that people got what they deserved was becoming less certain. I was just another sixties college student, being slowly drawn into the culture and practice of protest. But my first step into that world would cause a seismic shift in my faith in justice and fairness. Bookkeeping is one method of changing a mind—but there are more rapid ways to experience change.

In the summer of 1967, a white priest, Father James Groppi, called for demonstrations demanding the city of Milwaukee pass an "open housing law" to allow Black people to live anywhere they could afford. That seemed "right" to me. Residential redlining was still legal at the time. I decided to go to the first "open housing" march, but I was nervous. I had never been to St. Boniface where Groppi was priest. The Catholic Church was in what I thought of as "the ghetto," and I remember being cautious, yes, a bit scared, as I parked my car and entered the church. The streets were alive but the only white people I saw were a handful of protesters walking into St. Boniface. The first thing I noticed as I walked into the church was that all the stained-glass images of Jesus had been painted black. To my own lily-white Lutheran background, that seemed daring, bordering on blasphemous. But then, why should Jesus be white? My racial stereotypes were being given the shock treatment and crumbling.

That day, August 28, 1967, the march left St. Boniface and ventured about ten miles to the nearly all-white south side of Milwaukee where we were greeted by jeering racist crowds. Groppi's plan was to replicate Dr. King's marches of the year before in Chicago into Cicero and Marquette Park where mob violence exposed publicly the reality that racism didn't just live in the south. King intuitively grasped the power of the conversion technique to destroy stereotypes. Similarly, Groppi led us to Kosciusko Park where police estimated 13,000 angry white people were gathered. They held racist signs and threw garbage and worse at the 150 or so marchers, at most a quarter of us white. At one point I heard a cry, "There he is! Get Groppi!" from the mob, and I turned around and to my shock Father Groppi was standing right next to me. Joe McClain, one of the march security team told me, "lock arms," and we held back the charge. The struggle for justice in an unjust reality wasn't a world of words anymore. My body was on the line. And it would get worse.

In response to the white riot against the march, the mayor banned the marchers, not the rioters. We marched anyway, and I was arrested for the first time in my life. I spent an eventful night in jail, but the next day, flush with youthful rebellion, I was ready to march again. That next night turned violent. Police arrested the leaders of the march the moment we left St. Boniface and used considerable force. They smashed network TV cameras that were there to cover the marches in the city the national press had dubbed the "Selma of the North." I retreated onto the church parking lot, relieved that it appeared I wouldn't be arrested again. But without warning, police charged. One officer lunged at me, and I can still recall his billy club coming down and hitting me in the forehead. As I fell, I watched my broken glasses fly off in slow motion in two directions. Police were all over me, hitting me with batons. I covered my head with my hands as a billy club kept trying to bash my skull. One officer couldn't find any open spot to hit me, and I remember him smashing his club on the bottom of my foot. Throw the bookkeeping method of persuasion out! My views on a just world were undergoing "sudden and massive change." But this night of terror was just getting started.

After an exchange of angry words with Milwaukee's notoriously racist judge, Christ T. Seraphim, I was sent to the hospital. My hand was clearly broken but the lab techs said I was fine. On the way back to the jailhouse, I rode in a paddy wagon with another marcher—a young Black man whose name I never learned—and six police officers. We sat silently and something didn't seem right as I watched the nervous eyes of our guards. When the van arrived in the basement garage below the county jail, on cue the six cops jumped up and assaulted us. My newfound buddy stood up to them and was pummeled mercilessly. I rolled under the paddy wagon benches to keep from being directly struck. I then slid out of the van and immediately rolled under it, minimizing the damage of swinging billy clubs. I watched as my Black coprisoner was beaten across the basement floor. The officers lifted and sat him, butt down, in a large trash can where they hit him again and again.

Finally, someone said, "Enough, let's get them into a cell." As we waited for the elevator, my buddy was physically shaking from his brutal beating. I took my good arm, the one attached to a hand that was not broken and placed it across his chest to stop his shaking. One cop pulled out his gun and said, "Get your hand away from that n---- kid or I'm going to shoot you." I underwent a conversion. Law wasn't justice; it was power. It wasn't color blind; it was racist.

Those nights still live and pulse in my mind. They've stayed with me as fresh as ever like any recurring trauma. At the end of a police billy club, I arrived at an "injustice frame" that turned my just world theory on its head. I joined into the civil rights movement full throttle. Those nights in August propelled me to a lifetime of activism, sealing my dedication to confronting an unjust world. But, by design, most people who serve on juries do not so intensely experience such an interruption to their faith in a just world. These experiences have been hidden until now, with the advent of cell phone video and media. In-court conversion, Perry Mason style, is more for television and the movies than real courtrooms.

Conversion itself, I've recognized over time, also brings a cost for so much passion and clarity. The shattering of the idea of a just world leads to a struggle for justice but also can mean replacing one demon with another. When I insist on understanding information that doesn't fit with stereotypes about gangs, I don't want to create a new overly simplistic story that undermines the understanding of other human beings, like victims' families. We run the danger of stripping individuality from police, judges, or prosecutors, dehumanizing them and reducing them to stereotypes, inhibiting successful tactics. Confronting injustice and evil acts without demonizing your opponent runs against our psychological grain. To better understand this problem, and the nature of my work in court, we need to understand how stereotypes are turned into a story of good versus evil. Let's turn to the concept of frames.

4

Frames and Facts

Contesting the Gang Frame

Let me tell you a story about the day the Gangster Disciples invaded Mahnomen, Minnesota, population 1202 (see Fig. 4.1).

In 2000, Peter Cannon, a small-town lawyer from rural Minnesota, had been phoning around the country trying to find a "gang expert" that could help him make sense of what he thought was a bogus murder charge for his client, Timothy Shanks. He finally reached eminent gang researcher Irving Spergel from Chicago who said he didn't do expert witness work but suggested Cannon get a hold of me. There has been considerable reluctance among academic gang researchers, who receive much of their research funds from law enforcement, to take expert witness cases for the defense. Back then, it was very rare, and Irv knew I was skeptical of many law enforcement claims about gangs, so maybe I'd take the case.

A local crop farmer, Cornelius Rodgers, had been found murdered in a drainage ditch. The culprits, Anthony Eley and Elizer Darris, were quickly arrested. Incredible as it sounds for a small town in northern Minnesota, police alleged that they and other locals were members of a Mahnomen chapter of the Gangster Disciple Nation. Eley, Darris, and their companions copped pleas and agreed to testify to get reduced charges. They claimed the murders were done on the orders of the gang "Pharaoh," Timothy Shanks, a former resident of Gary, Indiana. It appeared that Rodgers, the soon-to-be-victim, had failed to pay for a beer at a party, and Shanks ordered him to be punished.

The Minnesota attorney general's office, however, saw the murder as much more than a deadly beer-related spat. To them this was no less than the first

Figure 4.1 Did Gangster Disciples really target Mahnomen, MN? (© 2021 Google, INEGI.)

example of violence by the Chicago-based Gangster Disciples in their state. They were less interested in Shanks's story than in a broader story they already feared, unsupported by fact, that gangs were expanding like a military force to occupy unclaimed territory in their home state. They were determined to stop the cancer of Chicago gangs from metastasizing to Minnesota and dispatched a team of assistant attorneys general to prosecute the case. They brought their own police "gang expert" from the Minnesota Gang Strike Task Force, Sergeant James Rugel, who informed the court that the Gangster Disciples were "moving into Minnesota cities" and were a "well organized, paramilitary" organization. On cue, codefendants Eley and Darris spun a tale to police that the murder of Rodgers was part of a gang initiation organized by Shanks for the Gangster Disciples, who were branching out from their Chicago roots into the hinterlands of Minnesota.

Shanks's court-appointed attorney, Peter Cannon, was called into the judge's chambers and informally advised to roll over. The judge and Peter were old friends, and the judge pointed out the obvious: a case of a Black gang member ordering the murder of a white local in a predominantly Scandinavian town, prosecuted directly by high-powered Minnesota assistant attorneys general, had an inevitable outcome. The judge privately advised Peter to have Shanks cop a plea like the others. Instead, Cannon, without any actual knowledge of gangs, thought something smelled rotten in Mahnomen. The facts as he saw them didn't fit the state's conspiratorial story line.

Mahnomen is an isolated village 235 miles north of Minneapolis, and the court had limited funds to provide for an expert witness and none to bring me to northern Minnesota. I doubt they ever had an expert witness testify in a case there. Cannon sent me transcripts of the police interviews of all the defendants and the indictment. Cannon arranged for a phone call where I could ask Shanks, who was in the local jail, about his gang ties and the supposed "gang-related" nature of this crime.

I quickly discovered that there were no facts to the case against Timothy Shanks, just a bunch of stereotypes that fit into the state's implausible fear of invading Chicago gangs. To me, it seemed ridiculous on its face that the Gangster Disciples would descend on tiny Mahnomen, Minnesota. The gang migration angle was ostensibly derived from several defendants who got immunity or vastly reduced charges for their implication of Shanks as the gang's Pharaoh. I suspected they were coached by Sergeant Rugel. How could such a story be proven beyond reasonable doubt? Perhaps because it invoked frames that bypassed investigators' doubts by confirming their fears. We would have to break them out of the frame, or at least show how poor a fit the story was to the gang frame.

Peter Cannon was right: the story didn't add up. The first clue that the so-called Gangster Disciple members didn't know what they were talking about was their claim that Timothy was the Pharaoh of the gang. There is no such rank in the actual Gangster Disciples, though their rival, the Black Disciples, have a title of that name. When Jeremy Langer, a seventeen-year-old local white kid, who received a plea deal in exchange for his testimony against Shanks, was asked who the top leader of the Gangster Disciples was, he said "King Hoover David or something like that." Another defendant-turned-witness was stumped when asked the significance of the number "six" to the gang he claimed to have insider knowledge of for the purposes of the trial. Almost anyone with even a passing idea of the Gangster Disciples knows that the Larry Hoover–led "Folks" gangs, including the Gangster Disciples, are represented by a six-pointed star in opposition to the five-pointed star of "People" gangs like the Vice Lords. David Barksdale was the founder of the rival Black Disciples. A formal chapter of a gang always has extensive written literature and demands mandatory memorization of various laws and prayers. This was no chapter.

What was going on? I discovered a more mundane story. Timothy Shanks was one of a group of African American itinerant laborers attached to a carnival traveling through northern Minnesota. Timothy had a faded six-pointed star tattoo on his arm from when he was growing up in Gary. He called himself an

"OG," which he tried to explain to police meant he was like an older brother to his younger coworkers. In the Scandinavian towns they toured with the carnival, Timothy and the other Black workers naturally came together as a social group, and they reveled in the tough-guy image of Chicago gang members—especially in order to appear more dangerous, masculine, and impressive to locals who would not know any better or be able to call them out.

What about the ordered hit? Asked by Anthony Eley what should be done about Cornelius Rodgers not paying for a beer, Timothy Shanks, among a coterie of teenage girls and boys at his side, huffed, "Do what you gotta do." That was it. No gang meetings were ever held, and no one reported Shanks giving any "order" other than tough guy words, "do what you gotta do." Eley and Darris were under no formal or organizational pressure in their errand to ask for beer money, certainly not to kill. No one seemed to have even rudimentary knowledge of the Gangster Disciples or their structure. The story I told was an old-fashioned tale of immature boys impressing girls and posing as cool tough guys to other males.

The entire fantasy of an invasion of Minnesota by the Gangster Disciples was a local version of a national scare story at the time by law enforcement. Police "gang experts" were claiming Chicago and Los Angeles gangs were trying to take over the entire United States to sell drugs and spread terror. In Mahnomen, this national story was crudely superimposed on a homicide that resulted from displays of masculinity, lots of beer, and a trivial disagreement over payment for a drink. The trial became a clash of two stories, or frames. The masculinity-based story conforms with a frame people recognize, one based in actual social behavior that most of us have observed firsthand. Luckily, these characteristics made my frame, what seemed to me the real story, persuasive.

In my testimony over the phone and in writing, I told a familiar story of men drinking heavily, showing off for girls, complicated by a volatile component of race and expectations. I argued the homicide was a tragic result of a drunken dispute gone wrong and had almost nothing to do with gangs or Timothy Shanks. I ridiculed the gang angle by zeroing in on the words of one codefendant. He told the court he knew Timothy was a "Folks" gang member because he often said to other workers, "You folks can take a break now." Timothy, he swore, often greeted coworkers by saying: "What's up, folks!" That common phrase and Timothy's faded tattoo from his hometown were the only evidence of a Gangster Disciple "invasion."

I testified that if "What's up, folks" qualified Timothy Shanks to be a gang member, then Porky Pig and his Looney Tunes gang should also be indicted for saying, "That's all, Folks!" At that point, the judge called all the lawyers to the bench, and everyone agreed to drop all the charges against Shanks. Peter Cannon dug into his pocket and gave Timothy bus fare to get back to Gary. The victory was complete when, on appeal, the Minnesota Supreme Court dropped first-degree murder charges against Elizer Darris, which had been based on the homicide being carried out on gang orders. The court concluded that the group's naive rendition of the Gangster Disciples "did not meet the statutory definition of a gang."

I hesitate to use this story because it is the exception. It is the only case I've been a part of where the client was completely innocent, and justice prevailed. It's as close as I ever got to Bryan Stevenson's ennobling victories or to a conversion experience in court. At the time, I had not begun my study of the literature on stereotypes or framing. I stumbled into "reframing" the police "gang invasion" tale by just retelling the story as Timothy Shanks told it to me. An age-old tale of masculinity, race, sex, and drinking, which leads to violence. My frame of what happened was simply more believable than Sergeant Rugel's story of Chicago gangs invading Mahnomen, Minnesota, not least because it was one that observers, even nonexperts, recognized. And Peter Cannon was a heroic, dedicated lawyer who did not give up.

This case also demonstrates all prosecutors aren't like Milledgeville's Fred Bright. Some can be convinced by reason and research, when a gang story is recast into common sense, one that explains, eliminates, or minimizes the gang angle. In Johnnie Norman's case in similarly sized Camptown, Alabama, in the face of a powerful story of a mentally challenged, confused young man, prosecutors had agreed to drop the death penalty and allow the possibility of parole. In Mahnomen, the case went so far as to go to trial. Unlike the hostile treatment by prosecutors I typically get when I testify, the Minnesota assistant attorneys general were respectful to me on the stand. They had read my first book, *People and Folks*, and gave my arguments credence. These assistant attorneys general held a belief in "doing justice" higher than winning the case and, when their case fell apart, had the grace and good sense to drop charges. On the other hand, the initial framing of a local dispute as a gang-related homicide and sending in assistant attorneys general to prosecute is a striking example of the power of frames and how they thrive on their own set of facts. The lesson is that all prosecutors are not stereotype-spouting demonizers, and their use of frames may not always be intentionally misleading so much as built on the same common misconceptions that plague juries and even defense attorneys.

"It is possible for a stereotype to grow in defiance of all evidence," psychologist Gordon Allport wrote (1954, 189), "developing where no real correlations exist." Thus the gang frame can flourish in courtrooms ipse dixit, just because a police gang expert or prosecutor suggests it.

Frames and Facts

What exactly is a frame? One simple way to look at it is as a picture frame, which focuses our attention on what is inside the frame and disregards what is outside. Another way to understand it is as a scaffold, a frame that holds up an entire building or argument. For my purposes, frames are stereotypes that are compiled together with assorted facts as stories, or as Leyens, Yzerbyt, and Schadron say (1994, 204), as "naïve explanations of the world."

The story that begins this chapter presents a gang frame of the Gangster Disciples invading Minnesota. To accept this frame lends meaning to actions that, in the words of Erving Goffman, are "rendering what would otherwise be a meaningless aspect of the scene into something that is meaningful" (1974, 21). In the tiny town of Mahnomen, an "invading gang frame" transformed what was a simple dispute over an unpaid-for drink into a gang-related murder. This is what the APRI manual means by how police gang experts can "explain the inexplicable." Police experts put the evidence given in a trial inside a "gang frame," which both makes sense to and frightens a jury.

Anyone living in the United States today has no trouble understanding frames. Our political discourse has been reduced to little more than clashing frames: "immigrants are criminals and rapists" versus "we are a nation of immigrants." Each frame marshals its own set of associations or examples. The MS-13 gang member who chops up his victims versus the immigrant DACA "dreamer" who graduated from college. Channel flip between Fox News and MSNBC, and the facts reported on each network come from seemingly different universes.

Former president Donald Trump understands frames. He demonstrated his understanding in his tweets. Here is one from July 19, 2019, about the Mueller Report: "NO COLLUSION, NO OBSTRUCTION, TOTAL EXONERATION. DEMOCRATIC WITCH HUNT!" He frames his base's response within what he would have them believe is the essence of the issue, telling his followers only what he wants them to understand as important. The Democrats didn't really have a counterframe that made sense of Mueller's conclusion in light of what Trump's base believed was at work in the investigation. What could they say, "COLLUSION, OBSTRUCTION, GUILTY, HONEST INVESTIGATION?" They tried to counter with facts. They scrutinized the 448-page report to find examples of collusion, obstruction, or corruption in vain hopes to find facts that would convince the public of Trump's corrupt intent. Without a frame to relate it to what their audience expected and recognized, investigators pointing out facts and examples did not carry meaning. Trump and his base didn't care. The frame or the story was set, and he repeated and retweeted it again and again. Trump's "witch hunt" frame cast his impeachment as an abuse of power. Senator Chris Murphy (2020) sums up Trump's first impeachment trial in terms of frames:

> That dichotomy, that contrast, has been growing over the last three years, but this trial really crystallized that difference. We were just speaking different languages, fundamentally different languages when it came to what this trial was about. They thought it was about the deep state and the media conspiracy. We thought it was about the president's crimes.

Use of frames is not limited to the powerful. During Trump's administration, a long-simmering conflict in how people understand tragically common events burst to the forefront of the national consciousness: race and inequality in policing. The powerful protest movement after George Floyd's death marshaled two conflicting frames: police brutality versus law and order. Systemic racism versus a few bad apples. As we see throughout this book, hard frames aren't easily dented by facts. Supporters seldom hunt for what is called "discrepant information"—facts that don't fit within their chosen frame. Once a frame or story is set, all the facts get interpreted by the frame. The ones that don't fit get discarded. It's not that either side is lying, it's that they are only selecting the facts that fit their frame.

Framing is a central concept in many literatures, including sociology (Goffman 1974), communications (Entman 1993), linguistics (Lakoff 1987), and social movements (Snow et al.; Benford 1997). For our purposes, this definition fits best: a frame provides "a central organizing idea or story line that provides meaning to an unfolding strip of events, weaving a connection among them. The frames suggest what the controversy is about, the essence of the issue" (Gamson and Modigliani 1994, 376). For example, Trump's "WITCH HUNT" tweets told his fans what is meaningful about impeachment and, in effect, don't bother with the details.

Likewise, contested politics over immigration boils down to a difference of frames rather than any particular issue or question. The "immigrant as violent, rapist gang member" frame is about threats to our physical safety and identity as homogeneous white "Americans." The essence of the "nation of immigrants" frame is about racial tolerance and cultural heterogeneity. Each side uses "confirmation bias" to select and emphasize facts that support their "frame" or beliefs. Most people's social media feeds are the epitome of confirmation bias.

A frame weaves together facts and stereotypes into a story that resonates with an audience, like voters . . . or a jury. Lakoff (2004, 17) explains that thinking in frames is how the brain works:

Neuroscience tells us that each of the concepts we have—the long term concepts that structure how we think—is instantiated in the synapses of our brains. Concepts are not things that can be changed just by telling someone a fact. We may be presented with facts, but for us to make sense of them they have to fit what is already in the synapses of the brain. Otherwise facts go in and then they go right back out.

The frames are the existing concepts we hold that we use to decide whether new information is meaningful to us. Therefore, when we present facts that we want our audience to account for, we need to try to fit them into an existing concept that is already built into the structure of our thoughts.

The Mahnomen story of migrating gangs was a common myth within law enforcement and initially frightened the Minnesota attorney general's office and caused them to take charge of the prosecution. The frame of gang migration as an imminent threat was firmly embedded in the way some law enforcement officials at the time thought. On my part, I countered with a slew of facts, but facts that also fit court officials preexisting understanding of how people behave. Cheryl Maxson (1996) had conducted research on behalf of the U.S. Department of Justice that disputed the attorneys general's conspiratorial, imperialist theory of gang migration. She found gang members' families mostly fled to new environments for economic reasons or from fear of gang violence in their original home. My own research also directly investigated the allegation that Milwaukee gangs came from Chicago. While there were a handful of migrating gang members and, certainly, some Chicago influence, *People and Folks* (Hagedorn 1988) found the origins of Milwaukee gangs could be found in the poverty and racist conditions of Milwaukee itself.

Gangs in cities like Milwaukee or Minneapolis were often called a virus, spreading out from Chicago or Los Angeles and infecting local youths. In my first book, I interviewed a Gangster Disciple and asked him about the virus metaphor. "No" he said. "Gangs ain't like no virus, jumping from city to city." My research backs up his assertion. But gangs as contagious diseases persist as a frame to explain how gangs diffuse from area to area.

But on reflection, my story of carny workers, masculinity, and drink, buttressed by academic research, cast more reasonable doubt on Sergeant Rugel's far-fetched gang invasion tale to a fair-minded judge than any one fact or assertion from all my research. What I've learned over the years is that while the facts matter, it is the stories or frames that matter more. Lakoff could have been talking about courts when he wrote in his book *Don't Think of an Elephant* (2004, 73):

It is a common folk theory of progressives that "the facts will set you free." If only you can get all the facts out then every rational person will reach the right conclusion. It is a vain hope. Human brains just don't work that way. Framing matters. Frames once entrenched are hard to dispel.

In court, one of the most difficult tasks for lawyers is to dispel the gang frame. We've seen that the mere mention that the defendant is a gang member means he is more likely to be convicted. Frames tell the audience what the story is all about. In any story, Lakoff explains, "there is a hero, a crime, a victim, and a villain" (2004, 71). The prosecutor embeds his case in a *story*. Gerry Spence, in his book on how to win a court case, calls the use of a *story* "the strongest structure for any argument" (2005, 113). The stories we've been told since childhood, buried not too deeply in our own subconscious, employ this basic structure where there is some big bad wolf or villain trying to eat us up, because, well, he is a big bad wolf. Lakoff (2004, 57) says, "Evil people do evil things. No further explanation is necessary." Because the story starts with a gang villain, a big bad wolf surrogate, the fact that he must be guilty of this crime or another evil deed follows from his character. As referred to earlier, this is called the fundamental attribution error. It was what convicted Arthur Dent in my Introduction, and I explore it in more depth later.

Former attorney general Eric Holder's Department of Justice manual on gang prosecution gives ample support for the gang frame (my italics):

> Unquestionably, the purpose of the law in making it an offense to [agree to commit a crime as a group] is to reach everyone who has participated in forming the evil plan irrespective of who or how many carry out the design, and well may this be a protection to society, *for a group of evil minds* planning and giving support to the commission of crime is more likely to be a menace to society than where one individual alone sets out to violate the law. (Originally from People v. Lupparello 1986)

Gangs as "evil minds" capable of greater destruction in concert than as any one person is one aspect of the gang frame. In Mahnomen, the evil minds of "King David Hoover or something like that" and his Gangster Disciples plotted an invasion of northern Minnesota. A frame, Castells (2009, 142) says, leaves "gaps in the information that the audience fills in with their preconceived schemas." Our folk wisdom of gangs as a collection of "evil minds" fills in the gaps in the prosecution's story of a crime. Thus an "inexplicable" motive can be easily explained, and we believe the absurd idea that the Gangster Disciples are marching on Mahnomen, Minnesota.

Another way to illustrate frames is to step on some politically correct toes. Trials are contests of frames, with each side picking out facts that support their story of the crime. What matters in a trial is the frame, convincing a jury or judge of your "theory" of events. The best story wins. I have testified in multiple Juvenile Life without Parole (JLWOP) resentencings. These are cases where a juvenile was originally mandatorily sentenced to life without parole, typically for a double homicide. In 2012, the Supreme Court's *Miller* decision ruled that such mandatory life sentences were cruel and unusual punishment and that courts at sentencing needed to recognize the immaturity of the juvenile brain and take into account the capacity of youths to change. The law previously had allowed prosecutors to frame such juvenile killers as evil, incorrigible monsters, so lock them up and throw away the key. The *Miller* decision reframed adolescents as having immature brains that encouraged reckless acts and noted that youths were likely to mature. Thus, they could be expected to lead a conventional life and should be given the possibility of release. Only "the rare juvenile offender whose crime reflects irreparable corruption," *Miller* found, should be sentenced to life without parole. In Illinois, more than a hundred youthful killers had been mandatorily sentenced to life without parole and had to be resentenced.

The first to be resentenced in Illinois was Adolpho Davis, a former Gangster Disciple who had killed two people in a drug dispute when he was sixteen. Adolpho was seen as the best candidate to be a model for resentencing, since he had reformed his life and demonstrated how a former gang member can change. The plan backfired when prosecutors said Davis had not left the Gangster Disciples in prison, which, they argued, meant he hadn't changed at all. An angry judge bought their story and resentenced Davis to life without parole again, claiming his gang affiliation in prison meant he was one of the "incorrigibly depraved." Attorneys representing JLWOP clients who had all maintained gang ties in prison for safety reasons suddenly desperately needed a gang expert to reframe what it meant for a young man in prison to maintain gang membership or, more tellingly, what it would mean to try to renounce your gang while jailed next to fellow members. Jaime Ruiz's story gives insight into the difficulty of undermining a frame with facts. My testimony took place at the same time as the Senate hearings on the confirmation of nominee Brett Kavanaugh for the U.S. Supreme Court. The disturbing lesson from both: frames rule.

I was exhausted from seven hours of court the day before. My arm was still in a sling supporting a broken clavicle from yet another bike accident. I had used up all the adrenaline I had waiting five hours in a Chicago court and then enduring two intense, combative hours on the witness stand. I was laying prone on the couch in front of the TV, watching the Kavanaugh hearings with half-open eyes and a dulled brain.

The stakes for Kavanaugh were a seat on the Supreme Court or a continued career as a powerful circuit court judge but for Jaime Ruiz, in the balance was natural life in prison versus an eventual release. He was a member of the Latin Kings and had killed two people in separate incidents as a teenager. At Jaime's original sentencing, in 1999, the assistant state's attorney (ASA) said a sixteen-year-old Mr. Ruiz should "never even be considered for early release" because "he is much too dangerous." The state's story or frame of evil gang minds had not changed since then. At his resentencing, nineteen years later, a new ASA was insisting Jaime was not just a gang member but a gang leader. No fewer than four "Confidential Informants" told gang intelligence officials in the Illinois Department of Corrections (IDOC) that Jaime was on the Crown Council, a secret leadership body of the Latin Kings. He was a candidate, they implied, to be included among the subset of juveniles Miller had referred to who were so incorrigible they deserved to have their young age at the time of their crimes discounted.

Jaime was a rough character and had a hard time trusting his lawyers—or anyone else. He appeared to sabotage his case by getting into a brutal fight in Cook County Jail while awaiting resentencing. His pro bono lawyers were very sharp and dedicated but had a hard time figuring him out, and the fight gave them second thoughts about his character. I met with Jaime three different times, in part to pin down his shifting stories but mainly to try to see his life and gang experience in prison from his eyes. Like all the gang members in prison I had interviewed, he maintained ties with his gang, which provided security in an environment permeated by rival gangs. On the other hand, he desperately wanted to be released and live a free, conventional life. The two aspects of his young life were in contradiction.

The frames contest at Jaime's sentencing was similar to that at the trial of Adolpho Davis. In this case, prosecutors argued, "once a King always a King." The announcement that the state had snitches saying Jaime was in gang leadership was intended to prove to the judge that Jaime was hard core and would never change. The fight in the jail also proved his incorrigibility. My counterframe was much weaker: Jaime was a flawed human being, doing what he could to distance himself from the gang in prison while maintaining gang membership for protection. My frame required the judge to see Jaime not as a stereotype—a "gang member"—but as a human being. I had to rely on facts, discrepant pieces of information, to undermine the ASA's powerful gang frame.

I had plenty of facts to build a scaffold to reframe the debate. The high-ranking Latin Kings I knew pointed out that rank-and-file gang members in prison would not be told who sat on a highly secret Crown Council. That four snitches would "know" Jaime was on this secret leadership body was implausible. The ASA lacked facts to support the contention that Jaime was a hard-core gang member. Jaime had no disciplinary tickets for more than a decade, since his first years in prison; no confiscations of gang literature; no incidents of participation in gang fights—Latin Kings are mandated by their constitution to "aid and assist" a fellow King in distress. There were uncounted fights of this nature in the two decades of Jaime's prison life, but Jaime was not involved or ticketed in any of them.

The ASA thought he had a "gotcha" moment when I testified Cook County Jail guards said that the fight he had recently been in was not gang related but "over the telephone." For Jaime, keeping in touch with family was his lifeblood. At his hearing, dozens of family members waited hours to be given a chance to tell the judge that Jaime was a good person at heart. But in Cook County Jail, when a rival gang member who was the self-appointed guardian of the cell block telephone told Jaime he could not call his daughter, Jaime lost his cool. The fight wasn't pretty and was captured on cell house surveillance video. The ASA insisted it was a gang fight and demanded I show him where in the jail records it said it was a fight over the phone. With a flamboyant gesture he gave me a copy of the jail records or "State's Exhibit #1" and challenged me to show him the exact quote. One tip in testifying: always know your material and come prepared for surprises. I paged through the records, found the quote from a correctional officer, and said "here it is." The ASA looked, unbelieving and silent for all of an embarrassing thirty seconds. He had missed it. I did my best to suppress a smirk. I enjoyed his silent stare as he figured out what he should do next.

But unlike on television, court cases are not always won by gotcha moments: at least not when the lawyer being got has the stronger frame on his side. And this ASA knew it. His response was "but he is a Latin King, right?" He kept it up, asking me to confirm a set of mostly irrelevant facts about Jaime's record, ending each with, "he is a Latin King, right?" All he had left was the frame, but that is what was most important. Lakoff says a frame gathers strength with every repetition, and the ASA repeated it over and over. Being a gang member outweighed any facts I could present to show Jaime was keeping to the straight and narrow in prison, at least as much as possible.

The power of frames hit me again the next day in watching the Kavanaugh hearings. The Supreme Court nominee framed himself as a hard-working guy "who likes beer" but is straight as an arrow. And, by the way, very conservative. Since Republicans had the majority in the Senate, all they had to do was keep the votes of their own members, and they'd end up with another antiabortion vote on the Supreme Court. To testify, the Democrats called Dr. Christine Blasey Ford, who had accused Kavanaugh of attempting to rape her at a party thirty years before when they were both in high school. The Democrats, and much of the country, had been moved by the #MeToo movement, a public reckoning that exposed the nation's stark failure to recognize how widespread sexual harassment and assault has been in this country, and the ways victims are disempowered and doubted under the status quo. Both in the Senate chamber and for the TV-watching millions, Dr. Blasey Ford represented all women who had been harassed or not believed. And she made an incredibly persuasive witness. Women saw themselves in her story, in the #MeToo frame (New York Times 2018). Kavenaugh said:

> This whole two-week effort has been a calculated and orchestrated political hit fueled with apparent pent-up anger about President Trump and the 2016 election, fear that has been unfairly stoked about my judicial record. Revenge on behalf of the Clintons and millions of dollars in money from outside left-wing opposition groups. This is a circus.

Democrats were outraged at Kavanaugh's self-righteous outburst and found it beside the point of their objections. Republicans were delighted that Kavanaugh had put his finger on what for them was the actual reason anyone would object to his nomination. What was going on was a bare-knuckled frames contest, "#MeToo" versus a "Circus" of unjust liberal accusations. Democrats had tried in vain to get the Republican committee chair to allow other accusers to take the stand and for the FBI to conduct a more detailed investigation into the attempted rape allegations. As they would reaffirm two years later in the Mueller report and consequent impeachment trial, the Democrats wanted more "facts" so they could break the frame. I'm not sure more facts would have mattered.

The confirmation hearing would not be a trial, and the truth of the accusations against Kavanaugh could not be confirmed. In the absence of facts, the Democrats heavily relied on the #MeToo frame. In a widely reported incident during the hearings, Senator Jeff Flake (R-AZ) was confronted at an elevator in the Senate office building by two women who also had been victims of sexual abuse. One of them said Flake's "yes vote" would be "telling all women that they don't matter." A New York Times Op-Ed, "She Speaks for All of Us" (Yellin 2018), reinforced how deeply this frame resonated with many observing the confirmation hearings and how the hearings had taken on a meaning beyond what they could establish factually. The Democrats insisted that we should "believe women." In the absence of relevant facts, it was the frame that counted.

As I lay exhausted on the couch watching this dazzling display of contrasting frames, I remembered Jaime Ruiz's hearing the previous day and my attempts to break the gang frame by pointing out "discrepant information" or facts of Jaime's life that didn't fit, for instance, the reality of life in prison for gang members who need protection from rival gangs and cannot easily give up their gang identity. But being "on the count" or a nominal gang member is a far cry from active gang life. The standard course of gang membership for incarcerated teenagers like Jaime was active gang participation in their first years behind bars, then settling in and "distancing themselves" from the gang. This meant staying out of gang fights, getting involved with educational or charitable programming, and finding an outlet for their frustration, like art or religion. The *Miller* decision accurately predicted most serious youthful offenders, including teenage gang members, would undergo such a maturation process.

Ruiz, like Kavanaugh, was being weighed within a frame created by his behavior and associations as a teenager. Jaime's life circumstances led him to join a gang and his reckless behavior led to two homicides. In jail, even awaiting a chance for release, he exploded in a fight where he couldn't contain his anger over the possibility of losing contact with family, reinforcing the violent gang frame in the eyes of his accusers. For Kavanaugh, his teenage years were passed in a wild upper-class peer group that drank heavily. A credible witness claimed he tried to rape her one out-of-control night. Though such behavior would constitute a serious crime, as a privileged white student at a prestigious school with a well-connected family, he was never charged, and he may have completely forgotten the incident. When the allegations surfaced at his confirmation hearing, he exploded in anger at the damage to his reputation, demonstrating to some that his temperament hadn't changed, and he continued to fit the "frat boy" frame introduced by the accusation.

In the absence of evidence introduced to corroborate Dr. Blasey Ford's testimony, all the Democrats had was the #MeToo frame. This frame would lead them to ignore or leave out the vast literature on the unreliability of even confident eyewitness testimony, like Dr. Blasey Ford's. Justice Sotomayer in her dissent in *Perry v. New Hampshire* noted that over the past several decades more than two thousand studies had been published on eyewitness identification, which is the single greatest cause of wrongful convictions. Memory of events, including serious assaults, is often distorted. As for Kavanaugh, Nietzsche could have been talking about him when he wrote: "Memory says, 'I did that.' Pride replies, 'I could not have done that.' Eventually, memory yields."

Both Kavanaugh and Blasey Ford's accounts depend on memory. Harvard psychologist Daniel Schacter, in his book on memory, says even serious trauma can "induce us to engage in what psychologists call 'counterfactual thinking'—generating alternative scenarios of what might have been or should have been" (2001, 165). In the Steven Avery murder case, made famous by *Making a Murderer* on Netflix, Avery was exonerated of raping *Penny Beerntsen* even though she clearly and without a doubt identified him as her attacker. DNA evidence cleared him, and I personally heard Beernsten regret her absolute certainty that it was Avery who raped her, recalling that police had compiled suggestive lineups.

My own crystal clear memory of trauma from my civil rights marching days inclined me to believe Dr. Blasey Ford's recollections. While my sympathies were squarely behind her, neither side had enough facts to prove their case for an independent observer. For the senators of each party and in the perspectives of their supporters, it was only the frame that mattered.

What also struck me after two long days of hearings was the difference between the Brett and the Jaime frames contests. The #MeToo frame, while vanquished in the Senate vote, powerfully resonated with women across the country. Given the history of minimizing or ridiculing women's testimony, the call to "believe women" made the Senate's debate once again painful to many and recalled Anita Hill and countless personal examples. Still, no one on either side changed their mind in the Senate hearing. The two sides argued their respective frames for the TV cameras, the history books, and a polarized nation. We ended up with what we expected.

For Jaime, I did not have a powerful frame with which to contest the states' gang frame. Unlike in Mahnomen, I didn't have a story of masculinity, research, and race to contest a far-fetched Minneapolis "gang invasion" tale. In Jaime's case, I had an impressive set of facts that disputed the frame of the state that "Jaime is still a hard-core gang member." My only frame was from the Supreme Court's *Miller* decision, that youths' brains were immature and able to change, thus they shouldn't be locked up forever. The ASA who challenged me to find the sentence that said "the fight was over the phone" easily gave up contesting the facts and switched to relying only on the gang frame. I had to settle with the bookkeeping method of piling up facts and subtyping Jaime as a gang member who valued family, matured, and demonstrated he had changed from his irresponsible youth. The judge tried to bail out the bumbling ASA by taking over the questioning of me. He asked mainly about how gangs actually operate, if gang leaders didn't sometimes stay out of trouble and get their underlings to do the dirty work? His questions were trying to fit my discrepant information about the lack of a record of Jaime's gang activity into his stereotypes and thus keep the gang frame intact. As in nearly all of my JLWOP cases, "the youth's brain can change" frame was trumped by the gang frame.

As in the Kavanaugh hearings, I don't think any minds were changed in Jaime's resentencing. While the court decided he was not incorrigible, the judge gave him sixty years, at that time the maximum for juvenile homicide in Illinois. He won't be free until he is an old man. I wrote the lawyers in despair that all my efforts, in the end, meant nothing.

A good bit of my pessimism on my work in court is contained in this case. The state concocted evidence to allege Jaime was a hard-core gangster, but, as their evidence fell apart, they just relied on the gang frame, and the judge went along. In Mahnomen, I realized my success was due to not only ridiculing the state's facts but presenting a credible, down-to-earth story that was much more believable than the "gang invasion" fairy tale of Sergeant Rugel. The Minnesota prosecutors were much sharper and more open minded than the sorry ASA in Chicago.

In a trial or sentencing hearing, the bookkeeping method of contesting stereotypes is sometimes all we have, but it doesn't work very well. The time is too short to change deeply embedded stories reflecting our internalized folktales of the big bad wolf threatening to devour little red riding hood. Lakoff's point is that if you get your opponent, or a judge, to accept your frame, your arguments become common sense, available to your brain through its preferred, System 1 fast thinking. If you don't, the old stereotypes rule and you lose. The court's acceptance of the gang frame meant Jaime will spend the vast majority of his life behind bars.

Now that I have retired from teaching, this book has prompted me to go back over my life and think about how my own stereotypes were formed and challenged through the years. The nature of any social movement is to stereotype and even dehumanize your opponent in order to encourage solidarity on your side. I was a dedicated activist and learned how to build solidarity by uniformly framing the opposition as monsters. Over the years, however, some cracks appeared in my "us vs. them" frame.

CASE LAW

Perry v. New Hampshire, 565 U.S. 228, 262–263 (2012).
State of Minnesota, Respondent, v. Elizer Eugene Darris, Appellant, S. Ct. Minn., No. C8-01-1587, July 25, 2002.

5

Cracks in the Frame

Subtyping and Stereotypes—
A Personal Story

F raming is a useful persuasion strategy in many areas of life. As I've looked back over my own life of activism and court advocacy, I've come to realize that social movements utilize framing in ways that are similar to how prosecutors use them. Both depend on framing an opponent in ways that highlight evils and minimize differences within the category being invoked. Both depend on stereotyping that can be useful in some circumstances but can cloud over reasonable thinking.

With regard to social movements, the concept of framing solves an old problem in understanding how people can be persuaded to rise in protest. In early studies of protesters, scholars theorized that participants in social movements were suffering from psychological maladies. The strains of society, they supposed, caused a kind of mental illness that prompted anger and rebellion. Authoritarians still call some activists "lunatics" and lock them up in mental asylums.

In the 1960s, as mass movements swept the globe, academics began to consider protest more as a rational response to racism, poverty, and war. Studies began to dissect the relative strengths of resources of both the activists and our opponents. Organizers, they noticed, could perform a sort of cost/benefit analysis of how, where, and when to protest. They could distinguish different trends and interests among their targets as well as within the movement. But still unexplained was how people are motivated to break out of their reliance on belief in a just world and take action against the powerful.

Organizer and scholar Saul Alinsky (1971) gave one of the early and most powerful answers. Brought up in the left-wing tradition of working-class struggle, he said people had to be *organized* to fight back. The thirteenth of his "Rules for Radicals" stated: "Pick the target, freeze it, personalize it, and polarize it." Alinsky's organizing was based on identifying a common enemy and, in essence, *framing* him as the personification of all that needs to be changed. The antidote to the power of the frame, wherein the powerful cast those who fail to fall in line as an evil enemy, Gamson and Modigliani (1994) later argued, was for people to instead accept an "injustice frame" and use it as the "seedling" for action. Accepting a frame of an overwhelmingly unjust world, Gamson and others argued, allowed people to break free of the ties that bound them to accept the status quo. Indeed, MacAdam (1999, 34) calls an injustice frame "cognitive liberation." Framing allows us to identify an enemy who is the target of action and build solidarity among ourselves as "woke" or "doing the right thing."

Manuel Castells adds a final piece to the puzzle when he identifies "outrage" as the key emotional response motivating social movements. The trigger for social movements is "anger," he says, which is needed to overcome the fear of repression (2012, 5). No better example can be offered than the mass outrage at the police murder of George Floyd. Many people are motivated to embrace the Black Lives Matter movement out of acceptance of a repeated frame that the police are too often brutal racists. We take to the streets out of anger, confident that this will drive change.

Of course, framing, like technology (after Ellul 1967), is neither good nor bad, nor is it neutral. Uniting people against a common enemy was the intent of "hate week" in George Orwell's novel *1984*. The masses in Oceania regularly came together to express their hatred of the personification of the enemy of the people, Emmanuel Goldstein, an anti-Semitic archetype. In the real world, the scapegoating and demonization of immigrants operates to frame them essentially as "rapists and murderers" in opposition to the American tradition of posing them as the tired and poor "yearning to breathe free." "Build the Wall" and "Make America Great Again" are the obvious actions the "immigrant as rapist" frame demands as it cements nativist unity through hatred of the other. Similarly, prosecutors often will call on a jury to convict a gang member offender by evoking the "entire community's" hatred of gangs.

An obvious problem with such framing of enemies is the reduction of all members of the stigmatized group to a single, simplistic, and hated stereotype. All immigrants, surely, are not rapists, nor are all gang members violent criminals. Neither, Gamson would say, is the "ruling class" just one thing. Not all social movements rely on demonization. Dr. King's Third Principle of Nonviolence explicitly states that the goal of the movement is to defeat evil, not people. William Barber's revival of King's Poor People's campaign is aimed at the fusion politics of uniting diverse constituencies around common issues and common obstacles.

But social movement leaders regularly frame enemies as evil and make simplistic generalizations that may excite their base but not accurately describe a situation. Consider this incident that taught me the dangers of framing. It occurred in the years directly following my 1967 violent encounter with Milwaukee police. After my conversion experience, I no longer had faith in a just world. My belief that the law protected the normal and good from evil others was replaced with a new frame, more woke, but still dehumanizing.

———

Like other activists in the 1960s, I was charged with the spirit. I had the boundless energy of youth and a passion to change the world. I testified in hearings about police brutality and had repeated conflicts with Milwaukee's finest. As the open housing marches slowed to a stop in the spring of 1968, I dropped out of school and began to work full-time as the project secretary of the Milwaukee Organizing Committee, a radical antiwar and civil rights organization.

I attended the big antiwar demonstrations in New York and at the Pentagon. I shouted out with gusto: "Hey, Hey, LBJ! How many kids did you kill today!" "Dump Johnson" was an early goal of the movement. If anyone was the personification of evil, it was the president who had escalated the war in Vietnam and was responsible for the deaths of hundreds of thousands of Vietnamese and Americans. His leadership in the war on poverty was discrepant information and dropped from consciousness. Johnson's ouster became a rallying cry for the antiwar movement.

I framed the war as immoral, but, as a draft-eligible former student, I faced my own choice. I considered whether to noncooperate with the draft. The consequences were a five-year prison term and $10,000 fine. I signed a "We Won't Go" statement in the local paper, a turning point in my life. Seeing my name high on the list in the newspaper ad both made me proud and left me with a queasy feeling in my stomach. What had I done?

I could tell dozens of "war stories," from those days, and they all buttressed my belief in the oppressiveness of the system. My anger was slowly overcoming my fear.

Then, in the summer of 1968, just prior to the tumultuous Chicago Democratic National Convention, I was approached to help an assortment of priests and activists figure out how to nonviolently raid the Milwaukee draft board and destroy their records. They were following in the steps of Dan and Phil Berrigan who had burned draft records in Catonsville, Maryland, and then submitted to arrest. This was a stirring act of moral courage, which hurt no one, a direct action against a senseless war, followed by accepting the legal consequences. With

Milwaukee Fourteen member Doug Marvy, I planned how to pull off the raid, and, in order not to implicate others in the local Catholic support community, I agreed to contact the press and bring them to the scene of the crime. The local journalists were able to film the burning of the records and the arrest of the Milwaukee Fourteen live for the six o'clock news.

While I wasn't arrested that day, a couple of months later, I was indicted on two counts of federal charges of conspiracy to "Hinder the Administration of the Selective Service Act" and "Destroy Government Records." I received notice of my indictment while in Boston, and my attorney said I should return right away and surrender voluntarily to avoid high bail.

I was twenty-one years old and not certain I'd even be released on bail. So, I delayed just over a week before I gave myself up at the federal court-house in Milwaukee. I learned there had been a national alert out for me, and the FBI had even traveled to my hometown of Clintonville to interview my mother. I was ready to go to prison, ready to continue my work, and ready to sacrifice more for my cause. In my mind, at this moment, taking on the law meant taking on the forces of evil.

One day several months later, I received a phone call from a high school friend, Scott Stromberg. He told me a telephone company machine he was driving had toppled over and severed his leg close to his waist. He was home from the hospital and swallowing painkillers, but he wanted something more effective to dull the pain and ease his mind. I've never been into drugs, but I knew how to procure them. I bought what then was called a "nickel bag" of fine Colombian Gold marijuana that would have the desired effect of al-leviating Scott's misery.

I didn't have a car, so I hitchhiked the 130 miles from Milwaukee to Clin-tonville with the weed in a gas mask bag I always carried over my shoulder. I got as far as Appleton, about forty miles away, when the blue and red lights on top of a state trooper's car pulled over ahead of me and stopped me in my tracks. As the officer slowly got out of his vehicle, clad in a bright blue police uniform, my stomach had that feeling of quiet terror. In my mind's eye, the trooper looked just like Broderick Crawford, the tough-looking star of a 1950s TV show, *Highway Patrol*. Arrest for possessing a "controlled sub-stance" would mean revocation of my bail and immediate prison time.

He asked me for my ID, and I gave him my driver's license. I didn't have a clue how to talk my way out of this jam. He looked at my license and re-treated to his car. He came back after a short while and said point blank: "Are you the John Hagedorn that we had an all-points bulletin out for a while back?" I felt like I had passed under Dante's gates that said: "Abandon Hope All Ye Who Enter Here." I looked nervously at the handcuffs he had hanging on his belt. At some times in your life, you just are prepared for the worst and all you can do is wait for it to happen.

I only had a feeling like this one other time. Decades later, after I was hit by a car riding my bike, I went totally black. No feelings, no sensation, just traumatic brain injury black. Waking up, I'd realized my life was about to change, and I'd have to adapt. Similarly, facing Officer Broderick Crawford, I helplessly realized, Oh oh, my life is about to completely change. Nothing I could do would alter what was about to happen to me.

In this one highway patrolman, I saw the personification of all police, of the cops who beat me on the church playground, the police who harassed us at our antiwar demonstrations, those who imprisoned my friends, and those who protected the unjust system I'd been working with righteous anger to overcome.

As I braced to accept the inevitable, Broderick Crawford implausibly said, "You know, some of us agreed with what you did." I can't remember what I replied to that. I was in so much shock. He morphed in my mind's eye from Broderick Crawford into "Officer Friendly the former altar boy," and he went on, "Hop in and I'll give you a ride home." He talked about his admiration of the Pope and his moral convictions about the war in Vietnam. He told me that, while other police officers would not talk about it, many held deep moral qualms about the war. I remember he talked nonstop for the whole hour. Sitting next to him with illegal drugs in my possession, I mostly nodded in agreement with his declarations. He left me at Scott's doorstep, aware he was aiding and abetting a draft resister but unaware he was also "delivering a controlled substance."

———————

At the time, to me, this was a story of luck: how many state troopers could I have encountered with such views? But over the years, and as I began my work in court, this story grew into a prime example of breaking a frame, of how we too easily assume all members of a group fit the stereotype. What this incident revealed was that frames obscure the existence of subgroups, members who do not share all the group's stereotypical characteristics. Research on police, like that of James Q. Wilson (1968) and William Muir (1977), have identified various subgroups within police. You can't assume all police are like Derek Chauvin, who murdered George Floyd, or the officers who refused to intervene. Similarly, my work has repeatedly argued that all gang members are not alike.

As the story of Jaime Ruiz, or Chester Niven in Chapter 2, shows, one way to combat stereotypes is to "subtype," admit the stereotype may be true of the group as a whole but doesn't apply to this person or every member of the gang. Like with my experience with the state trooper, subtyping humanizes individuals, forcing us to understand a specific, real human being and not dismiss him or her as nothing more than a category.

One of the main ways I subtype in court is to use a typology of adult gang members I developed in my Milwaukee research, published in the journal *Criminology* (Hagedorn 1994). This approach is especially important at sentencing, when the issue arises of whether a convicted offender is likely to continue gang membership and criminal behavior into his thirties or forties. My research found four types of adult gang members: Homeboys, Dope Fiends, Legits, and New Jacks.

At Jaime Ruiz's sentencing, I argued that Jaime was not a "Dope Fiend"— drug use did not define his life. Nor was he a "Legit"—one of a small percentage of all gang members who come from conventional family backgrounds and the only explanation for gang involvement is the temporary thrill of the local peer group. Legits typically don't last long in gangs. I argued Jamie was not a "New Jack," a type that is relatively closer to the stereotype of gang members. New Jacks are hustlers. They have trouble settling down, have weak family ties, and go from one woman to the next. There is an amorality about both their illegal businesses and their lifestyle.

Homeboys, like Jaime Ruiz, are centered on family life. They marry or settle down with one woman and want to raise a family. They aspire to conventionality. Their gang life is in contradiction to their family life, and, in prison, they desperately seek to maintain ties with family. The several dozen extended family members who sat through two days of court were punctuation to my characterization of Jaime as a "Homeboy."

Subtyping is in itself a kind of reframing. In order to argue with my typing of Jaime as a Homeboy, the ASA would have had to adopt my "framework" that there are individual differences among gang members worth considering. This dispute over which category fits a person undermines stereotyping. It "breaks the frame."

My typing of Jaime as a Homeboy didn't work. The gang frame was too strong, and Jaime ended up with a long sentence. But a subtyping approach creates logical problems for prosecutors. Jaime's ASA retreated into repeating "He is a Latin King"—repeating the frame—rather than engaging with me in argument over subtype. My experience with the Wisconsin state trooper had taught me to look for differences within all groups. This behavior is not always practiced among prosecutors, police, or activists.

Some prosecutors realize their case is weak and built on stereotypes. The stereotype lacks evidence, and they need help to make sure they get a conviction. Maybe the defendant doesn't easily fit into the stereotype of a gang member. One way to get around this problem is the popular definition of "framing": perjured testimony and outright lies. Let's turn to some cases of these malpractices as we close our discussion of the conscious use of stereotypes.

6

Crooked Frames

Giving Stereotypes a Boost

—————

Attorney Leigh Ann Webster was persistent. It was early in 2016. I was promoting my book, *The In$ane Chicago Way*, and had a full load teaching in the spring semester. I didn't have time or energy to do another gang court case. And this wasn't even a murder trial. It was for a hearing reconsidering a guilty verdict in an assault. Webster insisted on sending me transcripts and asked if I could read them and then give her a final answer.

My expert witness work necessitates that I practice triage, like a doctor or public defender. When the death penalty or life without parole are on the line, that's an immense motivation to act. But a trial where gang stereotypes are egregiously used to buttress a weak case, or even replace evidence, likewise carries a strong imperative to push back. As I read through the transcripts of the trial of Tadarius Williams, I became amazed at the brazenness of the prosecution. In order to get a conviction, a violent, out-of-control dispute over a romantic rivalry was opportunistically transmogrified into a gang-related assault. The prosecutor claimed, "The whole thing is about gangs and what was going on." It wasn't. Then the prosecutor's strained invocation of the gang frame had so many holes, he needed perjured testimony from a jailhouse informer to nail his case shut and send Tadarius Williams to prison. I joined Webster in Atlanta for the hearing.

In Georgia after a guilty verdict, defense attorneys need to litigate a motion for a new trial, where they raise procedural errors and, if there is a new attorney, as in this case, issues of ineffective counsel. They hope to uncover ways the case may have been improperly tried so that they can convince the court to give it another chance in a new trial. Prior to Tadarius Williams's trial, witnesses repeatedly failed to identify him as the shooter in a dispute over a young woman. Prosecutors had to go back three times in lineups before they could get witnesses to identify Williams as the shooter. Their case was shaky, to say the least. Then the prosecutor brought a "gang expert," a Sergeant Lyda, into the trial, with no notice to the defense. Sergeant Lyda gave a PowerPoint presentation to the jury about the gang problem countywide and regaled them with tales of violence and murder. Oh yes, and he told the jury FOLKS stood for Followers of Our Lord King Satan. The defense was denied the opportunity to call their own expert, and their objection to Lyda's testimony was timid. The prosecutor at the time defended the appropriateness of Lyda's testimony that was unrelated directly to the crime, stating:

> Judge, it's relevant to show the Gangster Disciples, the type of activities they engage in and the type of people they engage with . . . this investigator stated nothing specifically about the defendant. He stated generically about the Gangster Disciples. It's not a basis for a mistrial. (Superior Court of Butts County 2014, 637)

The prosecution was relying on "guilt by association" to introduce the crimes that local gang members had committed and hope that the court held Williams responsible by virtue of asserting his association. The prosecutor introduced the gang frame into the trial to shore up his case. All of a sudden, prosecutors turned a shooting rooted in a dispute among young men over a romantic partner into a trial of all the crimes of the Gangster Disciples based on the mere assertion that the shooting was gang related. After police decided Tadarius Williams was the likely culprit, they didn't have the evidence, beyond reasonable doubt, to convict. But, if the individual identity of the shooter was in doubt, the prosecution could put the amorphous menace of a gang on trial instead. Enter the gang frame and Sergeant Lyda's lurid tales of devil-worshipping gangs spreading violence and mayhem across the area.

Sometimes just declaring a crime gang-related isn't enough. In such a case, however, the availability of the gang frame and the confirmation bias such a frame introduces in the minds of the judge and jury allows the prosecution to bypass the critical faculties that might otherwise have reacted skeptically. Dubious evidence becomes a strong support when the mind's confirmation bias is engaged, meaning its tendency to look for patterns to fit an established frame,. The prosecution introduced Billy Budd as a witness, a man who was serving a prison sentence for identity theft, was habitually in and out of jail, and had made a deal with the prosecution for release without bail in return for his testimony. All of which might have made him a dubious witness had his testimony not served to confirm existing ideas and suspicions the court already had about how gang members behave and the danger one would pose if not confined for a long time. Budd came forward to testify that Williams had admitted to him he was the shooter, and claimed the dispute indeed was gang related. One study of confidential informants (Natapoff 2011) found that prosecutors are particularly likely to use incarcerated witnesses who take a deal to testify like Budd did in order to shore up weak cases. Budd claimed Williams then left a signed note under his bunk that said if Budd would snitch on him, Budd would be killed. The note was illustrated by a Gangster Disciples symbol, a six-pointed star. The introduction of this note provided the full evidence for the prosecutor's claim that this shooting was "all about gangs." End of story. Well, not so fast.

"Gang" crimes are complicated and Tadarius, like many of the people on whose cases I testified, deserved to be tried on the reality of the evidence and not on stereotypes, frames, and manufactured stories. Tadarius Williams was a short and lively young man with a trimmed mustache and beard. I told him of my relationships with leaders of the Gangster Disciples, including Larry Hoover Jr. coming to my classroom and the assistance its various leaders had given me in court cases. After that, he went out of his way to impress me, admitting he was a member of the Insane Gangster Disciples, a prison arm of the Gangster Disciple Nation. He excitedly said he would do anything for Larry Hoover. This wasn't what his enthusiastic attorney, Leigh Ann Webster, wanted to hear. His admission scrapped any defense hope that they could distance Williams from gang affiliation, but it did not mean that the shooting was gang related or indeed that Williams had pulled the trigger. But Tadarius's gang membership would work to our advantage as we pointed out the implausibility of the evidence Budd provided.

Tadrius was shaken when I described the fractured state of the Gangster Disciples in Chicago and that the national board no longer functioned (Hagedorn et al. 2019). The national edifice of the Gangster Disciple Nation, that once had a tangible presence even in Georgia, now was fractured. I told him gang members in Chicago no longer cared about what Larry Hoover said. Tadarius was honoring a myth from bygone days, not a present-day reality. He told me he didn't believe me but later asked Leigh Ann if he could get some of my articles or books.

Williams grew animated when we talked about Budd. He denied talking to him about the shooting at all. Guards found the note Williams supposedly had left threatening Budd's life under Budd's mattress in his cell adjacent to Tadarius's. The note admitted the shooting was not about a relationship but about the victim falsely claiming to be a Gangster Disciple. Tadarius's supposed note ended with "Take the stand and die, bitch." It conveniently made the prosecu-

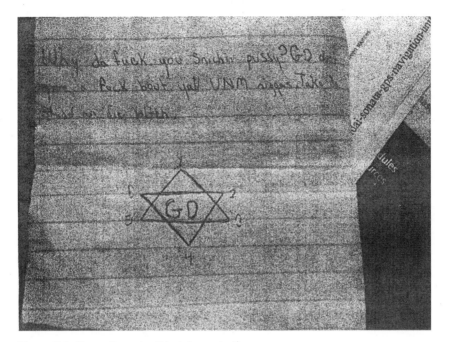

Figure 6.1 Phony Gangster Disciple symbol. (Case file.)

tion's case for them. But here my gang research expertise came into play. The death threat note was illustrated with a six-pointed star (see Fig. 6.1), which the state argued supported their claim this case was gang related.

Well, Williams was a gang member, but he didn't write that note and he definitely didn't draw that star. I examined other drawings by Tadarius of Gangster Disciples iconography. He was a fairly good artist, and his drawings, like the one in Figure 6.2, depicted the traditional Gangster Disciple heart with wings, pitchforks, and a six-pointed star. The numbers seven and four were around the star points, seven being the number of the letter G and four for D. But the note found under the snitch's bed had the six points of the star numbered, 1-2-3-4-5-6. I showed the note to a veteran Chicago Gangster Disciple, and he laughed at it, saying no "real GD" would number the stars that way. In other words, the star was drawn by someone who had insufficient knowledge of the Gangster Disciples, likely a correctional officer. Certainly not Insane Gangster Disciple Tadarius Williams.

Prosecutors come in all shades: some are truly "seeking justice" and have scruples about using tainted evidence, like using clearly perjured testimony. For this hearing, the state brought in a new prosecutor, Jaret Usher, specifically to cross-examine me. Usher fits the stereotype of the "win by any means necessary" prosecutor, aptly described by Daniel Medwed's (2012) book, *Prosecution Complex: America's Race to Convict and Its Impact on the Innocent.* She was

Figure 6.2 Actual Gangster Disciple symbol. (Case file.)

well coiffed and expensively suited and projected an air of confidence with a sniff of arrogance. Seeing me sitting alone in the courtroom before the hearing, she asked me to come into a room with her adjacent to the court. Out of politeness, I did, and she asked me to outline my testimony for her. Amazed, I declined to talk to her without defense counsel present. When later she asked me on the stand if I had refused to talk with her, I said, "I considered it improper of her to speak with me without opposing counsel." She snarled, "Just answer 'yes' or 'no.'" I laconically said, "yes."

My direct examination pointed out the lack of any credible gang-related evidence. Leigh Ann asked me, "In your expert opinion, what do you think is required to find that a crime is motivated by gang membership?" My reply was succinct: you need more evidence than the claims of a jailhouse snitch. I also testified that Sergeant Lyda's description of gangs across the area was interesting but irrelevant to this crime and his ideas of gang rituals was "far fetched." Of course, I once again debunked the inflammatory FOLKS canard. Webster had me on the stand for about an hour and a half. Her point was that if the state had allowed an expert witness like me to testify in the original trial, a key part of their evidence would have been substantially weakened, if not thrown out.

Judge Rueben M. Green appeared distracted during most of my testimony. He didn't seem to be closely paying attention and was fiddling with his phone and typing on the computer on the bench while I was questioned. It seemed his mind was made up that he was going to affirm his original decision. In some of my cases, I can tell the judge is listening to me. They make eye contact and will stop both counsels at various points to ask their own questions or follow up on points on which they need more information. Judge Green had a history of openly siding with prosecutors and was under official scrutiny for refusing to recuse himself in one case where he was caught on tape openly colluding with the prosecutor. But with me, his biases would pop up in an unexpected context.

Jaret Usher's cross-examination of me appeared to frustrate her. I repeatedly challenged her invocation of the gang frame as sufficient to convict Tadarius Williams by asking for evidence, aside from the pretty obviously compromised testimony of Budd. After about an hour of cross, she abruptly changed tactics and asked: "Where were you on April 23, 1967?" Leigh Ann Webster leaped up in objection as to relevance, but one measure of the judge was that he saw no reason to stop me from answering. For the life of me, I couldn't remember the date fifty years ago, and I guessed I might have been in New York City at an antiwar demonstration? She said "no" and showed me a picture she had found on my website, of me returning my draft cards in a Milwaukee church on that date. It was my irrevocable action as a nineteen-year-old that I would not cooperate with the Vietnam draft or take part in an immoral war. Webster rose in objection once more, and Usher countered, "This goes to bias." Well, yes, a bias was being invoked as the judge was a former Marine and hawkish supporter of the military. Draft resisters do have a bias against war. Would support of an unjust war make an expert witness unbiased? I don't think the positions of witnesses on war had any bearing on the truth of the accused's innocence or guilt. But Usher thought my politics fifty years ago would influence the judge.

Usher didn't have any other points. Her case was the gang frame, a witness who offered evidence that had clearly been planted, and a half-hearted attempt at demonizing the politics of the expert. All were poorly attempted. If she would have spent more than a few minutes searching on my name, she could even have turned up a recent mug shot from my 2014 arrest protesting the Milwaukee police killing of Dontre Hamilton. As a prosecutorial hit woman, she proved to be an amateur. As I finished this book, the Georgia Supreme Court overturned Williams's conviction and extensively quoted from my testimony, including my claim that some of the state's gang expert's ideas on gangs were "far fetched."

Throughout the book, I've been citing the research evidence that the mere mention of gangs cues deep-seated antipathy among jurors and makes them more likely to convict. Consider this sentence from one law review article examining the prejudicial impact of gang-related evidence:

> The words "gang-related" give rise to strong emotions in jurors. Many of us fear and hate criminal street gangs. (Eisen et al. 2014, 4)

Facts matter, but to make sense to a jury, judge, or anyone, they have to fit into a frame. In a criminal trial, another word for frame is story. What is the story of the prosecution, and how does it compare to the story of the defense? When frames are strong, like the gang frame, Lakoff (2004, 17) says, facts that go contrary to the frame bounce off the audience's information processing. To put a more precise point on it, a strong frame, repeated over and over again, colors facts and interprets them in light of the frame. It's not that the facts don't matter, but rather that we choose those that fit the frame. This is also called confirmation bias. Once we have swallowed the gang frame, even dubious testimony, like that of Billy Budd, becomes credible.

Frames work like conspiracy theories. Once you accept that the "government is out to take away your guns," every gun control bill is evidence of the conspiracy. For example, in 1986, Congress passed a bill prohibiting a national gun registry. Tracing a gun at the Bureau of Alcohol, Tobacco, Firearms and Explosives (ATF) central office is accomplished by a hand search of paper records. No computers are allowed to keep track of gun registrations. I had to double- and triple-check this amazing fact, because the frame that gun control is the first step to gun confiscation has been reinforced through constant repetition and record keeping has followed that frame. ATF's records of gun purchases are nonsearchable in any field except gun ownership, and a search for purchase records typically takes three to seven business days. The National Rifle Association, in its interests and the fears of its membership, has constructed a frame so strong that any proposal to regulate guns, like from the Parkland massacre survivors, is interpreted within the frame of "they are coming to take your guns."

So, it is with the gang frame. With Tadarius Williams, the prosecution's case was so weak, they needed to interpret the shooting in a way that jurors could understand. As previously noted, in the words of the APRI manual (2004, 7), they needed to "explain the inexplicable." In other words, by labeling the shooting "gang related," they could provide a consistent story, or frame, to jurors that shifted their focus from the confusing and inconsistent facts of the case to a story they recognized and feared. In the absence of facts to support the frame, they first brought in Sergeant Lyda to construct a gang frame out of the blue "with no mention of the defendant." Then they miraculously "discovered" Budd, who tied the frame directly to Tadarius Williams. The use of snitches is a common way to create facts that fit the prosecutor's frame, or story.

As Paul Butler wrote in *Chokehold* (2017a, 219), "Prosecutors are not sure they have enough evidence to get a conviction, so they basically bribe someone to be a witness." By contrast, Supreme Court Justice William Douglas once said, "The function of the prosecutor under the Federal Constitution is not to tack as many skins of victims as possible to the wall." The snitch is the key link in prosecutors tacking the skin of the gang frame to the wall of the courtroom.

It is tempting to digress into a history of snitching that goes back millennia. Paul Bloom (2016) reports that, in Athens in fifth century B.C., snitches were handsomely rewarded when their testimony was proved accurate. But when it was exposed as a lie, snitches were put to death. Can you imagine the impact of such a policy today on the industry of snitching that has grown in our nation's jails and prisons?

Snitching has been institutionalized behind bars and a professional class of snitches has arisen, some even compiling newspaper clippings of the details of crimes on which they might volunteer to testify so they can appear credible. The *Los Angeles Times* in 1989 wrote a major exposé of snitching in the Los Angeles jails with interviews with multiple practiced snitches (Stewart 1989). It still makes fascinating reading today. One famous snitch, Leslie Vernon White, told the *Los Angeles Times*: "The motivation to lie is too great." He recited ditties snitches might take as credos in a *60 Minutes* interview: "Don't go to the pen, send a friend" and "If you can't do the time, just drop a dime." The Los Angeles grand jury, investigating the use of snitches, found that prosecutions of snitches for perjury, unlike in Athens in fifth century B.C., were nonexistent.

The motivation to snitch recalls a basic theme of this book. As Steve Vulpis, an inmate snitch, told the *Los Angeles Times*: "The guy's guilty. Who gives a damn? I want to go home." This sentiment echoes the prison guard who assured me that if a defendant was not guilty of the crime he was charged with, surely, he would be guilty of something: a cynical attitude that ruins the life prospects of countless Americans. About one in five DNA exonerations, Northwestern's storied crusader against wrongful conviction and an old friend of mine Rob Warden (2004) found, could be directly linked to snitch testimony. In 2001, the Ninth Circuit in Northern Mariana Islands v. Bowie (2001) summarized in their Conclusion:

> Never has it been more true that a criminal charged with a serious crime understands that a fast and easy way out of trouble with the law

is . . . to cut a deal at someone else's expense and to purchase leniency from the government by offering testimony in return for immunity, or in return for reduced incarceration.

I've found snitches often play a role in buttressing the gang frame. Such behavior appears in studies of prosecutorial misconduct. In one San Diego case, Medwed reports (2012, 85), prosecutors were so keen on convicting four gang members that they gave a jailhouse informant a cell equipped with a color television and allowed conjugal visits to take place in a prosecutor's office. This dealmaking mirrors the misconduct in 1991 by U.S. attorneys obsessed with smashing Jeff Fort's notorious El Rukn gang. According to a *Chicago Tribune* 1983 editorial, "The witnesses, both El Rukn leaders, received clothing, money and other gifts, and were allowed to obtain drugs, have conjugal visits with their wives, and use government phones."

Given these examples, it is difficult not to be wary of the true devotion to justice of win-at-all-costs prosecutors. Some see putting a gang member behind bars as "doing God's work" and the ends justify the means. A. Davis (2007) says prosecutors develop a "willful blindness" or a "conviction psychology" that thrives on tunnel vision—they feel they have a categorical imperative to get a conviction no matter what.

Understanding frames is a helpful way to explain what motivates prosecutors when they are convinced a gang member is guilty and, unfortunately, lack the evidence. Paul Butler, in a remarkable reexamination of his career as a prosecutor, said (2017b, 105): "But one of the lessons of history is that it is hard to see the picture when you are inside the frame." Once the state has adopted a "gang frame," as with Tadarius Williams, evidence is reconstructed to support it. And if the evidence isn't there, the state can suborn it from snitches. If a prosecutor believes the defendant is guilty of something the temptation is great to manufacture or hide evidence or even to bribe a snitch to make sure "justice" is done.

I conclude this chapter with the story of Narseal Batiste's terrorism trial because it demonstrates the extent to which law enforcement can get so carried away in a demonizing frame they've invoked that they fail to keep sight of justice in the case before them. In this case, federal authorities brought the full resources of the war on gangs and on terror down on the head of one naive man they lured into claiming that he'd plotted a preposterous conspiracy. This trial carried national prominence since Narseal was charged with trying to blow up the Sears Tower in Chicago. In that case, I made the biggest mistake of my expert witness career by not testifying and, therefore, leaving the gang frame unchallenged. The U.S. attorney had been unable to convict Narseal as a terrorist in two consecutive prior trials. The third time was the charm, but only by claiming this young community activist was not only a terrorist but a gang member to boot. And you'll see I do mean "boot." The two overlapping frames, on top of a strategy of entrapment, convicted Narseal and his friends of conspiracy to commit an act of terrorism beyond their wildest imagination.

Ana Jhones, Narseal Batiste's attorney, told me she was a Republican but was offended by the Department of Justice's entrapment and relentless prosecution of her client. She asked me to come to Miami for Narseal's third trial—the first two had resulted in hung juries as well as the acquittal of some of the defendants. The indictment charged that Narseal and his handful of followers plotted with Al Qaeda to commit terrorist acts, including blowing up Chicago's Sears Tower, a claim that got national headlines. Narseal was the leader of the Universal Divine Saviors, a seven-member Miami Bible study group, with some linkages to the Moorish Science Temple of Chicago, a Muslim sect. The Universal Divine Saviors marched around the streets of their neighborhood and were seen as kind of community watch–like protectors of the community. The Department of Justice, however, was looking for the prototype of a domestic Islamic terrorist and must have decided that they could coax Narseal into an admission.

In the Tadarius Williams case, Georgia prosecutors needed to label Tadarius a gang member and manufactured evidence provided by a snitch to prove their shabby case. The FBI went to much more extreme lengths to ensnare Narseal Batiste in the war on terror. A federal agent posing as an Al Qaeda operative skillfully maneuvered Narseal to implicate himself in far-fetched plans to blow up federal buildings, from Miami to Chicago. When juries didn't buy the terrorist frame in the first two trials and were unable to reach unanimous verdicts, the feds added a gang frame to cement their case.

Before I met Narseal, I reviewed the transcripts of hundreds of hours of the FBI's fifteen thousand recorded conversations between Narseal and his followers with two FBI contractors who posed as Al Qaeda members. The FBI paid a total of $120,000—read that again, *$120,000*—to two men to engage in secret recorded banter that facilitated an FBI "sting" of Narseal Batiste. "Sting" is the prosecutor's term for entrapment. What I learned from plowing through the transcripts is that Narseal and his Bible study group, which doubled as a construction company as well as a community watch, were desperate for money. Narseal had a bit of the con man in him and was looking for an angle to support his wife and three kids as well as give his followers uniforms. Narseal understood through the men he didn't know were informants that Al Qaeda was flush with cash, and he thought maybe he might con them into supporting his band of associates. Bad idea.

In the post-9/11 world and early days of the "war on terror," the Department of Justice saw Muslim terrorists everywhere just as they had seen Communists behind every file cabinet in the 1950s. The two highly paid informants paid a Chicago member of the Moorish Science Temple, a convicted rapist, to encourage Narseal to commit acts of terror. No luck. All they had on tape were just the equivalent of religious "trash talk."

The rambling transcripts of rather mundane conversations were not enough to convict Narseal of anything. The FBI's frame of an Islamic terror plot needed a bit more help to get a jury to buy it and justify the very expensive work that they had put in to finding something on Narseal. The FBI needed a smoking gun and it came with a videotaped December 16, 2005, meeting between Narseal Batiste and a federal agent posing as an Al Qaeda representative, supposedly fresh off a plane from Lebanon. The transcript does not do justice to how the undercover agent skillfully waltzed a hesitant Narseal into specific incriminating statements so he could be charged with conspiracy. I watched the footage of the meeting, and I understood why two successive juries had trouble agreeing that Narseal was anything more than a flawed and gullible young man.

The video shows Narseal and the fake Al Qaeda representative sitting at a table. The footage is grainy, and I had to boost the audio to make it clearly heard. The fake Al Qaeda representative, a bossy, type A personality, keeps egging Narseal on to ask Al Qaeda for something incriminating. Narseal is clearly both nervous and reluctant. But in order to get the money, he senses he needs to tell the informant something to lead him to invest in his group. Then this incredible exchange occurs:

(Note on the transcript: CW stands for Cooperating Witness—the fake Al Qaeda guy. NB is Narseal Batiste.)

7	CW:	You don't tell me, let's, don't test me. You are
18		not capable of testing me. You don't test me. Go
19		straight to the point. Straight, straight to the
20		point. I put my life at risk because I like to go
21		straight to the point. So, here I'm here to
22		analyze. I'm here for you to give me something to
23		approve . . .
22	NB:	I'm exhausted financially.
23	CW:	Okay.
24	NB:	And everything I'm trying to do. We have nothing.
25		And the little bit that I have, I took to fix the
00027:01		mosque. The men trained hard. They don't have boots or

02		uniforms.
03	CW:	They don't have boots?
04	NB:	No sir.
05	CW:	You don't have what?
06	NB:	Uniforms.
07	CW:	No what?
08	NB:	Uniforms.
09	CW:	Uniforms. So, first point. First point, you want
10		boots and uniforms.
11	NB:	Yes sir.

At this point in the video, you could see the pained expression on the fake Al Qaeda guy's face. He was trying to get Narseal to ask him to provide weapons for acts of terror and instead Narseal said they needed "boots and uniforms!" Narseal was broke. He and his group paraded around the neighborhood regularly, and he wanted them to look respectable. So, he asked for boots and uniforms. But he quickly figured out what the CW wanted him to say in order to move forward:

12	CW:	What else?
13	NB:	We need artillery.
14	CW:	Like what? Give me a list of what you want. Give me
15		all the list what you want.

The fake Al Qaeda guy insisted that Narseal put in writing his incriminating request for "artillery." Of course, the paper that Narseal wrote out his list of needs on would be handed over to prosecutors as an overt act in a terrorism conspiracy. When I met with Narseal, he seemed like a gentle soul who had wanted to do his best for his group and community . . . and screwed up big time. If I was a federal agent concerned with justice, I would have stopped the tape, told this naive young man he was in over his head and needed to come back to earth. Instead, the feds elevated Narseal Batiste into a national symbol of Islamic terrorism.

Narseal and his Bible study friends were a timid, even respectable, lot. They were trying to do some good for the community but, as Batiste said, were financially exhausted. I suspect the hung juries in their first two trials had a hard time reconciling their well-meaning, if opportunistic, behavior with the government image of hard-core Islamic terrorists. Enter the gang frame.

The U.S. attorneys produced a proffer by Dan Young, an ATF agent who would testify as a gang expert. As it turned out he was an expert only in stereotypes and blatantly false information. A proffer is a synopsis of what his testimony would be, and Ana Jhones sent it to me. I would be called as a rebuttal witness. I suggested she retain Lance Williams, Chicago's leading expert on the Black P Stone Nation.

Dan Young's testimony was a rehash of old myths and stereotypes about Chicago gang figure Jeff Fort and the Black P Stone Rangers. Did you know, Young would say, the "P" stood for "Prince of Darkness?" No one in Chicago knew that either, as it was not true. Young also proffered the "little known fact" that Gangster Disciple leader Larry Hoover, principal rival of Fort's Blackstone Rangers, had actually been a Blackstone member? The claim is little known because it was a myth, confined to law enforcement conspiracy theorists, and demonstrably false. Young's estimate that the Rangers had fifty thousand members was unsupported by even Chicago law enforcement sources.

But Fort's Black P Stone Rangers were important to the government's case because they had transformed for a few years into the El Rukns, a group with loose ties to the Islamic Moorish Science Temple that Narseal also had ties with. The Al Qaeda impersonator was pressing Narseal in their video-taped meeting about how his tiny group of followers could pull off acts of terrorism. Narseal, clearly lying to get the investment he'd come for, boasted that he could call on the Blackstone Rangers for five thousand "soldiers."

(Note on the transcript: "(UI)" means unintelligible, a word that might describe this entire segment.)

07	NB:	This world war can be won if we win one city. You
08		know when (UI) in Chicago.
09	CW:	How many brothers we got down here.
10	NB:	Shew. (UI) Let me tell you something. I
11	(UI).	Ooc, you know I'm not kidding you. I can get
12		five thousand (UI) soldiers in Chicago.
13	CW:	So.
14	NB:	Five thousand . . .
15	CW:	Why you didn't mention anything about that
16		to me brother (Laughing)?
17	NB:	Cause I save the best things for (UI).
18	CW:	I heard that.
19	NB:	(Laughing) (UI)
20	CW:	I heard that. But seriously, we can get
21		five thousand soldiers going?
22		NB: Yep.
23	CW:	I'm serious brother. Brother this is real
24		guerillas or . . .
25	NB:	Shew . . . Nothing like you ever seen before.
00064:01		Crazy.

02   CW: (UI) four thousand. You have already five
03   thousand brother. Come on God.

Narseal goes on to ask the fake Al Queda guy if he has ever heard of Jeff Fort, who was convicted of trying to make a similar con of Libya's Muammar Gaddhafi and ended up convicted of terrorism. So, his comparison played into the government's hands as they would claim he was both gang leader and terrorist. By associating himself with multiple powerful frames in order to make his con more plausible to his audience, Batiste had also allowed himself to be walked into those same powerful frames in the minds of his jurors.

In Batiste's case, I screwed up. As the trial became heated, Ana and the team of attorneys debated about how to combat the government's claim that Narseal was a gang member. One view was that the claim was so ridiculous that we risked giving it credibility by putting me on the stand to rebut the uninformed testimony of ATF agent Dan Young. In this line of thinking, the gang link was already too incredible but by dwelling on it and repeating it, we would get the court thinking about it and repeat and reinforce the frame when they'd hopefully rejected it on their own. I also disclosed to Ana my prior conviction for conspiracy in the Milwaukee Fourteen draft file raid forty years before. She was certain the U.S. attorney would bring that up.

My testimony was more about facts than frames, focused on Young's lack of understanding of Chicago gang history. I didn't understand at that point that what Ana needed was expert testimony to discredit the gang frame itself. It was ridiculous to consider Narseal and his Bible study group a gang, much less allied to the Blackstone Rangers of Chicago. My testimony would put the gang issue up front before jurors, but it also might highlight how clumsily manufactured the prosecution's case was and refute head-on their phony gang frame. Instead, I sided with Ana and the lawyers who thought it better to belittle the gang frame but not call me to take it head-on.

Either I was wrong, or our strategy just failed. Narseal was convicted the third time around, at an expense of hundreds of thousands of taxpayer dollars for three trials that succeeded in convicting five of the seven Universal Divine Saviors. Narseal was given the longest sentence of thirteen and a half years. Readers of this book by now understand that, once raised, the gang frame persisted in juror's minds. Unless it was thoroughly rebutted, it would hang over the juror's deliberation. The combination or bridging of the terrorist frame with the gang frame was too much for the jury to ignore.

———

At that stage in my expert witness work, I lacked confidence and did not understand the psychological impact of merely raising a gang frame to jurors. More recently, I have been qualified as an expert in "gangs and the public perception of gangs," which allows me to confront the awesome power of stereotypes on a jury. Given the determination of the U.S. attorney in Narseal's case, I'm not sure my testimony would have made a difference. But I would have gone about my testimony much differently today.

So far, we've discussed the awesome power of stereotypes and how the gang frame provides a believable story line in a trial, how confirmation bias filters for facts that support that story line, and how unscrupulous prosecutors can manufacture evidence to fit the frame they've introduced. Unfortunately, the challenges to successfully rebut the gang frame get worse. The chapters in the next part explain how stereotypes and the gang frame are subconsciously "primed" and influence jury's verdicts. The prototype of a gang member is metaphorically related to deeply buried racist schema or beliefs and justifies the demonization of the other. I provide you with examples from my court cases of how these psychological processes supercharge our engrained "us and them" mentality. These are not insubstantial factors in how Americans have constructed a mass incarceration society.

CASE LAW

Northern Mariana Islands v. Bowie, 243 F.3d 1109, 1123 (9th Cir. 2001). https://caselaw
    .findlaw.com/us-9th-circuit/1364922.html. Unpaginated.
United States of America vv. Narseal Batistes a.k.a "Brother Nax," a.k.a "Prince Manna,"
    Patrick Abraham, a.k.a "Brother Pat, Stanley Grant Phanor," a.k.a "Brother Sunni,"
    Naudimar Herrera, a.k.a "Brother Naudi," Burston Augustin, a.k.a "Brother B.,"
    Lyglenson Lemorin, a.k.a "Brother Levi," a.k.a "Brother Levi-El," Rotschild Auguys-
    tine, a.k.a "Brother Rot." U.S. Dist. Ct. (S.D. Fla). 18 U.S.C. § 2339B18 U.S.C.
    § 2339A18 U.S.C. § 844(n)18 U.S.C. § 2384.

II

Dehumanization

7

There Is No Such Thing
as a Gang Member

Priming, Prototypes, and the Subconscious

The first thing the jury obviously noticed about Patrick Stout was that he was Black. I wasn't at the original trial, but, knowing Patrick, he was likely scowling. He may have appeared angry to the jury who would preside over his trial and, if convicted, his death penalty hearing. Simultaneously, the jury would have recognized that Patrick Stout was the defendant on trial for murder. The two observations combined to fit a story that was already available in the minds of the jurors: one more violent Black man in high-crime Memphis, Tennessee. Patrick was accused of killing an innocent young African American woman, Amber Hunter, and the jury waited for the prosecution to supply a motive for what seemed to be one more wanton, senseless "Black-on-Black" killing.

Eventually, another frame would fill in the remaining gaps in the story forming in the juror's imagination. It would come to the attention of the jury that this murder was gang related. The prosecutor would tell them Patrick was a Gangster Disciple. How did the jury know that was true? The prosecutor would dramatically buttress his allegation by demanding Patrick remove his shirt in front of the jury and show them his tattoos, including three teardrops and a six-pointed star, the emblem of the Gangster Disciples. The prosecutor labeled the tattoos as confirmation of the evil, violent nature of this hard-core gang member. This story, undoubtedly, resonated with jurors' preexisting fears and stereotypes of angry, dangerous, Black gangsters.

Patrick shook with resentment when he spoke years later, as his conviction and death sentence were being challenged. He had pleaded to the judge "no," when he was ordered to remove his shirt, and put up an anguished plea for dignity in front of the jury. He had been "eradicated" from the gang—kicked out—earlier while in jail and had tried to write over some of his tattoos. His attorney mounted little or no defense, one of the reasons the Tennessee Office of the Post-conviction Defender challenged his conviction on the grounds of ineffective counsel. No "gang expert" had been called at his original trial by the defense to contest Patrick's gang involvement, and I was brought in to assess how I would have testified had I been called as an expert.

Patrick told me he only allowed his shirt to be removed after the judge declared that if he didn't remove it, the judge would have it forcibly taken off in front of the jury. Patrick could hardly look me in the eye as he recalled being paraded—"like at a slave auction"—in front of a gawking jury. "It was like a macabre fashion show," he eloquently and grimly added. Patrick quivered as he described the scene, obviously an open wound still pulsing in his muscle memory. Defense attorneys learned later that the forewoman of the jury, a schoolteacher, had commented to her fellow deliberating jurors, without any informed knowledge, that "his three tear drop tattoos stood for how many people he had killed." The jury unanimously agreed on the death penalty.

Patrick Stout was presented to the jury as the quintessential violent Black male gang member. The memory of violent Black gang members was more than abstract for both the judge, Walter C. Kurtz, and William Massey, Patrick's original defense attorney. These two had been judge and defense counsel in the highly publicized Tony Carruthers murder case just one year before. Carruthers, also allegedly a gang member, had assaulted three people and then buried one alive. He had also threatened Judge Kurtz, who was so frightened he had asked to be relieved of the case. Carruthers also demanded Massey resign as his counsel. Now, to their eyes another gangster, James Patrick Stout, was in front of Judge Kurtz. The prosecutor said Stout, too, was a brutal murderer. No mention of Tony Carruthers, a murderous gangster who threatened judges and lawyers, can be found in the transcripts. But no one could seriously think that his frightening image did not still lurk in the minds of the judge and defense counsel, and perhaps the dozen Memphis residents sitting as jurors, as a memory from which they might draw their sense of what is normal and expected in a gang case.

I met with Patrick three times over the couple of days I spent in Nashville, preparing for an ineffective counsel habeas corpus hearing before Tennessee appellate judge Wedemeyer. I got along well with Patrick. Like me, he was intense and wore his emotions on his sleeves. He had his lighter moments in our conversation, but he was all business since his life was on the line in the coming hearing. He was the son of a prostitute and raised by his maternal grandparents. Most important, he observed repeated domestic abuse by his grandfather who directly followed up his brutality toward Patrick's grandmother with acts of kindness toward Patrick. Violence against women was both normal and confusing for Patrick.

I asked Patrick if he ever thought about the impact of his grandfather's violence on his life. He thought for a second then went on to explain that "people say I think too much." He said he often tried to think about the meaning of living with men whom he loved but who did horrible things to women. "The same man who took me to get ice cream was a monster with my grandmother." He said all his life he was "trying to figure this shit out," and he sometimes felt responsible for what happened to his grandmother. A psychiatrist later would testify that the abuse left Patrick with posttraumatic stress disorder and would diagnose him as bipolar. The defense counsel at his original sentencing presented no mitigating evidence whatsoever, giving the jury no understanding that trauma clearly played a role in Patrick's actions.

The murder was exceptionally brutal. According to codefendants, in cutting a deal for themselves, Patrick asked the victim, Amber Hunter, if she believed in God. When she answered, "yes," he said, "well, you're with the devil now." He then asked her if she wanted to hug "a real man" before she died. She hugged Patrick, and then, according to the gang members in the car with him, Patrick stepped back and shot her in the head.

Patrick vigorously denied being the shooter in Amber Hunter's homicide. Over our three sessions, he tried to convince me of his innocence and was frustrated by my "reasonable doubt." I could not testify that he was innocent. I wasn't at the scene of the crime, and Patrick's emotional makeup lent credence to the possibility of his involvement. But I pointed out in my testimony that he was just as likely to have observed such an act of violence and not interrupted or reported it—just like he did with his grandfather for years.

But, as with all my cases, my job basically was to make clear to the court the misleading character of the gang evidence and how that evidence and the defense's failure to contest it contributed to both his conviction and his death sentence. The tattoos were the prosecutor's visual proof that Patrick was a hard-core, murderous, irredeemable gang member—and evoked the jury's preexisting ideas of Black gang brutality. Patrick explained that he crudely tattooed himself as a teenager in Memphis, and his local gang was largely a circle of friends and kin. Years before, when he did some time in Shelby County (Memphis) jail for a car theft, he was shocked by the organization of the Gangster Disciples. They had rules and laws he had to memorize, and they demanded he pay dues. When he said he had no money, they demanded he give them his sneakers. This is something he would not do since the sneakers were a gift from his beloved grandmother. Patrick's neighborhood gang had been informal, with no written laws or rules. Like many gangs across the country, his neighborhood set identified with the image of the Gangster Disciples but was not a formal chapter. The gang in the Shelby County jail was another creature entirely.

Patrick told me that rather than give up his sneakers, he was "eradicated" from the gang in the Shelby County jail, beaten and stabbed, a potentially fatal wound. He wanted no part of this kind of rule-bound, cruel, and hierarchical Gangster Disciples gang in the jail. After his violent eradication, the notion that the murder of Amber Hunter was the product of Patrick carrying out some gang order was improbable. The Shelby County jail would later be put on federal oversight due to its out-of-control gang-related violence.

Patrick was released from jail for the car theft and a few months later was arrested for Amber Hunter's murder with four admitted Gangster Disciples. Gang-dominated Shelby County jail allowed Patrick's four codefendants to hold a cell block meeting to get their stories straight. Initially, prosecutors had placed two of the four, the higher-ranking gang members, at the scene of the murder and determined one was a likely shooter. But, after the cell house meeting, the story changed and the lower-level codefendants denied the leaders were at the scene and put all the blame on Patrick. This is a common gang practice to protect leaders and members, to blame a nongang "throwaway." On the stand, I recalled the Arthur Dent story I told in the Introduction, an example of how gang members blame someone not in their gang for a crime committed by gang leaders.

I testified that the tattoo was an amateurish depiction of gang symbology and showed that Patrick was not the dedicated Gangster Disciple the prosecutor claimed he was. I had brought colored pictures of the tattoos to Duffie Clark, a former member of the Gangster Disciple's national board and confidant of Gangster Disciple leader Larry Hoover. I brought a magnifying glass, and Duffie and I carefully examined each tattoo. Duffie was dismissive of the tattoos, telling me Patrick had little idea of Gangster Disciple symbology. For example, Patrick had a pyramid tattoo, but a pyramid is the symbol of the Gangster Disciple's most deadly enemy, the Blackstone Rangers. He also had a top hat and cane tattoo, which were the symbols of the equally hated Vice Lords. On one tattoo, the pitchforks were pointed down, meaning disrespect toward the Gangster Disciples. Teardrop tattoos are common and not just a gang symbol, Duffie said. They typically represent those lost to violence, not those killed by the wearer. Indeed, advertising one's murders would make one an easy target for law enforcement. I explained on the stand Clark's insider perspective: rather than demonstrate Patrick's dedication to the Gangster Disciples, the tattoos actually showed his shallow understanding of the gang. They represented his imagination and, in fact, his lack of commitment. Had I been called at the original trial, I could have undermined the prosecution's argument.

Patrick's hearing was the first time that I was qualified as an expert in both gangs and "the public perception of gangs." Brad MacClean, the Tennessee postconviction attorney defending Patrick, presciently decided that my exposition on stereotyping and the power of subconscious primes was the most important aspect of my testimony. Rather than lead with my research on gangs and Patrick's clumsy Gangster Disciple tattoos, Brad began his direct examination by asking me about stereotyping. We drew pay dirt right from the start as I testified that famed journalist Walter Lippman (1922) called stereotypes "a picture in your mind." The judge interrupted my answer to praise Lippman as a "generational authority." The judge was paying attention, and Brad's direct examination allowed me to point out that there was more at work in the prosecution's presentation of the tattoos than just poorly drawn gang symbols. The tattoo was also an example of priming latent fears and prejudices in the jury:

Q. What is priming?
A. Priming is when a stereotype or an image is interjected and it immediately prompts other ideas. In other words, in this case, a tattoo is a prime that people immediately think about gangs. And they would think about their initial image of gangs, the stereotype that's there of this scary Black guy who is obsessed with violence. . . . Is there any (other) way to deal with it? . . . yes there is and [to rebut] . . . you need authoritative testimony to say, wait a minute, there's another way to look at this. There's more to the frame, there's more to the picture. You'd have to combat that priming that evokes a false stereotype.
Q. Now, if there's priming in a situation, or cues that bring up stereotypic processes in a person and if that is not challenged, or counteractive, what is the effect of that?
A. It reinforces the existing stereotypes.
Q. Explain that?
A. It means that people have a stereotype in their mind . . . Walter Lippmann says . . . you've got this picture of a gang member and it's scary and if you're primed and cued of images that can be (scary too) . . . unless people have challenged, authoritative experts . . . that legitimate authority has said, wait a minute there's more to this, then that initial image is confirmed in your mind (and you say) "Oh yes, that's the way, that's just what it is." (15–16)

Judge Wedemeyer was listening closely to my testimony, and Brad's decision to begin with the theory of stereotyping and priming was effective. I had pointed out that stereotypes of gangs had been evoked by the tattoos and gang allegations that were not evidence in the case but part of the preexisting beliefs of jurors. This is what mid-twentieth-century psychologist Gordon All-port (1954, 21) meant when he said, "A person with dark brown skin will acti-vate whatever concept of negro is dominant in our mind." When a juror adds to the dark skin a gang tattoo and a homicide charge, an image of a violent dark-skinned gang member—perhaps a juror's worst nightmare, the prototype of the violent gang member—substitutes for the real-life person, Patrick Stout.

Patrick was earnest in trying to convince me he was innocent. I wanted to believe him. He was a person damaged from observing so much violence in his childhood. While all damaged people do not automatically become kill-ers, sometimes they are rendered helpless by extreme exposure to violence. In my testimony, I had cited Lt. Colonel Dave Grossman's (2009) comments on the severe impact of violence to onlookers in his book, *On Killing*.

At the habeas hearing, Patrick was no longer the nineteen-year-old who was arrested for murder. He was mature and thoughtful and fighting for his life. But even if he was guilty, I was enormously impressed with Brad Mac-Clean and his defense team's mitigation case before Judge Wedemeyer. The original attorney had put forward no mitigation case, and MacClean's multi-ple mitigation experts established the profound damage to Patrick of the violence in his early life. "Why," Bryan Stevenson says in *Just Mercy*, "do we want to kill all the broken people? What is wrong with us, that we think a thing like that can be right?" (2015, 288). Brad's mitigation case was over-whelming and proved persuasive.

But, as I returned home, I thought more deeply about the impact on ju-rors of the unchallenged stereotype of the threatening Black male gang member. Brad MacClean was successful with his extensive mitigation case in getting the death penalty overturned. But I wondered how the trial itself, even before the sentencing phase, could be considered fair given the uncon-tested fears of the judge and jurors, primed by the gang tattoos and false allegations of Patrick's "hard-core" gang membership. How could the jury look at Patrick and not see their prototypical image of the violent Black gang-ster? How could the judge in the original trial look at Patrick Stout and not see Tony Carruthers, who threatened him the year before and buried his victim alive? I didn't think Patrick's guilt and sentence could have been de-cided solely on the evidence, given all the associations haunting the trial. Scary stereotypes of gangs and race were subconsciously superimposed on the jury deliberations, making it impossible to disentangle what was evi-dence and what was prejudice.

That is why I do this work.

———

Patrick Stout's case illustrates the problem with instructing juries to decide a case only on the evidence as presented in court. To paraphrase and apply

Allport (1954, 20), "Strictly speaking, a trial on the evidence alone cannot occur." In this chapter, I briefly probe the meaning of priming and prototypes. I explore how the mind and brain work in metaphor to subconsciously associate a defendant with the category of violent gang member. And I tell a final story of a case where testimony of a "gang expert" for the prosecution was based on the prototype of a gang member that bore no resemblance whatsoever to the defendant.

In some ways, the testimony by police gang experts and the construction of a gang frame by prosecutors are hardly necessary. Just priming the idea of a "gang member" subconsciously brings our "Google Guy" into the minds of the jurors and inclines jurors toward a guilty verdict and a long sentence. As I argued in the Stout case, unless someone that jurors see as a legitimate authority, such as an expert on gangs, raises questions about the stereotype, jurors are, unfortunately, captive to them. Unless we are "motivated to go beyond them," Susan Fiske (1978, 363) says, all of us rely on thinking in the quick, associative methods of Kahneman's System 1 fast thinking. Jurors, too.

The Eighth Circuit's Roark decision recognizes the impact of priming and consequent confirmation bias. William Clinton Roark was a member of the Hells Angels, and reports about the havoc caused by the Hells Angels motorcycle gang, unrelated to the specific crime, were entered into evidence in the trial. The judge ordered the jury to disregard any mention of the Hells Angels, but the Eighth Circuit overturned Roark's conviction, saying "a bell once rung cannot easily be unrung." The circuit court thus established that by introducing a prime, even one that the judge had pointed out, the prosecution had irrevocably biased the jury and the trial had to be thrown out.

A label of gang member. An orange jumpsuit. A dark skin. A tattoo. All these are "primes" or "cues" that subconsciously evoke fear and stereotypes. Yes, the apparatus of the trial itself is a built-in advantage for the prosecution. The best explanation of priming is Claude Steele's (2010) *Whistling Vivaldi*, where he describes *New York Times* columnist Brent Staples running down a Hyde Park street in Chicago shortly after he moved there. As an unfamiliar young Black man in a running suit, Staples fit a stereotype, and residents crossed the street to avoid him and looked warily at him. That stopped when he whistled a tune from Italian composer Antonio Lucio Vivaldi, signaling he was someone familiar with classic European culture. Priming here worked both ways: Black man in a running suit primed, "Danger—he's one of them." Whistling Vivaldi primed, "Relax—he's one of us." Think of how hard it would be for Patrick Stout to have "whistled Vivaldi" and build that sort of trust in the courtroom. Can a jury filled with stereotypes of violent Black men and gangs really be trusted to consider a Black man in an orange jumpsuit, a gang member accused of murder, "innocent until proven guilty?"

Steele's book is filled with examples of the power of priming. Female students who are subconsciously primed with images of confident, professional women before a math test outperformed males on those tests. Those female students who were primed with images of housewives or traditional gendered images conformed to the "stereotype threat" and did worse than their male counterparts.

Malcolm Gladwell, in his book *Blink*, sums up Steele's research precisely (2004, 58):

> The results from these experiments are obviously quite disturbing. They suggest that what we think of as free will is largely an illusion: much of the time we are simply operating on automatic pilot, and the way we think and act—and how well we think and act on the spur of the moment—are a lot more susceptible to outside influence than we realize.

This means trials are often more confirmation bias than the reasoned judgments of System 2 slow thinking. We are simply not aware of our motivations. Apply law professor Adam Benferado's (2015, 17–18) observation to Patrick Stout sitting at the defense table in court:

> Research suggests that once we have summed someone up, we search for data confirming that identity in this regard or minimize evidence conflicting with it. . . . But really our minds are bending the facts, sawing off inconvenient corners, and tossing away contradictory information so that everything can be fit into ready-made boxes.

In Dennis J. Devine's (2012) seminal research on jury decision-making, he argues that this is, in fact, how jurors often act; they make up their minds early on and subsequent evidence is "adjusted" to support their initial beliefs. These initial beliefs can be easily primed by prosecutors, and jurors are not aware of the impact of their prejudices.

Brain research explains how priming works neurologically. Neuroscientist Dean Buonomano lays out this process as the central theme of his book *Brain Bugs* (2011, 20). First, "knowledge is stored in an associative manner." This means "thinking of one concept somehow 'spreads' to other related concepts, making them more likely to be recalled." This is the process behind Kahneman's System 1 fast thinking. Neuroscientists find that while the conscious brain can process up to forty different pieces of information a second, unconsciously, much, much more is going on. Our subconscious brain is processing up to *eleven million* pieces of information at the same time. How does that maelstrom of subconscious concepts, emotions, and experiences influence our conscious actions and thoughts? Buonomano sums up: "This unconscious and automatic process is known as *priming*."

How could the judge in Patrick's case not be influenced by the memory of Tony Carruthers burying his victim alive? More so, how could any of the jury not be affected by the avalanche of gang stereotypes pervading the media, including the headline stories the year before regarding Tony Carruthers? Priming means we subconsciously link our preconceived images of gangs to the gang member in front of us. Unless that linkage is somehow challenged, we simply do not use System 2, slow thinking, and rely instead on a process that uses no more than forty pieces of information at a time. Evidence is not neglected but colored by our existing stereotypes and fears of dark-skinned gang thugs.

In murder trials, fear has an overwhelming impact on how we think and consider evidence. Buonomano looks back over the evolution of the human brain and concludes (2011, 122): "We are hardwired to fear acts of aggression perpetrated by other humans more than most other modern dangers." Processing emotion is a function of the amygdala, one of the older evolutionary structures in the brain. Buonomano laments the exploitation of "amygdala politics" and fearmongering in our polity, a problem that has only grown more severe since the start of the Trump era. The prosecutors in Patrick Stout's case—like in so many other cases in this book—were advanced practitioners of "amygdala politics." They do it because the bell keeps ringing in the jury's head. One study (Greenberg et al. 1990) describes this process as "terror management theory."

The associative method of the brain is described in depth by linguist and cognitive scientist George Lakoff. He (1987, 118) argues that we all construct "folk models" that are "theories, either implicit or explicit, about every important aspect of our lives." These folk models correspond to frames, which I discussed in Chapter 4. Lakoff explains: "A folk theory defines common sense itself" (121). S. Winter (2001, 87) argues we never approach the world "sui generis" but through folk theories or frames he calls "stock structures." This use of stock structures resolves ambiguity and complements "given" information (evidence) with the preponderance of "assumed" information drawn from our past experience and beliefs. In other words, a jury uses their folk theory of gangs to fill in the blanks about how dangerous the defendant is, even with no supportive evidence, and looks to new information only to confirm their prior beliefs, leaving behind what does not fit the structure.

Lakoff points out (1987, 121) that we also have a "common sense" folk model of categorization itself that says: "things come in well-defined kinds" and have "shared properties." In other words, we all assume incorrectly that we know what a gang member is and that each one shares the violent, dangerous characteristics of the category "gang." So, by this system of processing, our minds assume Patrick Stout belongs to this violent category—gang member—and, therefore, is violent himself.

Our brains typically work by metaphor, by "conceiving one thing in terms of another." It is how we make sense of a specific gang member, like Patrick Stout, by comparing him to the picture in our head. The picture in our head provides an uninformed shortcut to where we believe we should begin making sense of who he is. In Fiske's explanation of priming (1978, 375), she points out that even subliminally priming faces of African Americans prompts white participants in a study to respond hostilely. Patrick Stout surely brought to the judge's mind a gang member like Tony Carruthers or another horrifying experience. Gilovich (1991, 37) points out the power of such simple comparisons:

> Asked to assess the similarity of two entities, people pay more attention to the ways in which they are similar than to the ways in which they differ.

The judge and jury would have continued to focus on the similarities between Patrick Stout and Tony Carruthers *unless* an expert or the defense attorney would have asked them to pay attention to how they differ. At that point, Gilovich says, "they become more concerned with differences than with similarities." This is why subtyping can work. It forces juries or judges, as in the case of Jaime Ruiz in Chapter 4, to consider different types of gang members and attend to differences not just similarities. That didn't happen in Patrick's original trial.

In Stephen Jay Gould's (1983) famous essay, "What, if anything, Is a Zebra?" Gould looked at the category "Zebra" and pointed out that it is not one thing. In fact, there are three distinct biological categories of Zebra, and no single Zebra represents the characteristics of all groups. Gould, in his usual provocative manner, disputes the applicability in most groups of universal characteristics. After he points out that a lungfish biologically has more in common with mammals than with a trout, despite its categorization in human classification systems, he concludes, "I regret to report that there is surely no such thing as a fish."

Instead of an individual who represents all the characteristics of a group, we construct "best examples" or prototypes, images shaped by a myriad of experiences and popular opinion. If we think fish, we likely think "trout" though the category of "fish" contains twenty thousand species of vertebrates that have scales and fins and live in water. We think "bachelor" and an unmarried man we know comes to mind, but we don't think of the Pope, though he fits the usual definition. Our prototype of a gang member is the "Google Guy" from the Introduction. In my freshmen classes, I asked students to close their eyes and imagine a gang member and what they were doing. My students always laughed when they opened their eyes to my PowerPoint image of a young white blond woman doing the dishes. "Aren't some gang members females, I asked? And aren't many gang members white? Don't gang members do more dishes than drive-bys?" The point is that prototypes are not representative. As with Gould, I regretted to inform my class that there was no such thing as a gang member, just as there is no such thing as a zebra.

Most prototypes, Lakoff goes on to say (1987, 85), "are not models of categories; they are models of individuals." Meaning a prototype ought not to be taken as a guide to the category, even though that is how our mind uses them. Lippman (1922) was absolutely correct when he said a stereotype is a "picture in your mind." That picture, "Google Guy," is the prototype of the gang member. Unless that scary image is challenged, it influences or even replaces in the jury's mind the real human being sitting at the defense table.

In my very first expert witness case, I had to confront the scurrilous claims of an unprincipled pseudoacademic "gang expert" that a real-life defendant, Keith Harbin, was nothing more than an evil, murderous prototype. This case angered me and encouraged me to set out to use my research experience to add rationality and humanity to gang-related court cases.

It was 1995 and would be another year until I took a faculty position at the University of Illinois–Chicago. I was working full-time running a follow-up research study to my book *People and Folks*, which I wrote in collaboration with Perry Macon, a Vice Lord who became a good friend. In this study funded by the National Institute of Drug Abuse, we were tracking what happened to the 404 founding members of Milwaukee's gangs as they neared thirty years of age. This study was amply funded, and I was able to hire former gang members as "community researchers" to help design the study, interview their homeboys and homegirls, and participate in the analysis. Following the example of my mentor Joan Moore, I called this "collaborative research."

My research experience dispelled any notion that "gang member" stood for one thing or type of person. My staff all had different family backgrounds and personalities. Going through the life histories of the founding cohort of Milwaukee's male and female gangs, we found a bewildering array of people: from college students to drug addicts; from union workers to drug dealers; from down-and-out to up-and-comer. Overall, their life chances were dim, but most were busy chasing the American Dream in a variety of different ways.

The typology of adult gang members, the subtyping I used to describe Jaime Ruiz, derived from this study. My staff argued with one another as we created the Homeboy, Dope Fiend, Legit, and New Jack categories as a way to describe the different life trajectories of hundreds of adult gang members and former gang members. We constructed the categories by discussing real gang members from the founding members of Milwaukee's gangs and we applied them to my staff as well. I remember a nearly out-of-control argument between community researchers Jerome and Lavell about whether Jerome was a Legit or a Homeboy. Clint, another of our community researchers, wanted desperately to settle down but had a drug problem he couldn't shake. Drugs were the center of his life. Angelo considered himself a New Jack while he was on the streets but had settled down with Mona, had several kids, and, after he left our study, worked steadily before dying prematurely of natural causes. He was as Homeboy as you get. Looked at closely, the 404 founding gang members had unique personalities and life trajectories. There was no such thing as a "gang member."

I was both intrigued and disturbed when I got a call from David Zessin, a lawyer from Holland, Michigan. I don't remember how he got my name, but he represented Keith Harbin, a Vice Lord who was facing murder charges after escaping from a Michigan prison. As he fled, he had shot and killed Grand Haven public safety officer Scott Flahive. There was no dispute that Keith was the shooter, and Michigan law mandated a life sentence. But the problem was that the ATF had filed a motion to move his trial to federal court on the basis that the murder was a "hate crime." That would allow the feds to pursue the death penalty.

In order to persuade the Michigan court to give up jurisdiction to the feds, ATF hired George Knox, a professor at Chicago State and the head of the National Gang Crime Research Center, a right-wing antigang center that does "training" for law enforcement officials. His "research" on gangs consisted of reinforcing stereotypes, not dispelling them. Zessin asked me to critique Knox's affidavit.

Knox wrote in his report that Harbin's shooting of Officer Flahive was motivated by racism, making it eligible to be categorized as a hate crime, therefore, making Harbin eligible for the death penalty in federal court. Knox stated that Flahive was killed in a "ritual execution." Harbin, Knox claimed, was "predisposed to kill" in order to "increase his status in the gang."

I was flabbergasted. On a basic level, Knox had never spoken to Keith Harbin and had no idea what his motivations might be. In my own letter to the court, I pointed out that Knox committed the "ecological fallacy" of (falsely) claiming the Vice Lords were a racist organization, then deducing, therefore, that Keith Harbin shot Flahive out of racism. You can't draw conclusions about individuals from group characteristics—remember from Chapter 1, the Irish drunk stereotype and its inapplicability to Timothy Dolan, the New York Cardinal?

Another way to look at the ecological fallacy is that Knox presented Keith Harbin as the prototype of a gang member, a vicious Vice Lord, "predisposed to kill." "Racist beliefs," Knox asserted, "are literally written into their 'gang constitution and by-laws.'" As a Muslim, Harbin conducted a "ritual execution" of a white law enforcement officer, which combined Black racism with what Knox called a "warrior personality" based on an "urban freedom fighter combative personality syndrome," according to Knox's storytelling.

No evidence about the real person, Keith Harbin, ever appeared in Knox's hysterical, tendentious diatribe. There are no racist concepts in the Islamic-shaded literature of the Vice Lords. I noted that Vice Lords were members of my research team, and white researchers and activists had long documented histories with various Vice Lord sets, including white activist David Dawley's in-depth involvement with Chicago's Conservative Vice Lords in the 1960s. There was no evidence of any "ritual" relating to what was clearly a spontaneous shooting during a prison escape. As far as "urban freedom fighter combative personality syndrome"—that was completely made up to sound scary and only pretended to be scientifically based.

Knox superimposed his fantastical prototype of a Vice Lord onto the real-life Keith Harbin. I interviewed Keith by phone. We talked about the likelihood that he would spend the rest of his life in prison. Keith referenced his Muslim faith and solidarity with other Muslim inmates and was preparing himself for life behind bars. I asked him about what happened when he escaped from prison and why he shot Scott Flahive. He considered what he did as wrong and "immoral" and deeply regretted his actions. He was in the back seat of a car driven by some local girls in his ill-advised getaway. As the squad car closed in on him, he fired out the window with a gun he had been given, and somehow his wild, hastily fired shot found a victim. He had no idea whether the officer was white or Black in the car and was in a state of extreme agitation. That his shot would have hit and killed someone had only a minuscule chance. Rather than a couple of extra years in prison for escape, Keith would, consequently, never leave prison, and Scott Flahive's family and colleagues would grieve an untimely and unnecessary death.

When the car was pulled over, Keith was arrested, and Knox claimed Harbin expressed satisfaction with having killed a cop. Keith told me he said to the arresting officers that he "didn't care" that he had shot anyone. Such declarations of placidity, I pointed out in my letter to the court, are classified by social psychologists as "neutralizations" or coping mechanisms to mitigate the severity of the emotional reaction to the violation of deeply held beliefs. They are typical of offenders immediately after a homicide. Statements like "I don't care" do not characterize actual unconcern but quite the opposite: an emotional brain attempting to return to stasis. They neutralize the guilt that goes with violating one's morals. Cold-blooded murderers, like hitmen, don't say anything when arrested.

Keith asked me to send him my book, *People and Folks*, as he began to accept that he would never be released from prison. I sensed an inner con-

tentment as he realized that he would have to make meaning out of life behind bars, and he strongly relied on his Muslim faith. We corresponded for a
while. The real-life Keith Harbin was nothing like the prototype George Knox
had constructed in court.

I spent most of my report rebutting the falsehoods in Knox's letter to the
court. Even today, it is hard for me to imagine Knox writing a report to get
someone killed. But one allegation by Knox was especially meaningful.

Knox claimed Harbin should be executed because assaults by Black gang
members on white prison guards were increasing, and he cited Minnesota as
an example. Two problems. First, I contacted Mark Thielen, the deputy director
for corrections for the state of Minnesota. He denied Knox's allegation that
white correctional officials had been targeted for attack by gang members.
Thielen told me there had not been any racial murders and there have been no
race-related attacks by gang members, generally, or Vice Lords, specifically, on
correctional officials in Minnesota. To put it simply: Knox lied.

Second, Knox may have referenced Minnesota prisons because of personal experience. In 1971, Knox had been convicted of conspiracy to bomb
two Minnesota prisons. Knox was a left-wing activist at the time and had
been cited by the House Committee on Internal Security's (1974) report on
terrorism. Perhaps this was the origin of his imaginary construction of an
"urban freedom fighter combative personality syndrome."

My letter to the court dressed Knox down as disreputable and the "research" he conducted as shoddy and not peer reviewed. I did not mention
his terrorist background, which he understandably wanted to keep private. If
he thought about it, George Knox might have seen himself as an example of
how people change, even those who commit grievous acts like terrorism or
murder. Such a thought might have caused him to empathize with people
like Keith Harbin. When the judge refused ATF's motion to transfer Keith's
case to federal court, Knox was furious with me. Absurdly, he made a public
threat to mobilize Chicago police to picket me every time I spoke in Chicago
after I accepted a faculty position at the University of Illinois–Chicago.

––––––––––

Knox's conversion from left-wing terrorist to right-wing fanatic is rare but
not unprecedented among former activists. Facing the consequences of
one's actions, particularly if you are arrested or looking at serious prison
time, can prompt a "conversion," a radical shift in outlook. In Knox's case,
he became a defender of the unjust world and over time built a career based
on demonizing gangs for law enforcement. His National Gang Crime Research Center continues to train law enforcement officers in stereotypes. My
own journey took a different road, from my 1967 conversion at the hands of
police into more serious left-wing activism: to protesting police killings in

Milwaukee; to working with gang members on the streets; and then all the way to China and back to solid ground. I still do not believe this is a just world, but I have changed in how I fight for justice.

CASE LAW

James P. Stout v. State of Tennessee. 2012. Death Penalty Post Conviction. Case No. P-26091 and/or 26091. Criminal Ct. Tenn. (30th Jud. Dist. Memphis, Div. II).

United States of America, Appellee v. William Clinton Roark, Appellant. No. 90-1334WM, U.S. App. (8th Cir., submitted December 13, 1990; decided January 30, 1991).

8

Course Correction

Police, Racism, and China—
A Personal Story

When a person is certain that they know something is evil and exactly how to oppose it, it can lead them to lose self-awareness. As the 1960s advanced to the 1970s, its social movements faced a turning point, as did I. An era of protest was realizing some successes, like the Civil Rights Act, Voting Rights Act, and policies to address urban poverty. The Vietnam War wound down to an end. For some in the movement, these successes took the edge off of their motivation to continue to organize, and, for the others who remained, their targets became more abstract and fundamental. Spurred on by a certainty in the rightness of our cause and unmoderated by less committed participants, we began to fracture over strategy and tactics. Looking back, I realize that we failed to see we had many of the same human failings as our "enemies."

Like many thousands of sixties activists, I went from protesting specific policies of racism, police brutality, and the war in Vietnam to making a deeper critique of capitalism itself. Stereotypes about the working class as "revolutionary" and capitalists as uniform reactionaries were taught in "study groups" across the country. Violence was justified as the only way for "us" to end our oppression by "them." Marxism was all about working-class solidarity, but the sharpest debates were always over race, what Marxists called "the national question." Many white activists considered race a distraction from the root problem of capital—no struggle but the class struggle they said—and ignored the specific issues raised by their Black allies. I was uncomfortable with this divide and interested in learning more about the particular harms of systemic racism. Feminist critiques likewise were acknowledged but largely given lip service. The debates of the time actually complicated the issue of who was "us" and who was "them."

The revolutionary turn had broad appeal to sixties radicals: one commentator pointed out that polls showed in 1968 more than three hundred fifty thousand people favored the creation of a mass "revolutionary" party. George Knox's flirtation with terrorism was adopted by only a few frustrated leftists, and those few were quickly incarcerated, killed, and demoralized or flipped to the right wing like Knox. The lessons I learned in the movement pushed me away from idealizing or romanticizing the working class and encouraged my curiosity toward gangs, which were then emerging in Milwaukee.

Working as a community organizer in a changing Milwaukee neighborhood, I looked on firsthand as African American and Puerto Rican gangs formed. I saw them as frustrated and angry young people, cut off from mobility by the loss of factory jobs. For most Americans, however, gangs were evil. For the U.S. government and law enforcement, gangs were criminal conspiracies, and the role of the courts was to send gang members to prison. For mainly white property owners, gangs destroyed property values and needed to be crushed to save owners' investments. For Marxists and activists, gangs were "lumpen proletarians," criminals and enemies of working class or community solidarity.

I thought gang members should be won over, not locked up. I got to know gang members as human beings in my community work in Sherman Park in Milwaukee. They were not one sort of person, but nearly all shared a basic human desire to settle down in a good life. The jobs they needed just weren't there, especially in segregated neighborhoods of concentrated poverty, for them to escape a dog-eat-dog lifestyle. I didn't see gang members as qualitatively different than other residents, just more alienated, variably organized, and destructively rebellious. I didn't believe our then-fading movement should ignore so many angry urban minority youths, nor should they be dismissed as merely criminals. The waning of social movements in the 1980s and a corresponding increase in urban violence led me to work directly with gangs in Milwaukee and, eventually, to turn to research and contest stereotypes in court.

Back in 1974, I had left Milwaukee for Boston to look for a larger group of activists in sympathy with my then still revolutionary views. Looking back at my five years in Boston, what was most remarkable about those days was not the heated and largely irrelevant theoretical debates and formation of revolutionary "parties." Rather, the Boston working class and entire city was transfixed by the 1975 white riots over busing Black children to formerly white schools. In defiance of some anticapitalist theories of class solidarity, it wasn't class but race that mobilized thousands of working-class white and Black people—on opposing sides.

While the left debated whether busing "divided the working class" or not, there didn't seem to me to be any question that Black kids had the right to go to any school they wanted. White rioters from South Boston and Charlestown throwing rocks at buses was just wrong, so I willingly went to a Charlestown factory to agitate against white violence. My fiancée at the time, Kathe, and I handed out leaflets and tried to talk to workers about opposing the violence. Sensible idea; foolish plan.

Charlestown was a bastion of white supremacy. Irish neighborhoods were run by white cops, workers, and gangsters, like the infamous Whitey Bulger. As we handed out leaflets, I noticed a police car drive by and disappear around the corner. Shortly afterward, two men, one large and one small, both wearing long coats that barely covered their police uniforms, came around the same corner walking toward us. The shorter guy came up to me and told me to throw my leaflets away. Filled with bravado and moral righteousness, I said to this guy, who was maybe only two-thirds my size, "You gotta be kidding." Those were the only words I got out of my mouth before the bigger guy pulled out a baseball bat from under his long coat and smashed me on the head. I went down like the proverbial rag doll. The two thinly disguised cops snatched our leaflets and ran back to their squad car.

Kathe called an ambulance, and I was taken to a local hospital. This was the second time racist cops had taken me out. I could tell all sorts of wild stories from my five years in Boston about organizing workers at several local factories. But class issues like wages and working conditions did not inspire in Bostonians the intensity of the race-based passions that erupted into the streets in 1975. It was clear to me that something deeper was at work and not understood well by Marxist ideology. For thousands of white workers, Black people, not capitalists, were their most hated enemy. Marx wanted to divide the world between "them and us," meaning workers and capitalists. But it became clear to me that W.E.B. Du Bois (1989) had a deeper insight that race—he called it "the color line"—was the fundamental problem of the twentieth century. The next one, too.

Soon after the Boston busing crisis, our "antirevisionist" movement began to crack up. The United States was not even vaguely in a revolutionary mood, and a strategy of organizing mass production workers in deindustrializing cities made little sense. The racism of white workers in Boston also didn't fit well in Marxist thinking. I decided it was time to go home.

I moved back to Milwaukee with Kathe and began to do practical organizing in a city I knew well. By 1979, the huge factories like Allis Chalmers, AO Smith, and American Motors were closing or had already locked their gates. Workers were scrambling for jobs that were disappearing. Young Black kids growing up in Milwaukee would not be able to mature out of teenage gangs into a factory job like generations before had. As frustrations mounted across all communities, racial tensions flared. Like in Boston, race would polarize the city and mobilize both Black and white people. Busing plans and school integration stirred up antagonism among the newly formed neighborhood gangs, and fights broke out at every bus stop.

Police violence was all about race as well. Along with Mike McGee, who was a local African American activist and former Black Panther, I cochaired the Coalition to Oust Breier, Milwaukee's police chief who was granted that position for life by state law. He was a noted racist. Police killings had risen over the years with Harold Breier at the Milwaukee Police Department's helm, and he was much hated in the Black community and among youths of all races. Uniting all the left activists with McGee's old Panther core, we gathered tens of thousands of signatures on a petition to have a "vote of no-confidence" on the fall 1980 ballot. Our efforts frightened the Democratic Party who went to the State Supreme Court to block our petition from coming before the voters. They were probably right in fearing the petition would bring out an overwhelming tide of racist voters.

Then on July 9, 1981, Milwaukee police brazenly killed Ernie Lacy, a twenty-three-year-old Black youth, with an illegal choke hold. Enough was enough. The Black community organized and roared. A new Coalition for Justice for Ernie Lacy formed, led by Mike McGee and Howard Fuller. One march mobilized ten thousand people to demand "a measure of justice." This was especially remarkable since it was during the Reagan administration and the broader movement was in steep decline. I was part of an ad hoc strategy committee to set the agenda for weekly mass meetings of hundreds of multiracial, but mainly Black, protesters. I had just begun to work with neighborhood youths and was observing the beginnings of gangs in Milwaukee. These alienated youths watched the Lacy demonstrations but did not take part. They also hated the police but were wary of the community leaders who supported our boycotts and marches but also called the cops on them. The local youths were angry and undisciplined, not welcome in the organized, peaceful actions of our coalition.

In the midst of the Lacy campaign, an unexpected event occurred that became instrumental in shaping my outlook. As our national revolutionary organization was breaking up, the leadership decided to send a delegation to China. My experience in uniting left-wing groups in mass organizing in Milwaukee prompted them to add me to the delegation as an afterthought. I left the Ernie Lacy struggle for a couple of weeks as we toured Beijing, Shanghai, Nanjing, and a small rural village.

This was 1981, in the days just preceding China's capitalist turn. I wasn't impressed with what I saw. The factories were dirty and dangerous. The vast

Figure 8.1 Hagedorn meets China's vice premier.

majority of people lived in the countryside on little more than a survival econ-omy. I got to tour the Great Wall and enjoyed seeing the Ming tombs and other tourist sites, but it was clear China's workers had a long way to go to catch up to conditions in the West (see Fig. 8.1).

Then one of those moments occurred that would gradually alter my think-ing and transform my outlook about the merits of righteous anger. Our group met the vice premier of China—my memory says it was Communist Party veteran, Gu Mu. As we shook hands for the photographers, the vice premier asked me if I was the organizer who was trying to oust the police chief? Breier would have been mortified to know that his notoriety had spread all the way to China. I said, "yes," and the vice premier smiled and said, "We have officials like that in China. But now that we have power, we just shoot them."

That exchange never left me. If our movement succeeded in the United States, would we just shoot those we opposed? Do we kill our enemies if we are given the opportunity? The dehumanization and frames that motivate people to bring down the powerful and unjust can be too easily reproduced. Is the U.S. landscape of Black and white, of "us and them," where we exe-cute or disappear young men in dismal prisons, really that much different than Gu Mu's stark statement?

9

"Us" and "Them"

Racism and the Psychological Basis
for Mass Incarceration

I f the state of Illinois doesn't carry out Ike Easley's death sentence, correctional officer David Knight solemnly warned, "he will kill again!" Knight's stone-cold words echoed the sentiments of a raucous crowd of correctional officers gathered at an October 24, 2002, hearing. Illinois Republican governor George Ryan had called for testimony of people for and against the death penalty in each case of a convicted offender who had been sentenced to death. Ryan was distressed to have learned that many people on death row had been sentenced based on evidence obtained under torture by Lieutenant Commander Jon Burge and other Chicago police officers. He ordered a moratorium on carrying out death sentences pending a reconsideration of the death penalty itself statewide. Since the death penalty had been reinstated in 1976, Illinois had executed twelve people but thirteen more who were on death row had been exonerated as actually innocent. The physical torture of African American gang members in murder cases to coerce guilty pleas severely shook the governor's belief in a just world, at least concerning Illinois's criminal justice system.

Ryan called for hearings to advise him on what to do with each of the convicted murderers on Illinois's death row. This unprecedented consultative action sharply divided the state. The Illinois legislature would later abolish the death penalty and Governor Ryan's successor would sign the bill. But, at the time, conservatives, and especially law enforcement, condemned even the possibility for clemency for any convicted killer. They thought their best case to make their point for the continued need for the death penalty, even with torture-tainted evidence, was twice-convicted murderer Ike Easley. Uniformed correctional officers showed up at the hearing in droves to demand Ike be put to death. As you might guess, Ike was an African American gang member. I had written a report sharply criticizing his sentence. On the day of Easley's hearing, I was the sole supporter of clemency for Ike Easley, sitting by myself surrounded by a sea of vengeance-seeking IDOC officials.

Ike's most grievous sin was that he had killed one of theirs, and not just a guard. On September 3, 1987, Ike had stormed into the office of Robert Taylor, the deputy superintendent of Pontiac State Prison. After an intense struggle, Ike had stabbed and killed Taylor. As he was apprehended, he shouted: "All you h----y m-----------s want is a n----r donkey to pin this case on, and I am your donkey, I am your killer." Not words intended to evoke sympathy. Nor did they.

At the hearing, after gruesomely displaying photographs of Taylor's blood-soaked office, Correctional Officer Knight pointed out that Taylor was one step under the warden. "If you can kill a superintendent, you can kill anyone," he said, in equally pained and reverential tones. The correctional officers in the audience groaned and nodded in agreement. Several testified that Ike must be put to death, and all agreed he was a "monster," the embodiment of evil. I don't remember all the epithets hurled at Ike that day, but, to those who testified, Ike Easley was considered barely human, more like a beast. Animal metaphors abounded; one speaker said Ike needed to be "put down." The crowd of correctional officers arrived intent on convincing the governor that Ike Easley, Black gang member from Chicago's south side, essentially was subhuman and nothing less than his death would satisfy their thirst for revenge—or, as they called it, justice.

Ike Easley was everyone's deepest fear, the racist prototype of the murderous Black brute, and a gang member as well. To make matters still worse, this wasn't even his first murder. He had killed his mother's boyfriend, William Paschal, after a loud argument years before. He had been sentenced to twenty years for that first killing, which shocked Ike, who told me he believed he had acted in self-defense and would get little or no jail time.

At the hearing, witnesses repeatedly claimed that Ike, along with Roosevelt Lucas, had "assassinated" deputy superintendent Taylor "pursuant to gang orders." The image of Ike as a "gang hitman" permeated the hearing just as it had permeated his trial years before. As with all of my cases, the gang label evoked stereotypes of evil monsters, animals thirsting to kill, and, at the same time, contradictorily, cold-blooded hit men. And, as with my other cases, there are three fundamental problems with the image of a thoroughly dehumanized gang member: first, Ike Easley was in reality a damaged person with all-too-human emotions, nothing like either the bloodthirsty monster or the cold automaton he was called. His tragic and lethal actions could be understood in the context of his traumatic family history, his consequent struggles with mental health, the circumstances, and his unyielding loyalties to friends. Second, the gang-related aspect of the murder was quite different than authorities claimed. Finally, as in my other cases, the gang label transmogrified the defendant, Ike Easley, human being, into Ike Easley, stereotype, the "other," a dark-skinned, soulless gang brute. Since we know what "brutes" actually are, and Ike is one of them, the frame tells us we don't need to investigate any facts of Ike's real life or the actual circumstances of what happened. This process of dehumanization allows officers like Knight to conclude that we must kill Ike Easley because his nature will lead him "to kill again."

My testimony to Governor Ryan's hearing aimed to tell a different story of Ike's life, or "reframe" him as a living, breathing human being, a person like us, with struggles and faults, not a monster like some imagined fantasy of "them." This is the defense task of mitigation at sentencing in court and was missing in Ike's original trial. Such pleas don't excuse murder, but, after conviction, they provide context and understanding of how such a horrid deed could happen as the court decides on how to punish the convicted. Done well, juries can see themselves in a defendant's shoes and categorize him as human, not as monster—one of us, not one of them. Good mitigation suggests to a jury that, given the circumstances, all of us are capable of murder and dares them to look at the homicide through the killer's eyes.

On the other hand, labeling the defendant a "monster" obliterates any attempt to find a kind or warm side to a person or to admit human frailty. It freezes his life in a photograph—that of Taylor's blood-drenched office—when our lives are actually motion pictures, with a childhood "set up," adolescent "turning points," and many possible "climaxes." Indeed, the legal notions of criminal responsibility depend on the defendant being able to exercise free will and on the crime being not fated or in a person's nature but a choice. But, when it comes to capital punishment, especially the death penalty, prosecutors often find it more compelling to paint a picture of an inhuman defendant who deserves death because they will be unable to help but kill again. The epithets at Ike's hearing reduced Ike, a human being, to no more than a brute, instinctually and inevitably following his essential animal nature. One of the most deep-seated lies in the global history of white supremacy is that those of African descent are evolutionarily closer to apes than to white people. The conclusion of this racist logic is that you can't reform monsters or animals . . . or Black people. You can only kill them or lock them away forever. It's like how if you see a snarling wolf nearby, you are justifiably frightened. You don't ask why the wolf kills, and you don't care. You immediately shoot it, without having to think about it, "before it kills again."

Ike Easley is not a wolf, nor a monster. The facts of Ike's childhood and the context surrounding the two murders for the state are called by social psychologists "discrepant information," facts that aren't congruent with a simplistic narrative, like that of Ike as a monster. The facts of Ike's life were discarded because they didn't fit into the prosecutor's standard "big bad wolf" story line. Let me add the discrepant information and explain Ike's violence, not as justified, but as the act of a damaged human being who was then sentenced to death in a trial where stereotypes, racism, and demonization ran wild.

First, Ike was an abused child. The court noted the abuse but pointed out that it didn't really matter:

We take as true defendant's allegations that he suffers from mental impairments. . . . However, that does not necessarily mean that he was unfit for trial. The issue is not mental illness, but whether defendant could understand the proceedings against him and cooperate with counsel in his defense.

The "mental impairments" originated from a childhood of abuse. Ike had been bullied by his mother and made fun of at school, often for wearing old or mismatched clothes. The social science literature, I cited in my report, "shows a strong correlation between childhood abuse and adult violence." Ike's childhood was filled with explosive anger and fights, amplified by his large and powerful body. Violence at such a stage, I wrote, is seen by developmental psychologists as "expressive" not instrumental. Expressive violence "expresses" inner rage, like that displaced from child abuse, and is less manageable, tied to universal human needs that an individual lacks. Instrumental violence, on the other hand, is the result of a conscious decision and better fits the prosecution argument that Ike was dutifully carrying out a gang order. Even as they made him out to be a monster, they claimed Ike was a "rational actor." On the contrary, little about this murder was rational, but that doesn't mean it wasn't human. One purpose of this book is to show that we all, far from rational beings, are subject to the errors of human behavior and are not always successful in controlling our emotions.

For Ike, the record shows another effect of his inner rage: he developed a protective sense toward those around him, and he often used his powerful physique, rightly or wrongly, as a weapon of justice. As a child in school, he saw himself as someone who could protect others and was strong enough to take the blame. Even much later in prison, there were many documented instances of Ike acting as a peacemaker.

Studying court records, I learned the earlier murder of William Paschal was also far from a cold-blooded killing. Ike angrily confronted the victim after Paschal abused Ike's sister and threatened his mother with a butcher knife. Ike, indeed, had a nearly uncontrollable temper, and I could see in his first homicide how his violence was expressing a burning inner rage as well as his protective tendencies. I had read all this, but it did not prepare me for my moving interactions with Ike Easley, the man.

Ike's dedicated and highly skilled lawyer, Aviva Futorian, drove me to Menard prison on August 26, 1996, to interview Ike. Aviva and Ike had a complicated relationship, which often accompanies male inmate/female lawyer interactions. Many a vulnerable male inmate has found himself uncomfortable in a match with a passionate, dedicated female legal advocate. Aviva left me to be alone with Ike as I had only a few hours to make a connection and get him to reveal thoughts and feelings to me that went beneath superficial answers to questions from lawyers, social workers, and police. Goffman calls this going "backstage," as opposed to the performances actors do for audiences. It is the essence of good research but, done well, can violate the most personal feelings of a defendant, even if it can help in his defense. My interaction with Ike stripped my own defenses bare as I got a glimpse of his inner torment.

Aviva had researched Ike's childhood and the murder of William Paschal. She explained to me the deadly circus that posed as Ike's trial. But Ike wouldn't talk to her about the murder of Taylor. Since Ike was being portrayed as a monster, I decided I needed to understand exactly what happened that day and why: the good, the bad, and what would prove to be the very, very ugly.

The immediate motive for Ike's rage was the killing by correctional officials of Ike's friend Billy Jones, also known as Zodiac. The Illinois Supreme Court explained the official view of the motive:

> The State's theory of the case was as follows. Defendant was a member of a street gang. The gang blamed the prison administration for the death of Billy Jones, another gang member. Defendant murdered the victim to avenge Jones's death.

The broader context, Ike told me, was that prison officials were cracking down on the Gangster Disciples control of drug trafficking in Pontiac. The administration, Ike said, had built an alliance with the rival Vice Lords and was maneuvering to take over the profitable drug trade. Fantasy? No. In fact, the year after Ike's conviction, sixteen guards were indicted for drug trafficking at the prison, and Pontiac was described as a "battleground." Jones was one of Ike's best friends, and Ike firmly believed his murder was about the administration's war to control the drug trade. He took Zodiac's murder personally and was outraged at his best friend's death and felt compelled to personally strike out to protect his circle. His emotions were not unlike the correctional officers at Ike's clemency hearing who sought to revenge the death of their comrade.

I spent four intense hours that day with Ike. He explained the war between the corrupt prison officials, Vice Lords, and the Gangster Disciples. He denied there were any gang meetings ordering retaliation for Jones's death. Rather, Zodiac's death left Ike emotionally devastated. He tragically displaced his rage onto Taylor, a well-liked African American administrator who was apparently not involved with prison corruption. Taylor's office was usually left open, and he was accessible to inmates, making it easy for Ike to get to him. Taylor was, in Ike's mind, a scapegoat for the correctional officers who had killed Zodiac. Ike depersonalized Taylor, as the officers at the hearing would do to him, turning him into a symbolic enemy, no longer a real person. Taylor was an innocent victim, which intensified Ike's grief later on. In his blind rage at the time, Ike wasn't killing Taylor, he was killing one of "them," adding another victim to the body count, which is a by-product of "us and them" thinking.

I took a deep breath and asked Ike point-blank what happened and how he felt about killing Taylor. "I can't believe you asked me that," he said, looking me straight in the eye. And then he told me. Here are my field notes:

In one of the most emotional exchanges of my life, Ike talked about the "uncontrollable" urges that streamed over him once the violence had begun and he and Taylor fought for their lives. Afterwards Ike said he blacked out and "I threw up like a m----------r." These are emotions, triggered by extreme events—the killing of Ike's best friend and his revulsion toward his own violent act.

I learned a really important lesson that day. Ike's out-of-control emotions were not those of a monster, an animal who kills without soul. They were also far from the cold-blooded lack of emotion of a hit man who kills for money or duty and proceeds calmly on to the next hit. They were the emotions of a real human being, like you or me, absolutely appalled and emotionally destroyed by the act of taking another person's life. Violence is hard, sociologist Randall Collins (2008) says, and Ike Easley is living proof of the truth of his words. My notes don't describe Ike's contorted face and agonized eyes, which drilled his feelings into my inner being. His body alternately shook and tensed as he relived how both men fought for their lives. The last two hours of our visit passed timelessly, in another dimension, walled off from reality by waves of intense emotion. Later, in my more composed, reflective field notes, I wrote:

Therapists say people like Ike can be responsive to long term treatment. To me Ike's emotional response to his violence was an indication of his humanity and an example of how killing violates deeply held norms.

But my own feelings about what to do with Ike's display of emotion were more complex. What Ike expressed to me was private, while he gave me insight into how to understand his actions and argue against his death penalty. I'm not sure I have the right to take these feelings of his and write and speak about them, though he told me at the time to go ahead. After all, his life was on the line. But I still question whether anyone should take from someone else such primal memories and emotions and share them. As Aviva and I left Menard, we went to a local bar so I could unwind, and she worked sensitively to soothe and calm me. She had been through death penalty cases before and had a long history as a civil rights activist. She was teaching me about the legal injustices of what had happened to Ike and understood my reaction to Ike's technicolor description of his violence. She said she was sure it was the first time he talked about it to anyone.

I can only hope these words help the readers understand the humanity of Ike Easley and others like him and the harm and untruth of reducing human beings to unfeeling monsters. My revealing these private emotions intends to show that Ike is actually one of us, not one of some imagined, frightening, nonhuman "them." Aviva and I wondered, given his abused childhood and the circumstances surrounding the killing of his best friend, would it really have been too difficult for a judge to have seen himself in Ike's shoes? Such violence should never be excused. But was it too much to ask of fellow human beings, like the Illinois Supreme Court, to understand how this violent crime could have happened and to cross what Haney (2004) calls the "empathic divide" and exhibit a smidgen of sympathy? Probably. You don't empathize with monsters.

Ike and I had also discussed his life behind bars, and his fear of being killed by correctional officers in retaliation for Taylor's death. Ike surprised me when he told me that he refused to have a television in his cell. He said the mass media brainwashes African Americans, lies about their history, and portrays them as nothing but thugs. Nothing too radical in those observations, but his response was to isolate himself from these "whitewashing" messages and immerse himself in African American history and literature. He was part of a cultural resistance in the prison, though the cost was losing the diversion of TV entertainment in the never-ending dead zone that is incarceration. I found Ike eloquent and courageous.

He also was compassionate and an artist. At that time, my youngest son was in his drawing phase, and Ike was interested in his efforts. Ike had a deep empathy for children, wanting to protect them from the traps and dangers of life. He was especially sensitive to young kids since his own childhood had been so torturous. Later, he sent my nine-year-old son a picture he had drawn, and my son sent one back to him.

Even this human exchange has a sad ending. At my next visit with Ike, he told me to apologize to my son. As a disciplinary measure, Ike's colored drawing pencils had been taken away and replaced by a rubber ink pen that made drawing impossible. My little nine-year-old was heartbroken, and Ike felt that he couldn't follow through and sustain a human connection with a child who he only wanted to help. I didn't tell my son that my latest visit with Ike was also marred by Ike having not only his wrists in chains but his ankles chained together to a heavy iron ball, like a movie character in a chain gang. Aviva and I could have no physical contact with him either and had to have our legal visit through thick glass and a tiny speaker hole. Ike was humiliated to be chained up like a slave and displayed as if in a zoo and told us he did not even want a visit. Aviva and I cut our business short with him, out of respect for his feelings. As a proud Black man, the last thing he wanted to do was ask favors of white people while he was in their chains with any exchange of feelings intercepted and flattened by a glass wall.

Perhaps consider the image of Ike in chains for a moment before you move on. Dehumanization distorts our understanding of a human being, reduces him to an animal in a cage, just like Ike. The instruments of the justice system, literal balls and chains, then work to realize our ugly fantasy. But this book argues that such dehumanization also distorts a trial and makes a reasoned judgment of guilt and innocence and a proper sentence improbable. If you think some of the trials I've described before were bizarre, well the circus is coming to town. And Ike Easley was on trial for his life in the center ring.

The Trial of Ike Easley

I wasn't there but received descriptions of Ike's trial from Aviva, Ike, and court records. Ike had killed Robert Taylor in Pontiac State Prison, which is in the city of Pontiac in central Illinois. His trial was moved due to intense pretrial publicity and because so many families or friends of correctional officials who lived nearby might be in the jury pool. So the state moved the trial to Joliet in Will County, home of Stateville, the oldest prison in Illinois. Incredibly, during pretrial motions, Stateville Prison had a highly publicized violent attack by inmates who also killed a guard. Like Ike, the assailants were Black Chicago gang members. Ike told me jurors passed around a newspaper during the trial that discussed the murder. I've explained priming already.

Two rulings by the judge were remarkable. First, the prosecution struck every Black juror from the jury pool "for cause." Prosecutors argued that African Americans live in neighborhoods with gangs and might be subject to threats and intimidation by Ike's gang. This would later be recognized more generally as little more than a racist excuse to keep Black people who might be more resistant to the prosecution's racist and dehumanizing frames off a jury, but this judge found no fault in the prosecutor's race-based challenges to seating jurors at Ike's trial in 1996. Then the court wisely forbade the prosecution from claiming that the murder was ordered by the Black Gang-ster Disciples. It seems there was no evidence of any meeting, conspiracy, or testimony of any actual gang orders. Ike also firmly denied any gang meet-ing had ever taken place. Despite the judge's order, the prosecutor men-tioned the "gang-ordered conspiracy" in his opening, during testimony, and again at closing. The Illinois Supreme Court ruled that while the allegation of a conspiracy was "improper," Ike "suffered no prejudice therefrom." Read-ers of this book may tend to differ. Do you think this "harmless" error may have contributed to Ike being sentenced to death? The social psychology studies I've cited do.

I listened in disbelief as Aviva described to me the environment surrounding the trial. The jury was sequestered, and their motel was surrounded by sharp-shooters. When jurors asked why police with rifles were on nearby roofs, they were told Ike's gang might try to shoot them. What kind of reasoned judgment could the jurors make, nervously checking out the window to see if anyone was aiming a gun at them?

Terror Management theory (Greenberg et al. 1990) says when people confront the possibility of their own deaths, they hold even tighter to stereo-types and prior beliefs. Recall that System 1 fast thinking takes less mental energy, so when the brain cuts back on critical thinking to shift to action in fight-or-flight mode, it defaults to this easier system. We want security and certainty and can't spare the emotional energy to take on new challenges to old thought patterns when we are worried about our lives. "Gang members are irrational monsters," says the stereotype. Also, "gangs are tightly orga-nized, like a corporation, with trained killers carrying out orders."

It does not matter to the juror's primed, frightened, and hurried mind that the metaphor of monster contradicting the metaphor of hitman cold-blood-edly carrying out orders was not considered inconsistent. Both metaphors connoted "the other" to the all-white jury, conjuring images of members of a clearly racialized construction whose motives and psychology were un-knowable, dangerous, and did not conform to "our civilized" behavior.

The court found there was no evidence the gang ordered an "assassina-tion," but the power of the gang stereotype apparently compelled the pros-ecutor to belabor this falsehood from the beginning of the trial to the end. It filled in the blanks and provided a motive consistent with the stereotype, if not the facts. The Illinois Supreme Court ruled the prosecutor's behavior "harmless error." Once primed by the prosecutor, those images and words recall stereotypes and fears that can't be extinguished. Remember the *Roark* decision that said a bell once rung can't easily be unrung? Like Fred Bright in the Butts and Wilson trials, the gang stereotype wasn't necessary for con-viction but was an indispensable weapon for ensuring a death penalty. Once in the jurors' heads, the stereotypical bell kept ringing. Nervously peering at nearby buildings that could hide a shooter, Ike's jury took only one hour to come back with a death sentence. Are you surprised?

This line of argument was the essence of a report I earlier had written to the court arguing for a new sentencing hearing for Ike. The Illinois Supreme Court disagreed despite sharpshooters putting on a performance of protecting jurors from the defendant's gang; prosecutors ignoring court orders and insisting the murder was ordered by that same gang; and striking all Black jurors from the jury pool. The Illinois Supreme Court defied common sense and the well-established science of human behavior by saying such actions had no practical effect on Ike's sentencing. Why do prosecutors use the "gang frame"? Because it works, regardless of the evidence presented. The fear of a racialized "other" is deeply ingrained into our psyche, and prosecutors understand they can always mine these emotions for convictions and the most severe penalties.

Back to the Hearing

At the end of the Illinois clemency hearing called by Governor Ryan, I had my chance to contest the gang frame and the stereotype of Ike Easley as a "beast." Ike's brand-new court-appointed attorney for the hearing gave what must have been a record for a minimalist defense of any defendant, as he appeared in front of the hostile crowd. "Here is Professor Hagedorn," he quickly said. "He has something to say about Ike Easley." That was it. No other defense. No exhibits. No relatives or mitigation experts testifying for Ike. No arguments. He was either just lazy or wanted to give the floor over to me and get the hell out of there as quickly as he could.

I knew nothing I would say could change the panel's recommendation. And anything I could say in support of Ike would be met by hoots and yells from the hostile correctional officials pressed up directly in front of me at the podium. The lawyer was clearly intimidated. Ike was lucky he was in his cell a hundred miles away at the time. It wouldn't have taken much to turn that crowd into a lynch mob.

I have to admit that in times like these, politics and sound judgment don't always win the day with me. My oppositional tendencies kicked in and the situation got my adrenaline running. I started by talking about how child abuse led to Ike's explosive temper and about Ike's adolescence and his felt need to protect others. I talked about Ike being abandoned by his family once he went to prison and the recent death of his dear sister. To hisses, I mentioned corruption at the prison. But none of those facts made a dent in the gang frame. I was sure they flew in and out of the heads of the members of the sitting panel. So, I spent most of my time establishing a different frame, one with which some listeners might identify. I talked about Ike's sensitive relationship with my young son. I talked about their exchange of drawings and Ike's distress over having his colored pencils confiscated.

Then I brought the house down. I said that the Ike Easley they heard about so far was a scary monster. I told them that is not the Ike Easley I know. "If Ike was released today, I would feel perfectly comfortable having him babysit my children." Shrieks rebounded across the room and a few reporters ran to file stories by phone. I was gratified when one local paper headlined, "Witnesses Portrayal of Easley Vary Widely." The article treated my remarks as naive and gave more credence to the official, "Ike is a monster," line. But the headline framed it correctly.

Ike's story, fortunately, doesn't end with him being executed. Governor Ryan, confounded by how widespread Burge's torture of Black defendants was and other clear injustices in Illinois murder trials, decided he could not judge a systemic problem case by case. It was too complicated, and he didn't want the responsibility of playing God. Instead, he bravely commuted the sentence of each and every death row inmate to life without parole. That was the only way Ike could have been reprieved from a death sentence. The correctional officials were right: Ike was their best candidate for why there should be a death penalty, a double murderer whose second murder victim was an administrator in the "safety" of his own prison. If the governor had to decide case by case, Ike would be dead today. Governor Ryan's (2003) stirring talk at Northwestern University Law School about his decision is as fine an indictment of the death penalty as I've ever read.

Dehumanization and Mass Incarceration

This chapter gets to the heart of my thesis. The first section of this book argued that we all think in categories and that stereotyping is normal. The second section so far shows how stereotyping is subconscious. Two more steps are required. First, the most salient of cognitive categories is "them and us" and we classify gangs, of course, as "them." Race is a principal marker of humankind within American culture, a primary "them and us" category. Second, our American criminal justice policy—and, indeed, much of Western culture—marks "them" or those who are different, as evil, as a threat, not merely members of a separate category. This baseline judgment of the other as evil is neither inevitable nor simply evolutionary. It is a cultural adaptation, one that is coldly functional for maintaining those in power. Political leaders use it to rally a nation to war against what they inevitably imply are "subhuman" enemies, incapable of peace or reason. White Americans have lynched Black men since the establishment of plantation slavery, ostensibly for various crimes and sins. But surely it is Blackness it-self that serves as the decisive "Mark of Cain" that has allowed white Americans to slip the rope around their neighbor's neck. Influenced by the "us and them" frame, good men "go along" as police officers, soldiers, or prison guards just do their job or duty and preserve the status quo by subduing "them." Prosecutors similarly tell stories evoking big bad wolves so they can be seen as the protector of little red riding hoods. They portray themselves as the heroes who will plop the wolf into a kettle of boiling water, while we who they represent cheer the extermination of evil. The scarier and more vicious they can portray a defendant, the easier the conviction and the longer the sentence, if for some reason the death penalty is off the table.

This dehumanization is mainly but not solely about race. We think of race, David Livingstone Smith (2012) says, as "natural human kinds." Our cultural upbringing adds meaning to race and much of that meaning in white culture is deeply pejorative and dehumanizing to Black people. Americans' deep-seated racial stereotypes cannot be separated from our internalized psychological dichotomy of "them and us."

The dehumanization of nonwhite gang members underlies the logic of mass incarceration. How can we justify that one in five African Americans in prison are serving a life sentence, as the Sentencing Project reports? How can we conceive as "just" trials like Ike Easley's, or Marion Wilson's, or any of the other cases I've reported on here? Why are stereotypes and lies and sensationalized claims like the erroneous "Follower of Our Lord King Satan" label accepted by judges and not thrown out of court as absurd? Why are prosecutors allowed to bribe snitches to lie and purchase false testimony like George Knox's to put someone to death? These should be national outrages, but instead they are standard operating procedure for too many prosecutors and complicit judges. Courts decide "they" belong behind bars, or strapped down on the lethal injection gurney, because "they" by definition are "not us," and it is, therefore, somehow okay.

If the defendant is less than human, the jury, the court, and the law itself washes its hands of his fate. If he is inherently evil, he can't be reformed so, of course, we should lock him up forever if we can't "put him down." When any nonwhite defendant is on trial, jurors see only the "Google Guy" prototype of the gang member. When George Knox alluded mendaciously to Black African terrorist guerrillas (a homophone he surely recognized) in the escaped prisoner case discussed in the previous chapter, that image took the place of the real Keith Harbin. Through the power of prototypes, while an actual human being stands before the court, the prosecution frightens the jury to see instead a scary monster or bloodthirsty animal. Some trick, but it works because it takes advantage of the way we think in categories along with an exaggerated fear of "the other," expertly primed by prosecutors.

This mentality and court practice has laid the psychological foundation of our mass incarceration society.

To understand this better, let me take you on a short journey through the research on identity up to and including David Livingstone Smith's seminal history of dehumanization. His book, *Less Than Human* (2012), helps us understand why demonizing stereotypes are so easily accepted by jurors and enthusiastically promoted by prosecutors and have led us to our mass incarceration state. Smith argues that dehumanization is based on a concept of essences—the essence of the other is understood to the human mind as subhuman. The next chapter tells the story of Jacqueline Montañez and explains how this dehumanization results in the fundamental attribution error and justifies mass incarceration.

I'm using these literatures not to academically dress up my argument but as a mirror to expose an ugly side of the American character and the human mind it reflects. I'm hoping the shock of story after story in this book awakens in the readers a recognition that the practice in U.S. courts regarding stigmatized groups, like gangs, routinely relies on stereotypes and fear of the other *outside the evidence.* These studies explain the realization I've come to, after forty years of gang research, that the reason we have a mass incarceration society is more because of "us" than "them."

Categorical Thinking and Identity

All good people agree,
and all good people say,
all nice people, like Us, are We
and everyone else is They.

—RUDYARD KIPLING, "We and They"

Nothing is more natural than us and them. We all categorize ourselves as belonging to a particular humankind and are more favorable to our kind than other kinds. This is especially true for death penalty jurors, Fleury-Steiner (2004) says. Race is clearly one of the most salient of the dividers between us and them. The central point of Berreby's (2005) *Us and Them: The Science of Identity* is that "kind sight" is innate; it flows from the very construction of the human mind. Categories, he says, "are not lists at all but explanations." Thus, the category "gang" popularly explains that its members are violent creatures who break the law by definition. Historian Khalil Gibran Muhammad (2010) explains the long history of how criminality and Blackness are associated in the white mind. To whites, the category "Blacks" connotes creatures "less than human," the title of Smith's (2012) book. And the category "policeman" has explained to the white mind how "peace officers" enforce the law to keep us safe. To think of dark-skinned gang members in some ways as "good" or police as capable of "evil" just doesn't fit the mind's established categories and these notions are, therefore, typically dismissed from our thought process or deliberations. Hopefully, the on-screen evidence of the realities that lie outside the cultural fantasy, such as the murder of George Floyd by a police officer, will permanently undermine "the police as always good" stereotype, even to white people.

Humans naturally categorize people into groups and then tend to treat all members of the group the same way, which saves time and energy. Indeed, if primitive man did not treat every member of the category "wolf" in the same cautious manner, he might have been eaten rather than survived. Once we have a sense of a category, say, "wolf" or "gang," we know a lot about its members from our understanding of the category, which is what cognitive scientist Marvin Minsky (1975), using mathematical language first called a frame. So, it's not so hard to see why stereotypes of gangs are so dangerous. That stereotype of a gang member as a "limb of Satan," a monster, or a wild animal allows us to fill in the blanks about him and his character, even if we know nothing else about him. Whatever the mind recognizes that he does expresses his nature as a member of that frame. Like a wolf, he kills because, well, that is what a wolf does. The full humanity of Ike Easley requires we should question this simplification.

The meaning of the word "category" itself, Aristotle pointed out, is from a Greek verb that means "accuse." Primitive life was fraught with danger, and "them" meant a threat to "our"—Greeks—food or survival. As civilization spread, "others" were called barbarians, again from a derisive Greek term "bar bar" or nonsensical speech. We can't have a concept of civilization, we learned from Joseph Conrad (1899), without its opposite: the "uncivilized." This notion developed in Western imperial culture from our understanding of what we called the "civilized" behavior of colonists, compared to the "uncivilized" resistance by native peoples—"the brutes"—to colonial rule. Among other things, this imperial notion of civilization, still a prominent frame in our culture today, justified American chattel slavery, since the slaves were not considered "civilized," and barely, if at all, human. And, of course, genocide of native peoples could be overlooked since, according to the imperial mindset, they really were just savages. Thus, the purest form of "them and us" is white supremacy.

The most gripping exposure in European literature of the distance between colonial fantasy and reality was Conrad's novel *Heart of Darkness* (1899), which laid bare the attitudes of colonialists as they committed mass violence to secure their rule. I don't think it is a reach to say that echoes of the colonists chilling cry to "Exterminate all the brutes!" could have been heard in the correctional officers' cries to kill Ike Easley. I invite you to read Lindqvist and Tate's (1996) book by that same name. We can follow the cultural influence of this "exterminate all the brutes" attitude in the support for the death penalty as well as how courts handle dangerous Black men, like Ike Easley or other gang members. More broadly, this is why Michelle Alexander (2010) defines mass incarceration as an extension of slavery and Jim Crow, a means for "us," the white Americans in control of the instruments of law and order, to continue to control "them." Criminal justice is designed to sanction destructive, criminal behavior. The stories in this book are about violence and murder, horrific acts that themselves also require dehumanization on the part of the people committing the crime, as in Ike's murder of Robert Taylor. Dehumanization also underlies Gu Mu's cavalier statement that bad officials should just be shot. What my stories are trying to show is that what goes on in court is more than adjudications of legal or illegal or even right or wrong. In our own American heart of darkness, stereotype-laden trials of gang members really boil down to issues of "them" and "us."

The Other as Evil

Mankind has always feared the other: animals threatened lives and outsiders raided crops and livestock and often wantonly killed, raped women, or took captives. Primitive life was "nasty, brutish, and short," according to English philosopher Thomas Hobbes (1651). While this view minimized the cooperative behavior that was also necessary for survival in those times, it became the model for capitalism's credo of "every man for himself." Life is dangerous and taking care of "us" requires protection against "them." We build walls and prisons, raise armies, and yes, if necessary, we "exterminate all the brutes." This thinking has evolved out of the structure of our minds over millennia. You can see in these pages how prosecutors take full advantage of our fight-or-flight reptilian brain.

This evolutionary emotional and cognitive response, however, is not inevitable. We have choices. We have the same responsibilities for our choices that we try criminals for disregarding. However, proposals for more humane penalties or a renewed emphasis on rehabilitation run foursquare into our internalized folk myth of how the big bad wolf is out to eat us—these categories are persuasive, and we don't want to be fooled when our lives are on the line. In the battle for policy and public opinion, as well as in the courtroom, the most effective arguments rely on our fear of the other. Prosecutors particularly play on our cognitive biases and fear of being killed by evil and dangerous brutes. They convince us that, like Ike Easley, we have to kill monsters before they kill us. After all, isn't killing what monsters do? The gang trials in this book are ceremonies of the victory of us over them, rather than simply rational assessments of individual guilt and a sober weighing of the proper punishment.

My own academic life has been concerned with understanding violence. My questions have searched beyond simple motivation. I asked myself, what allows us to treat other human beings violently? For me, this meant understanding the gang members who killed in Chicago where I did my research and in my many court cases. But I also extended my inquiry to ask how we justify what is called the structural violence of concentrated poverty and mass incarceration? Seeing firsthand the extreme hardships and humiliations of racism and poverty, of police violence and the impact of incarceration, as I have over the years, I asked myself how we could so easily accept all of this systemic violence? In the court cases I've presented here, a judge or jury hands out a death penalty or locks up a defendant in a cage for the rest of his or her natural life. Is this only about "justice"? Criminologists may better define it as just deserts, "They get what they deserve." Or is there some underlying attitude needed to justify both interpersonal violence and the violence done by persisting poverty and our mass incarceration society? To put it provocatively: do legislators, soldiers, police, prosecutors, judges, and gang members have some common psychological motivations?

David Livingstone Smith's (2012) *Less Than Human: Why We Demean, Enslave, and Exterminate Others* offers an explanation for all kinds of violence. I think it exposes a deep kinship between the stereotypes of gang members and the win-at-any-cost behavior of prosecutors. It is also an unsettling glimpse into today's ethos in American and other authoritarian-leaning societies. Smith states his thesis baldly:

> We are innately biased against outsiders. This bias is seized upon and manipulated by indoctrination and propaganda to motivate men and women to slaughter one another. This is done by inducing men to regard their enemies as subhuman creatures, which overrides their natural, biological inhibitions against killing. So dehumanization has the specific function of unleashing aggression in war. This is a cultural process, not a biological one, but it has to ride piggyback on biological adaptations in order to be effective. (2012, 71)

And racism? David Smith (2012, 8) points out: "Dehumanization feeds on racism; without racism, it probably couldn't exist." Race, he goes on, "isn't primarily about what people are called—it's about what they are thought to be" (185). And a deep strain of Western thought has characterized Black people as "less than human." N. Winter (2008) explains the power of what he calls gender and race schema in detailing how public opinion is captured by "dangerous frames."

Deeply embedded in our thinking, however, are the prime categories, "them" and "us." Some of the "them" categories are labeled and smeared as evil, subhuman, or dangerous, and we conform our opinions about them, like at a trial, to what we know about what we consider their nature to be, which is different than ours. Haney (1995, 549) argues:

> Our system of death sentencing instead leads us to view capital defendants as genetic misfits, as unfeeling psychopaths who kill for the sheer pleasure of it, or as dark, anonymous figures who are something less than human.

This labeling is not natural or scientific but cultural and taught to us from a young age by many sources, as it was in my own upbringing. The existing frame of "them as evil" is primed by prosecutors in the courtroom, taking advantage of jurors' internalized fears. Thus, enhanced penalties on gangs are accepted as obvious since gangs, we're told, are categorically "collections of evil minds."

The Nazis are the easy-to-accept model for this dehumanization. Here is Joseph Goebbels, the Nazi propagandist speaking of the Jews: "They are not a people but a conglomeration of animals" (Smith 2012, 137). Goebbels enthusiastically promoted the Nazis' favorite film, *The Eternal Jew*, which grossly depicted Jews as rats. The main point of Smith's book is that dehumanization is a necessary prerequisite for us to commit violence. And not just the Nazis. In order to kill a human being, that person must be depersonalized, turned into an animal, a beast, or an absolute evil. An article about a seventy-one-year-old parishioner who gunned down an active shooter at his church in 2019 exemplifies this. The parishioner, Jack Wilson, told reporters: "I don't feel like I killed a human. I killed an evil. That's how I'm coping with the situation."

Precisely. "That's how I'm coping with the situation." Margaret Atwood, in *The Handmaid's Tale*, has a similar description of dehumanization (1986, 192):

> I'll take care of it, Luke said. And because he said it instead of her, I knew he meant kill. That is what you have to do before you kill, I thought. You have to create an it, where none was before. You do that first, in your head, and then you make it real. So that's how they do it, I thought. I seemed never to have known that before.

Smith (2012, 250–51) explains the emotional dilemma inherent in an act of violence as a struggle between identifying the victim as "them" or "us":

> On one hand, we are disposed to carve the world into them and us and take a hostile stance toward outsiders. On the other hand, we

think of all people as members of the human community and have a powerful aversion to harming them. Dehumanization offered an escape from this bind. By a feat of mental prestidigitation we discovered a method for counteracting inhibitions against lethal violence by excluding our victims from the human community. . . . If I am right, dehumanization caught on because it offered a means by which humans could overcome moral restraints against acts of violence. (2012, 250–251)

This internal battle between frames explains why Ike Easley "threw up like a m----------r" after killing Robert Taylor. He dehumanized Taylor as he stabbed him to death in a desperate fight for life, but afterward he recognized that Taylor was a fellow human being and he had violated the most sacred of his own internalized moral codes. Similarly, during Roderick Harris's sentencing phase, he was called "unstoppable evil." I consulted in his case after the judge sentenced him to death, in part for having committed a gang crime that I discovered was nothing of the sort. It's hard to kill a fellow human being. Much easier to kill "unstoppable evil" or creatures with animal behavior, like gang members. For some officials, an execution is seen as mandatory and made more palatable if the victim is "less than human." I think if I killed another person, like Ike I might "throw up like a m---------r." What about you?

I love reading detective stories. One way I divide them is between those who see the world as good against evil versus those who see humans as more complex. I enjoy Lee Child's Jack Reacher novels. Child is a great storyteller, and his tales are hard to put down. But Reacher is a sociopathic serial killer. He has no compunction killing the "bad guys," is restrained by no rule of law, and expresses no remorse. Consider this line from *Killing Floor* (2012, 216). Reacher expresses his disdain for due process as well as lack of regret after killing, not one, but several bad guys:

I wouldn't have to think about Miranda, probable cause, constitutional rights. I wouldn't have to think about reasonable doubt or rules of evidence. No appeal to any higher authority for those guys. Was that fair? You bet your ass. These were bad people. They'd stepped over the line a long time ago. Bad people. . . . As bad as they come.

I've interviewed mafia hit men. In their "cold-blooded" lack of response to killing they are like Jack Reacher but very unlike Ike Easley or you and me. Contrast Reacher's outlook with that of my favorite detective, Henning Mankell's Kurt Wallander. Here, the Swedish detective expresses views very close to my own. In *The Fifth Woman* (2004, 322), a friend asks Wallander:

"All this violence," she said. "Where does it come from?" "There aren't many people who are truly evil," replied Wallander. "At least I think they're quite rare. On the other hand, there are evil circumstances, which trigger all this violence. It's those circumstances we have to tackle." "Won't it just get worse and worse?" "Maybe," said Wallander hesitantly. "If that happens then it's because the circumstances are changing. Not because there are more evil people."

I hesitate to dig deeper into how we so easily turn the other into the personification of evil. I don't want to stray too far from my court stories. I was brought up Lutheran and was raised to believe in the devil and the reality of evil. My minister nearly every Sunday threatened us with eternal damnation if we broke from the Lord's path. At my grandfather's funeral, which occurred right after my arrest in the civil rights marches, my righteous Uncle Herb thundered at me as we both stood next to the open casket: "The Law of the Lord is the Law of the Land." I had *sinned* when I was arrested for an act of civil disobedience. To my father's brother, I had slipped into the category of the other.

America's Christian heritage has shaped our criminal justice policy by its demonization of lawbreakers. Elaine Pagels explained in her *The Origin of Satan* (1995) how early Christians turned the old Hebrew concept of Satan as a generic adversary into an actual person, a fallen angel, living now among us. The battle against Satan, these early theologians wrote, was part of a cosmic battle between good and evil, not just a battle against a local enemy. This moralistic interpretation of good versus evil has inspired countless people, Pagels writes, to fight against insuperable odds for justice and against persecution. For example, millions, including my father, were willing to sacrifice their lives in the war against the Nazis and Fascism.

But such Manichaean thinking has had some severe, unintended effects. If criminals, gang members, or other defendants do "evil" deeds, they are not just thought of as driven by circumstances, as Wallander concluded, but their crimes express an evil character. The biblical idea "to pray for one's enemies" is one of our great humanizing virtues. However, we are also taught we are waging a cosmic battle against Satan, who is evil incarnate. Within this outlook, criminals or gang members don't just do evil deeds, they are carrying out orders of the devil. Perhaps we might call them "Followers of Our Lord King Satan." You don't turn the other cheek to Beelzebub. Indeed, in 2008 Harris polling surveys found 59 percent of Americans believe in the existence of the devil. For comparison, only 47 percent accept Darwin's theory of evolution. Unfortunately, what is actually evolving is the ways in which we apply the concept of the devil in order to "exterminate the brutes."

Within our cultural categories, gang members, criminals, or other enemies not only do evil; they *are* evil. And our categories are not getting smarter as we learn more. Criminologist Frank Tannenbaum added back in 1939 that in the United States (17) "There is a gradual shift from the definition of the specific acts as evil to a definition of the individual as evil, so that all his acts come to be looked upon with suspicion." He called this process "the dramatization of evil."

Thus, our mass incarceration society has jettisoned the concept of rehabilitation: you can't rehabilitate evil or animals. And prosecutors invoke demonizing and dehumanizing language to fill our prisons to overflowing capacity. There is one final psychological trick that prosecutors play that underlies the logic of mass incarceration. To prosecutors and the assembled mob at Governor Ryan's clemency hearing, Ike was essentially a monster. This label was psychologically required to justify his execution. "For dehumanization to occur," Smith writes, "the target group must first be essentialized" (2012, 186). This applies what psychologists call "attribution theory" and leads to what is called the fundamental attribution error, and it is the link between our "them and us" mindset and our mass incarceration society. I want to explore Smith's concept more closely in the next chapter through the case of Jacqueline Montañez.

CASE LAW

Ike Easley, Jr., Petitioner-Appellant, v. Sheldon Frey, Respondent-Appellee, No. 04-1614. U.S. App. (7th Cir., decided January 11, 2006).

People v. Easley. S. Ct. Ill. 148 Ill.2d 281 (1992). Available at https://caselaw.findlaw.com /il-supreme-court/1487247.html.

United States of America, Appellee v. William Clinton Roark, Appellant, No. 90-1334WM, U.S. App. (8th Cir., submitted December 13, 1990; decided January 30, 1991).

10

"I Did What You Said I Did. But I'm Not Who You Say I Am."

*Jacqueline Montañez and the
Fundamental Attribution Error*

C ould fifteen-year-old Jacqueline Montañez really be, as prosecutors said, a "cold blooded assassin who would make Al Capone proud?" Judge for yourself.

I first met Jackie Montañez in 2008 at Dwight Correctional Center, a now-closed Illinois correctional facility for women. She was then thirty-one years old and came out with a big smile into a private meeting room for a legal visit with Patricia Soung, her talented and dedicated Northwestern University lawyer, with me in tow. Other times when I visited her with Aubri McDonald, my grad student at the time who was writing her dissertation on Jackie's case, we met in the large common room with visitors for other inmates at one of the plastic rectangular tables reserved for family and visitors. Only formal legal visits are granted privacy. The vending machines allowed us to buy her popcorn, her favorite blue Mountain Dew, and other food that spiced up the drab grub she was served at mealtimes.

I had been contacted by lawyers from Northwestern University's Bluhm Legal Clinic to consult on a possible clemency case for Jackie. On May 12, 1992, in an incident that made local headlines, fifteen-year-old Jackie and two female members of the Maniac Latin Disciples were reported to have "lured" two Latin Kings to a bathroom in Chicago's Humboldt Park with the promise of a party and instead shot and killed them. Sexualizing the murder,

---

This chapter is indebted to Aubri McDonald and the research she did for her dissertation *Framing in Criminal Trials: The Murder Case of Jacqueline Montañez.*

one syndicated columnist wrote: "First she kissed him. Then she killed him." Another tantalizingly called the murder the "Gang Woman's Kiss of Death."

Jackie Montañez was just seventeen days from her sixteenth birthday, and her first trial judge complained the law allowed her to escape the death penalty, which she would have been eligible for had she only been two weeks older. He was telling the truth. Her twenty-two-year-old codefendant, Marilyn Mulero, was sentenced to death in the same case. Seven years later, the Illinois Supreme Court vacated Mulero's death sentence and commuted it to life, citing her small children as a mitigating factor. Mulero is a free woman today, granted clemency by Illinois governor Pritzker as I write this in 2020. Jackie's other codefendant, sixteen-year-old Madeline Mendoza, was paroled in 2016. In 1993, Jackie, as a juvenile, was mandatorily sentenced to life without parole for the commission of multiple homicides. After the U.S. Supreme Court ruled such mandatory sentences unconstitutional, Jackie was resentenced with a mandatory release date of July 7, 2023.

My interest in Jackie's case was sparked because she had been thoroughly demonized in the media and at her trial. All of my other homicide cases at the time had been males killing other males. Female homicide was rare but not completely unknown; one out of every seven homicides is committed by a woman. The relative rareness and potential salaciousness of a female killer in a highly publicized trial inspired Jackie's prosecutors to grandstand with feats of gendered gymnastics. They alternately sexualized teenage Jackie to paint a picture of a femme fatale, then desexualized her when it came to the question of punishment, implausibly arguing that her age and gender, which they'd just highlighted to tell their story, "didn't matter." As we saw with Ike Easley, demonization ignores contradictory facts and arguments as long as they fit the "them" frame, in this case a gang frame. That a fifteen-year-old girl might be something more than a "cold-blooded assassin" seemed obvious to me.

I knew the research on "women who kill" someone other than their spouse or child. These women often have one thing in common, Ann Jones (2009) says: child abuse and likely child sexual abuse. An astounding three quarters of all female prisoners, the Sentencing Project (2019) reported, had a background of sexual abuse. Despite this disturbing research finding, at her original trial, nobody ever asked Jackie in detail about her childhood: not the prosecutors, not her judges, and, most important, not her own attorneys at the time. Jackie's prosecution occurred during years with some of the highest homicide totals in Chicago's history of gangs and gang wars, with media floodlights focused on putting a fresh and different face on one more gang murder with politicians pontificating about "super-predators." This context gravely diminished the court's capacity for objective analysis and extinguished any hint of compassion. To the court, Jackie was not an individual but the personification of gang violence.

The image that dominated Jackie's trial was played over and over to the jury. It was a clip from local TV of Jackie, under arrest, entering the local police station after the murders. She smiles and rebelliously gives a gang hand sign and mouths "Maniac King Killer." This clip would later feature in the History Channel's *Gangland*'s 2008 episode, menacingly named "Maniacal." Prosecutors verbally annotated the video by advising jurors to note: "None of this will show any contrition, any sorrow at all." They explained Jackie was "still reveling in the glory of her kill . . . on that videotape." The connotation was clear; an animal roars in the glory of her kill, not a human. Left unsaid: "If she is an animal it's okay to put her down." Jackie was a cartoon character, not a real human being: a she-monster, according to prosecutors, who slaughtered her victims.

Today, after nearly thirty years in prison, Jackie is still a rebel but long past her gang phase. Her history of prison tickets, or "violations," is a problem in clemency hearings, parole, or early release. The last time I saw her in person, her eyes still flashed with the charisma that made her "Loca D" on the streets. She prefers "Jacqueline" or "Jackie": her Loca D and Jackie identities have competed over the years for control over her behavior. Even in Illinois prisons, Jackie's life was endangered by both incarcerated rival Latin Queens and guards influenced by the Latin Kings or bribed by them. As a young girl, Jackie's killing of two male Latin King soldiers was a threat to the Latin Kings and their macho self-image. If she returns to Chicago when she is released, Jackie will never be completely safe. She is controversial in prison as well, which was one reason her present lawyer Ali Flaum got her transferred to Florida to serve the final years of her sentence. When released, she will have served thirty years in prison, twice as long as she had previously lived in the "free" world.

She is a constant focus of attention from correctional officers. I recall one visit where she and I exchanged a brotherly/sisterly hug and kiss as the visit started. A correctional official with graying hair and granny glasses adroitly sprang to our side a foot or so from us. She bent her knees and craned her face to within a few inches of our heads, eyeballing us to see if I had passed drugs or any other "contraband" from my mouth to Jackie's. Very little Jackie did in prison would be unobserved, and, if she violated a rule, she would be reliably ticketed, compiling a record that would be used against any early release. She seemed to be constantly restricted from various activities as a result of yet another ticket. It was never certain when we visited her in Illinois whether she would be allowed visitors. She vacillated between being a "Cool Hand Luke" and a woman who picks her battles. I sympathize. My own temperament is strongly oppositional and at times gets me in more than a little trouble. But I think my passion is one reason I always got along well with Jackie.

Aubri McDonald, a bright new Ph.D. student from the University of Colorado, was a good candidate to research Jackie's case for her dissertation. Aubri's background was in communications, not criminal justice, and could bring that perspective to understanding the demonization surrounding Jackie's trial. Aubri also came from a white middle-class background that was in many ways the polar opposite of Jackie's. Let Aubri tell the story of her meeting Jackie for the first time (2016, 51).

> I wasn't sure what to say during that first visit. What do you say to a double murderer who has spent more than half her life in prison? How could I relate to her? I wasn't sure that I could. At one point during the visit she turned to me and asked if I had ever seen those magazines with a page that has a flap you can lift up and it smells like perfume. I was struck and immediately humbled. "Sure" I said, with a rush of guilt as I envisioned the growing pile of unread Allure magazines on the floor in the corner of my apartment I had come to despise. They had come to represent time I didn't have. By some glitch I was sent one every week, they took up space and I wasn't going to read them. . . . She lit up when I told her I'd send her some magazines with that perfume flap. This had a profound impact on me long after I left the prison that day. There are few times in life when you have this abrupt realization followed by frantic recalculation about how much in life you take for granted. It put so many things into focus—the larger picture of liberties lost, things I took for granted, the vast space between us bridged by perfume inserts in magazines.
>
> She was not this "cold-blooded" monster like the prosecutors, the Chicago *Tribune* and Gangland had made her out to be. She is a girl like many of my friends who likes to read about makeup and clothes and those perfume inserts in magazines that I usually ignore, that's special for her.

Aubri had a sister Jackie's age, and the similarities between Aubri, her sister, and Jackie shaped Aubri's understanding of Jackie as a young woman who was of a kind with Aubri's peers, not a monster. Aubri has maintained a relationship with Jackie now for more than a decade. But how did a young woman like Jackie end up in prison, after killing two gang members, and not, like Aubri, in graduate school at the University of Illinois–Chicago?

Jackie grew up Puerto Rican and poor in Humboldt Park in Chicago and not white and middle class in a Kansas City suburb. As Northwestern Law School students researched her case, it turned out that Ann Jones's analysis applied: sexual abuse also defined Jackie's youth—unlike Aubri's. It became obvious that the prosecutor's claim to the jury that the murders occurred "for one reason and one reason only, and that's street gang violence," was false. In the frame introduced by the prosecutors, Jackie, like Ike Easley, was a monster, consumed by doing the evil deeds gangs do. "Street gangs," the prosecutor argued, "have their own set of rules. When someone does them wrong, they go out on missions and they take out revenge. Well, we don't do that in a civilized society. We have rules of law. We have due process."

Was it really that simple? The court thought so. Before the trial began, the judge accepted a motion in limine, which set the contours of what would be permitted to be discussed at trial. Aubri describes the scene in her dissertation (2016, 82):

> The judge determined that Montañez's mental health history was relevant only as far as explaining her gang name, "Loca D" which stood for Crazy Disciple. In the following excerpt from Montañez's trial, the judge stopped the trial to assure that Montañez's mental health history would be limited to explaining her gang name (*Montañez v. Illinois* 1993):

> Defense: Now, are you familiar with Jacqueline's history of hospitalization?
> Mother: Yes.
> Prosecution: Objection, Judge.
> Judge: Excuse us, ladies and gentlemen.
> Judge: We are in chambers. Objection by the State. Basis?
> Prosecution: Judge, first of all, relevancy . . . we made a Motion in Liminae [*sic*] prior to starting this trial and the only reference to her mental health would be to show that [*sic*] she got the nickname of Loca D. And to have her mother go in and testify about her mental health, I don't think that is relevant. I think it is outside her knowledge.
> Judge: Objection to the form of the question is sustained. What are you going into?
> Defense: That she has been hospitalized a couple times in the emergency rooms for taking drugs and that is it. That is all.
> Judge: What has that got to do with this case?

What, indeed, does Jackie's mental health have to do with this case?
As Jackie was interviewed by Ali Flaum, Patricia Soung, and other top-notch Northwestern lawyers, along with a host of law students, her childhood story leaped right out at listeners like a 3D horror movie. The story

begins with her stepfather, a Latin King and drug dealer. Preadolescent Jackie was put to work delivering (on the streets, it's called "serving") drugs curbside to customers. But, as Jackie recalled her early life, it was clear the hurricane-like terror of it had literally propelled her to teenage violence. She told of being her stepdad's favorite and having sex with him as early as nine years old. Of course, this is rape in any sense of the word. She said in a recorded interview with her lawyers that "I woke up to screaming every morning. I thought it was normal." She added forlornly to Aubri McDonald, "There was no child in that childhood." (See Fig. 10.1.)

She ran away repeatedly, only to be returned to her stepfather by police and social workers. As she headed toward her teenage years, her stepfather's abuse continued, and she continued to try to escape. Then, at age twelve, she succeeded and—surprise, surprise—joined her father's Latin King gang's blood rival, the Maniac Latin Disciples. The trauma of her childhood would find violent expression through two dead Latin Kings one night in Humboldt Park.

As I had with Ike Easley, I risked going behind the veil that covered up Jackie's vulnerable memories of the act of killing. As we talked in Dwight prison in a private legal conference room, I asked her to walk me through what happened that night, step-by-step. She talked about walking together with Hector Reyes and Jimmy Cruz at the Humboldt Park restroom with her hidden pistol. Her voice softened, and she began to whisper how she pulled the gun out and shot them, one and then the other. Then with tears flowing, she told me, "It wasn't them I wanted to kill. It was my stepfather."

Figure 10.1 Nine-year-old Jackie Montañez. (Courtesy of the subject.)

This was the revelation that needed to be understood by anyone seeking to truly understand what happened, although I was surprised it emerged so dramatically. The roots of what Jackie did that day went far beneath the prosecutor's claim that the killing was "only" the product of gang violence. Jackie's mental health was a mess. Her stepfather's abuse took away her self-worth, her trust, and warped how she viewed others. Her gang membership and her violence were both conscious decisions on her part but also a by-product of a life of cataclysmic, out-of-control emotions. These two threads, her decisions and her traumatic childhood, were stitched together to form the whole cloth of the homicide. You can't have one without the other.

Jackie's reality would complicate the narrative even more. Jackie told many different stories of the shooting over the years. During trial, she said she shot Cruz, then gave the gun to Marilyn Mulero, who shot Reyes. To me in Dwight, she vividly relived her shooting both young men. Mulero wasn't present in her tense narration of events. This later version provided a basis for Marilyn Mulero's claim of actual innocence, which would win her clemency in 2020. Jackie, serving life without parole, was motivated to help her friend and her statement was crucial in Mulero's claim of "actual innocence." Experience has taught me that Jackie's intense, whispered words recalling what happened that night can't fully be trusted. In many other cases, I've been told stories of murder that are shaped by both trauma and legal self-interest. I'm not clear if Jackie knows herself which version of that night's horror was "real." In one sense, it doesn't matter. Both she and her two homegirls were legally and morally culpable for both murders. But if Jackie's claim about how many Kings she shot can't be trusted, what about her horror story of child sexual abuse?

Ali Flaum located her stepfather and got him to come into the Bluhm Legal Clinic, where he agreed to be video recorded while he answered questions. I watched the video, seeing Jackie's stepfather nervously twitching as he gave halting answers to Ali's pointed questions about whether he did, in fact, have sex with a child. "If Jackie says I did, it must be true" was the closest he came to an admission. I learned from my Latin King friends that Jackie's stepdad was not the big-time gang leader he posed as but an unstable hype, a user, and a penny-ante dealer who was not trusted even by his own gang. Jackie's allegations of her stepfather's sexual abuse had no outside confirmation—few children's stories of sexual abuse get that—but were far from preposterous to those who knew her stepdad.

What do I think? I think Jackie's emotional life was severely distorted as a child by her family life, including sexually abusive acts by her stepfather. She also was pushed into behavior, like serving drugs to raucous men, that would damage something deep inside of any nine-year-old. Think of a girl in the fourth grade you know, or yourself when you were that young. Like the girl in the picture in Figure 10.1. Bringing a bag of weed or coke to rough characters who likely hooted at the pretty girl-child with a put-on smile. What violently conflicting emotions must this nine-year-old have had: pleasing her father, dressing up and being hooted at, and worst, having to keep "daddy's secret." Jackie was emotionally damaged and her hostile motivations toward Latin Kings were displaced from sources much deeper than gang rivalry. Whether she shot both or just one of the two Kings or whether she remembered exactly all the particulars of her stepfather's abuse is beside the point. The prosecutor claimed the crime was only about gang violence to get the most severe sentence. But this claim also banished from the courtroom any consideration of young Jackie as a real, emotionally fragile, damaged, and volatile human being. The jury saw her as inflicting pain but never caught even a glimpse of the pain that was searing inside her.

What about her provocative throwing up of gang signs and "King Killer" words upon arrest? Here is the "teen queen of criminals" as the media dubbed her describing to her attorneys her actual reaction to being arrested and put in a holding pen: "I wasn't a big bad wolf. I was scared to death."

Jackie told Aubri that the nihilism of gang life meant she was "just trying to fit in. . . . I never thought I would live to see my 16th birthday." As with Keith Harbin and Ike Easley, Jackie Montañez's bravado-sounding words after taking a human life are what Matza (1964) calls neutralization, a porous patch over the palpable rip in one's protective moral fabric. These angry posthomicide words get used by prosecutors against defendants like Jackie, Ike, or Keith to paint them as unfeeling monsters. But, in reality, they are a psychological window into these young killers' anguish over self-inflicted damage to their own humanity. Their outrageous words are a desperate and losing attempt at justification of their fatal deeds, too horrifying even for themselves to rationally face.

This returns us to the argument of this book. We can never forget that Hector Reyes and Jimmy Cruz are still dead, no matter what Jackie's motivations. I was in contact with members of both victims' families through comments on a YouTube video I put up as Jackie was seeking clemency. Some were still furious and understandably vindictive twenty years after the murders. Others saw no point in keeping Jackie locked up for her entire life. It wouldn't bring their loved one back. I concur with both: no one should get away with murder and Jackie's life without parole sentence brings no real relief.

At the same time, what happened at Jackie's trial, beginning with the state's decision to charge her with two counts of gang murder, represents the power of the gang frame to blot out any other motivations, any human understanding of what had happened. As we've seen throughout this book, the categorical logic of the gang frame, the public fantasy of what gang membership means, and the othering and dehumanizing inherent in the frame make it all too easy to ascribe Jackie's murder to what the juror imagines as her essential, monstrous nature and conclude that execution is the natural solution. Or in Jackie's case, if the technicality of her being seventeen days shy of her sixteenth birthday prohibits the death penalty, why shouldn't we lock her in a cage for life and throw away the key? Jackie said it best: "I did what you said I did but I'm not who you say I am."

Prosecutors have enormous discretion, and, in Jackie's case, the prosecutor's decision to charge her with two homicides made her life without parole sentence mandatory under Illinois law at the time. They instructed the jury not to consider her age and gender. Even if the court had known about the sexual abuse, legally, it would not have mattered to the determinations our justice system asks jurors to make. The prosecutor's decision to charge her with both homicides took off the table any judicial discretion at her sentencing. Had they charged her with one homicide, as the evidence at the time indicated, the judge could have set a sentence of something other than life without parole. The prosecutors knew what they were doing. Since they couldn't get a death sentence—as they would get with Marilyn Mulero—they settled for life without parole. They didn't want to take a chance with a jury who might wonder what happened that led a fifteen-year-old girl to kill? They planned to let Jackie die in prison, and they could guarantee it with the proper charge. They thought: "Isn't the maximum possible sentence what gang members deserve?" The defendant during that trial was not really Jacqueline Montañez. She was in essence, and no more than, "Loca D," a gang member who killed. The prototype replaced the person.

Craig Haney and the Fundamental Attribution Error as Criminal Justice Policy

Psychologist Craig Haney is best known for his work on death penalty cases and scholarly articles on mitigation. His 2006 book, *Reforming Punishment*, takes us on a psychological journey of retrograde changes in the criminal justice system. He explains the punitive lurch of our sentencing policy in psychological terms consistent with the argument of this book.

In these pages, I only briefly recap the story of how the United States ended up with a regime of mass incarceration. The reader can look to David Garland (1990), Michelle Alexander (2010), or Michael Tonry (2016) among many others for explanations of this dismal chapter in our nation's history. I'm interested in the role stereotypes play in our frenzy for mass incarceration. David Livingstone Smith's (2012) book *Less Than Human* argues that the use of a demonizing stereotype like those defining gangs, depends on belief in a category's "essence," a folk understanding of what a "gang member" really is. This essence, to use Smith's phrase, defines gang members as "less than human," and, therefore, it is permitted, nay encouraged, to use violence against them— whether through the death penalty or long terms of imprisonment.

In other words, to a mind primed by the gang category, Jackie Monta-ñez's history of sexual abuse was beside the point. Her killing of two Latin Kings was about her "nature" as a gang member. Even her confession was dehumanized, called by prosecutors the squealing of "a rat in a corner." Her smile, her throwing up a gang sign, and her mouthing "Maniac King Killer" were all confirmation that this fifteen-year-old girl was not one of "us" but one of "them." The psychological process that ignores context and biography is called the "fundamental attribution error," and Haney makes it the centerpiece of his criminal justice history.

Haney relies on attribution theory, which Fiske and Taylor (1991, 64) explain is how a "social perceiver" (say, a juror or judge) "arrives at causal explanations of events" (say, the motive of a murder). We all need to understand why something happens, so we can stop bad things from happening again and exercise some control over our world. In Haney's book, American correctional policy has long been characterized by the attribution that the cause of crime lies in defects in the criminal's character more than circumstances like poverty, racism, or situations of crisis or confrontation. The prison itself was established as a "correctional" institution, to correct human nature like the "reformatory" was to reform the character of youths. For example, Haney (2006, 36) quotes noted prison reformer and signer of the Constitution, Benjamin Rush, who believed that criminal behavior is a form of "moral derangement." Long terms of imprisonment and solitary confinement were initially justified as ways to "rehabilitate" criminals who were "sick."

The early twentieth-century Progressive Era faith in the perfectibility of man had many unanticipated consequences, like indeterminate sentences that relied on the good faith of prison officials and social workers to decide whether a prisoner was sufficiently reformed. In the 1960s, African American ghetto rebellions and riots brought a new appreciation of the influence of the environment on human behavior. Haney reports this realization resulted in more attention being given to the lessons of psychologists on the impact of poverty and racism. What they learned encouraged legislators to propose a war on poverty, an array of antipoverty programs aimed at changing the conditions of poor children and their families. That era, says Haney, echoing well-known history, was cut short by the Nixon era "white backlash" and war on crime, which led to a sharp increase in the number of prisoners in American prisons, an increase that continued even as crime rates fell or stayed constant. Punishment became an end in itself, rather than a means of "correction." More and more prisoners were "incapacitated," meaning warehoused in cages for decades at a time with little or no access to education and "reentry" programs. Criminal justice policy lost a professed concern with "correcting" and replaced it with "punishing."

Haney notes the racialization of punishment as the incarceration body count of nonwhite people mounted. For example, by the 1970s, Haney reports, nonwhite people made up two-thirds of California's prison population while making up only one-third of the total population. How is it, he asks, that an overwhelmingly white criminal justice system could so easily lock up for so long so many people who were nonwhite, who white policy makers, judges, prosecutors, and voters saw as the other? He repeats a line right out of David Livingstone Smith: "It is easier to punish people more harshly if they already have been demonized, are perceived to be somewhat less than fully human, or are regarded as fundamentally 'other'" (2012, 94). White culture stigmatizes nonwhite, and, particularly, Black, people, as having an essentially violent nature as well as other despised character traits. The pain they endure by incarceration is hidden from the majority of white citizens who consciously or subconsciously share the racist assumption that these dark-skinned malefactors deserve it or that somehow punishment affects them less because of who they are.

Haney says this belief in the less-than-human nature of nonwhite defendants allowed the "decontextualizing of crime" to go down more easily—perhaps like a spoonful of sugar lets the medicine go down. The medicine for white citizens, in this case, is the perception of being safe, and the "sugar" is the relief of knowing the dark-skinned people they assume to be bad guys are getting their just deserts. Sentences became harsher and "mandatory minimums" sent people automatically to prison regardless of circumstance.

Haney argued (206, 97) that the "sentencing reforms that began in the mid-1970s greatly constricted judicial discretion and eliminated the opportunity for social context to be considered at all in these types of legal proceedings." Determinate and mandatory minimum sentences disregarded the context of a crime and set a punishment based on legislators' judgment of a crime's severity, interpreted mainly by prosecutors. Thus, Jacqueline Montañez was mandatorily sentenced to life without parole because the prosecutor decided to charge her with two homicides, not separate counts—even though it was well within his authority to have charged her that way. And such a determinate sentence attached to a given crime, regardless of circumstance, makes it understandable how her judge could say with a straight face about her history of mental illness, "What does that have to do with this case?" This may also be why her original defense attorneys failed to research her family history. They may have realized her childhood, no matter how severe her problems, would not have any legal weight against an automatic sentence of life without parole. So why bother to investigate? In fact, no one did. Haney's point is that the sentencing regime in the United States since the 1970s has minimized context and elevated an "evil self" as the operative criminal motive. Sentences would be standardized, not individualized. Reform or rehabilitation of monsters, this line of thinking goes, is not possible so incapacitation is the only way to keep "us" safe from "them."

Haney argues that criminal justice policy has been characterized by the "fundamental attribution error," or the systematic disregard of situation and biography and an overemphasis on attributing a crime to a person's "supposed unmodifiable criminal dispositions" (2006, 96). American culture has attributed disparaging character traits to a disproportionately non-white population, and persisting racism and poverty are not permitted to be included when a court calculates punishment. In a separate essay on capital punishment, Haney (1995, 549) says defendants like Ike Easley or Jackie Montañez are seen by prosecutors and the public alike as "genetic misfits, as unfeeling psychopaths who kill for the sheer pleasure of it, or as dark, anonymous figures who are something less than human."

The post-1950s growth of the nation's nonwhite population and their concentration in largely poor urban areas fed white people's and politicians' natural "them and us" tendencies. In order to justify policies of violence— long sentences, the abolition of parole, the revival of the death penalty— prosecutors and law enforcement officials attributed blame to "them" not to the conditions that surrounded them. And as both Smith and Muhammad point out, the category "them" had an essence and that essence is criminality, violence, and the "Blackness" of sin. The sentencing reforms of the 1970s, Haney (2006, 113) says, "institutionalized" fundamental attribution error in the criminal justice system. In other words, crime and justice was about right and wrong, legal and illegal, but it became more and more about "us and them." This brings us to the trials of Jackie Montañez. Yes, trials, plural. It took more than one for the courts to get it "right." Or wrong.

The Trials of Jacqueline Montañez

The prosecutor in Jackie's trial in effect served as the judge and jury as well as specified the exact length of sentence. Conviction on the specific charges the DA indicted her on automatically meant life without parole. The outcome was determined from the start by the prosecutor's decision on what charges to bring. But in a scenario by now familiar to the reader, during the trial, prosecutors still went over the top to demonize Jackie and persuade the jury they need not consider anything in the case that might humanize the defendant. What does a history of child sexual abuse by a member of the rival gang of the victim have to do with this trial? "Not relevant," said the motion in limine. The jury and judge can pass judgment and sentence against the gang member, "Loca D," the prototype of a she-creature who kills, not Jacqueline Montañez, a real, damaged human being. "We" can safely do harm to her, David Livingstone Smith (2012) explains, because she is not really one of "us."

This dehumanization of Jackie permeated the trial and allowed for so many irregularities I don't have room to discuss them all. Aubri McDonald's dissertation recaps both trials in rich detail. Certainly, the gang stereotype was drilled uncontested into the heads of jurors. For example, prosecutors labeled Jackie "a gang murderer . . . a cold-blooded killer . . . with utter disregard for human life" (*Montañez v. Illinois* 1993a). But Jackie was a sixteen-year-old girl at the time of trial. Prosecutors had to work to demonize a pretty girl sitting in a "Heidi dress" at the defense table. They leaned into misogynistic stereotypes of women as manipulators and deceivers in order, ironically, to argue that Jackie as a killer was not so female as she appeared to be, in a feat of "gender gymnastics" that was a wonder to behold.

They started by getting the jury to question their own eyes. Here is Aubri's description (2016, 5):

> Prosecutors accused Montañez of masquerading as a female in court by wearing a "Heidi dress" in an attempt to "deceive" the jury just as she had her victims when she "lured" them to their death. A gendered and racialized "gang frame" was so tightly constructed during Montañez's trials it's argued that prosecutors, judge, defense attorneys and jurors were unable to see outside this frame.

The prosecutor argued the "Heidi dress" was part of a deceptive "masquerade." He warned the jury that Jackie had used her female wiles to get close enough to murder two young men, and now she intended to "seduce" the jurors so she could get away with murder. She was a "femme fatale" in the exact sense of the term but, at the same time, a "gender outlaw." A young girl killing two men is "something you don't see every day," one journalist wrote. In this way, her ability to break into and out of her gendered box sat in observers minds alongside the idea that a woman who commits acts of violence must be doubly dangerous because women don't commit violence. She was in the wrong whether she broke the category or stayed in it. When considering the other, the human mind does not demand consistency—you really can have it all ways. Then, as the trial ended, prosecutors abruptly changed course and urged jurors to "disregard" the fact that Jackie was young and female. It is only the cold-blooded murder by a gang member that counts, and the broader context of Jackie's life history should not enter into jury deliberations. This is the perfect example of what Haney means by the fundamental attribution error of correctional policy.

Jackie's guilt was so clear that due process niceties could also be disregarded. Her confession, for example, was coerced by detectives with a long history of threatening witnesses and manufacturing evidence. Her mother was not allowed to be present as fifteen-year-old Jackie was interrogated. Constitutionally, an accused juvenile is allowed to have a parent or guardian present. This egregious violation of how the Fifth Amendment applies to juveniles caused the Illinois Supreme Court to overturn her first conviction. Police claims to have observed due process, the court ruled, were no more than a "tragic charade." They ruled that the confession should not have been admitted and ordered a new trial. But when gangs are involved, the Constitution is often little more than an afterthought. With no confession, there wasn't any evidence to convict Jackie. So, the judge in her second trial simply said the Illinois Supreme Court was wrong. Jackie's mother wasn't at the police station waiting after all, he claimed, and her mother lied about not being allowed into the interrogation. The Illinois Supreme Court put "too much weight" on Jackie's mother's words, and the trial judge said the confession would be admitted, even though the Illinois Supreme Court said it should be thrown out.

Aubri McDonald's comment about the gang frame was on point: the court was unable to see outside of the frame of absolute evil gang violence, and all the evidence would be interpreted through a lens of Jackie as a "cold-blooded gang assassin." Jackie's childhood of abuse, her history of mental illness, her very young age, and her gender just didn't matter. Respecting a fifteen-year-old's right to have a parent present at a police interrogation really wasn't important either, and police could blithely lie and get away with it. Why? Because thanks to their fundamental attribution error, Jackie wasn't really a fifteen-year-old girl, she was a cold-blooded gang killer, and gang retaliation was all that was involved. The gang frame put blinders on every party in the trial except a bewildered and frightened Jacqueline Montañez. The fundamental attribution error in the mandatory minimum system and in the eyes of the prosecutor linked the gang stereotype of cold-blooded killer to the inevitable maximum punishment. Damn any discrepant information that would get in the way of what prosecutors called "justice" being done.

The Movement against JLWOP

Unfortunately, in the 1990s, Jackie's case was not unique. The rhetoric of superpredators dominated the public's understanding of juvenile crime. These were not children, within that public understanding, but unfeeling monsters, a wolf pack as the Central Park Five was called. Back in 1989, Donald Trump was among those who demanded the return of the death penalty for these five accused teenagers who were ultimately exonerated by DNA evidence.

Around 2009, a national movement arose to reclaim the early principles of juvenile justice, which acknowledged that children were different than adults. Using new brain sciences, scientists argued the obvious that juvenile brains were both not as "well-formed" as and "less fixed" than those of adults. In a throwback to court decisions in an earlier era of rehabilitation, *Miller v. Alabama* was a gasp of air for young delinquents drowning in a demonizing ocean of retributive justice. More than two hundred thousand children, disproportionately nonwhite, are prosecuted every year as adults. At the time of the 2012 *Miller v. Alabama* decision, more than twenty-five hundred youths had already been sentenced to life without parole—a slow death behind bars. *Miller* overturned laws, like the Illinois statute affecting Jackie, that had mandatory provisions that gave no consideration to a juvenile's capacity to mature.

Demonstrations against JLWOP broke out across the country. In Chicago, I steered my Gangs and the Media and graduate seminar in Research Methods classes to address JLWOP and Jackie's case specifically. Students wrote to Jackie and attended a University of Illinois–Chicago teach-in, which featured parents of JLWOP offenders and speeches humanizing the offenders. As JLWOP young men and a few women were lining up for resentencing, Aubri McDonald and I mobilized students to attend hearings and demonstrate support.

Jackie's attorneys, like most lawyers, were not crazy about public protests. The very real danger would be that such publicity would mobilize a much stronger, and larger, punitive reaction. Like elected DAs everywhere, the state's attorney in Cook County was susceptible to pressure, but the strongest pressures come from victims and reactionary law-and-order groups, not supporters of human rights. The impact of protests in the streets is also unpredictable and might backfire. Defense lawyers are taught to play it safe and trust their legal arguments to win the day compiling more facts and hoping for better stories to prevail.

What I think readers of this book have seen is that the impact of the stereotyping and demonization of gangs is often unbeatable in court. Mere words in a courtroom are nearly always insufficient to carry the day against the subconscious prototypes of killer gang monsters primed by conviction-hungry prosecutors and a white supremacist culture.

However, when looking at a trial, we have to realize the fundamental attribution error also works in the opposite direction. Police may have seen their reputations among much of the public permanently soiled by the George Floyd murder, but, in court, they have been historically assumed to be good at heart, truthful, and protectors of the public. This is the clear assumption of prosecutors at a trial—police are the good guys; gangs are the bad guys. These assumed character traits trump any evidence of misconduct, excuse lying, and overlook histories of illegal and corrupt police behaviors. The fundamental attribution error is a form of stereotype whose power to influence juries is the central theme of this book.

One way to understand the power of stereotypes and the fundamental attribution error is to consider police killings of civilians. Police kill about a thousand people every year in the United States: about 40 percent of them nonwhite. The *Los Angeles Times* reported that one out of every one thousand African American males can expect to be killed at the hands of police. And what happens in court when police kill a young Black man?

A National Public Radio analysis found twenty-four hundred people were killed by police between 2015 and 2017. Only twenty officers out of twenty-four hundred fatal shootings faced any charges at all. And, of those, a grand total of six were convicted of any criminal offense. Like in the gang cases I've been describing, on the rare occasion when police officers are indicted for a crime of lethal force, it's not the evidence that matters most but the power of stereotypes and the fundamental attribution error. While gang members are assumed to be demons, police officers have in the past received the benefit of the doubt. As I write, protesters have taken to the streets protesting the police killing of George Floyd with cries of "Black Lives Matter." Our protests have reframed the issue of police violence and pressured DAs to prosecute. These protests also often demonize police and prosecutors. I think this is a mistake. I believe demonization of any group undermines the cause of justice and defines justice as a battle of frame against frame instead of a pursuit of truth and remedy. But it is also true that prosecutors, who are so zealous in gang cases, are considerably less eager to prosecute police. The history of allowing police violence to go unprosecuted means that we have no other course to get justice but to go outside the courtroom and into the streets.

We are turning now to the final part of my story: What is to be done? I hope you don't expect these courtroom experiences to conclude well. But whether you think me pessimistic or realistic, such attitudes are no excuse for inaction. The criminal justice system may seem to be all powerful. However, I believe resistance is not futile but necessary. In the final chapters, I want to explore various means of struggle against the awesome power of stereotypes. Our culture of demonization is far broader and more menacing than in its legal application by prosecutors against gang members. Demonization is also a difficult burden to overcome for those of us who are protesting in our struggle for justice.

CASE LAW

Montañez v. Illinois, 92-CR-13088, Tr. of June 9, 17, 18 (Cir. Ct. 1993a). [Motion to Suppress Statements]

Montañez v. Illinois, 92-CR-13088, Tr. of August 5–6 (Cir. Ct. 1993). [First Trial]

Montañez v. Illinois, 652 N.E.2d 1271 June 30 (Ill. App. Ct. 1995). [1st Appellate Decision]

Montañez v. Illinois, 517 U.S. 116 S. Ct. 2514 (S. Ct. 1996). [U.S. Supreme Court Decision]

Montañez v. Illinois, 92-CR-13088, Tr. of November 1–3 (Cir. Ct. 1999). [Second Trial]

III

The Struggle for Justice

*Reframing Stereotypes
and Overcoming Demonization*

11

Don't Start Acting Human on Me Now

Prosecutors, Police, and Jail—
A Personal Story

I n the court cases you've read about in these pages, prosecutors have been more than eager to bring charges against gang members, insist a crime is gang related, and enhance the charges with statutes like Georgia's Street Gang Terrorist Prevention Act. And even when conviction is assured, I've shown that prosecutors often go into overdrive and demonize the defendant, making sure they get the maximum sentence allowed—if possible, the death penalty—for crimes that would have earned lesser sentences if not for the gang association. This "prosecution complex," to win at all costs, is an article of faith among many prosecutors. I've also pointed out gang demonization is occupationally useful. Being a gangbuster can get you elected and reelected. In the case of the gang member, it becomes possible to pursue a maximum sentence at all costs because the gang stereotype brands the gang member as an evil thug—the actual crime is hardly relevant. But, when the criminal is stereotypically seen as good, does the prosecution complex to win at all costs, invoke the most punitive statutes, and pursue the maximum sentence still apply? (See Fig. 11.1.)

For example, what about prosecuting a police officer for murder? The data say that an officer is charged in less than 2 percent of all police killings. For example, in 2017, 1,095 people were killed by police, and 13 officers were charged with a crime. Police shootings are also examples of what the term "presumption of innocence" should really mean. Prosecutors and city officials give police officers more than the benefit of the doubt in charging decisions. The public's stereotype or folk wisdom of police being the good guys tilts the evidence toward prosecutors not charging police at all. In the rare case of a trial of a police officer, there are seldom any convictions. In one way, prosecutions of police and gang members share the same psychology: decisions to prosecute and which charges to bring are decided by stereotypes and occupational self-interest with, at times, only a passing connection to the evidence. The results, however, are as different as . . . oh, say, black and white. One of the most important developments from the George Floyd protests has been the public questioning of the stereotype of police as good guys. (See Fig. 11.2.)

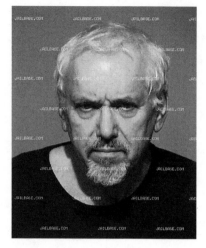

Figure 11.1 Your author.
(Photo accessed from JailBase.com.)

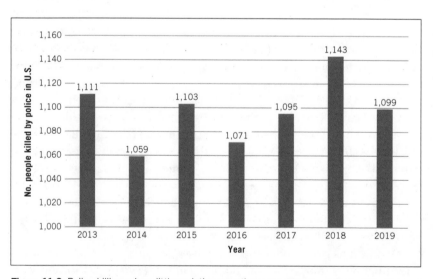

Figure 11.2 Police killings show little variation over the years. (Data from Mapping Police Violence.)

In the early evening of December 19, 2014, I was on my way to jail because a prosecutor, Milwaukee DA John Chisholm, was about to decide not to charge a killer at all. The killer was a white police officer, Christopher Manney. The victim was African American, Dontre Hamilton, a thirty-one-year-old man with a history of mental illness. On April 30, 2014, Dontre had been sleeping in a park in front of the Starbucks café across Wells Street opposite Milwaukee's City Hall. Starbucks employees were offended that some unsuitably attired Black man would be resting in a public park outside their store and called police. The first pair of officers who responded told them there was no law against sleeping in a public park and left Dontre alone. The Starbucks manager was not to be deterred and called in a second time, which brought this pair of officers to the park again to rouse Mr. Hamilton again, and to produce the same conclusion. Finally, the angered Starbucks manager contacted the local beat officer who had given the store his cell phone number. Milwaukee police officer Christopher Manney responded immediately. Manney, who had a history of excessive force—he had once beaten up a circus clown—demanded Dontre get up and vacate the park. Dontre laid there, and Manney began to poke him with his baton. Startled, Dontre grabbed the night stick. Manney wrote in a memo defending his actions that Hamilton had a "muscular build and most definitely would have overpowered . . . me or pretty much any officer I can think of, to tell you the truth. He was just that big, that muscular . . . I would say he would be impossible to control if you were one man." His memo was intended to document that he was justified in using lethal force because he feared for his life. It invoked a long history of white people's exaggerated racist fears of large menacing Black men as *New York Times* columnist Brent Staples wrote (2018). During the struggle for the baton, Manney claimed, he had been forced to pull out his handgun and shoot Dontre in self-defense. In fact, he felt compelled to shoot him fourteen times.

Dontre's autopsy makes for gruesome reading. Manney's description of Dontre in near "apelike" terms fits racist stereotypes of Black men but did not fit the autopsy's description of the actual person, Dontre Hamilton. The big, muscular man that one man could not possibly control was described by the medical examiner as a "169-pound, 5-foot-7, well developed, overweight . . . adult-black male." Manney's racist fears of Black men, and his own self-interest in justifying his use of lethal force, transformed Dontre in his own mind and in his official homicide report into the prototype of the dangerous Black monster.

The autopsy undermined Manney's claim of self-defense. Seven of the shots had a downward trajectory, meaning Dontre was on the ground and Manney standing a few feet away and above him. One of the bullet wounds entered

Dontre's back. The wounds showed no "stippling or unburned or burned gunpowder particles" meaning they were not fired from close range during a struggle, as Manney claimed. Toxicology found no illegal drugs in Dontre's body. Whatever happened, the evidence suggests Manney shot Dontre based on imagined fears, fed by racism and forward panic, not any actual threat to his life.

In response to the killing, the Coalition for Justice was formed, led by Dontre's mother, Maria Hamilton, his brother Nate, and their grieving family. My wife, Mary, became very close to Maria and later coordinated a national Million Moms March on Washington, DC, to protest police killings. Our local Unitarian Church would sponsor Maria, Mary, and me to travel to Ferguson, Missouri, two years later, to commemorate the first anniversary of the much more widely known police killing of Michael Brown, which had taken place just three months after Dontre's murder.

You already know the rest of the story. Just like gang members are certain to be charged, convicted, and sentenced, police officers don't often get charged and seldom go on trial and, therefore, do not run any risk of being convicted and doing prison time. The Milwaukee County DA, John Chisholm, a liberal champion, had sat on the charges for Manney for nearly eight months, in part because of city officials' fears that Milwaukee could become another Ferguson. In the cold of December 2014, Chisholm's decision was imminent, and the Coalition for Justice had little doubt where the Chisholm trail would lead.

John Chisholm found Manney's shooting of Dontre, fourteen times, "privileged and justifiable." Chisholm attempted to describe how it was understandable that Manney fired fourteen shots into Dontre's body with his Smith & Wesson M&P semiautomatic handgun. Manney had already been fired in the fall of 2014 by Milwaukee police chief Ed Flynn, not for killing Dontre, but for not following correct procedure in patting down a mentally ill person. Manney would retire on "duty disability" due to the stress caused by the homicide. He would earn more on disability and his pension than with his police salary. No criminal charges were ever filed.

Protest is risky and unpredictable. The Hamilton family led the Coalition and all sorts of activists and adventurists competed for their attention. Both Mary and I were in the group that had decided we would not tempt arrest the night of December 19 but would turn out in support of a group of younger, more daring protesters who planned to disrupt traffic. It didn't turn out that way. As the planned disruption occurred, and as rush hour was beginning, we were led by inexperienced and rash leaders onto the freeway downtown. The Milwaukee Police Department, in fear of inciting a high-profile standoff with citizens, as in Ferguson, had pursued a "velvet glove" strategy throughout the fall and early winter months, allowing us to march in the streets, almost wherever we wanted. But, when we went onto the freeway, we were no longer on city but on county land, the turf of flamboyant, conservative, cowboy-hat-wearing Sheriff David Clarke. Clarke saw right-wing glory in getting tough with Black Lives Matter protesters, whom he had publicly called "urban terrorists" and falsely claimed were led by "outside anarchists." Within a worldview like that, where protesters were not concerned citizens but dangerous enemies, what distinction could there be and what could the police force gain through toleration of protest?

Nervously, I watched the sheriff's deputies massing on the freeway ramp behind us, cutting off any easy retreat. Logistically, we were screwed. We had all believed we would be warned to leave before we would be arrested and, Mary and I at least, would have had the sense to quickly remove ourselves from traffic. The warning never came. Unbeknownst to us, the order had come down directly from the sheriff: "Arrest them all." Meaning all seventy-four of us. One young woman panicked and ran to try to escape. She was quickly grabbed by a pair of officers and wrestled to the ground. I was just standing there thinking that maybe if Mary and I could keep our cool we could avoid arrest, when a sergeant pointed at me and said to a group of waiting police, "Grab him." Adrenaline ran through me, but I had been there before. Truthfully, though, I had last been arrested in 1973, a distant forty-one years ago. I peacefully submitted to arrest, plastic handcuffs clamped on my wrists, as I was led to a waiting bus.

Rather than process us quickly, or just give us tickets or municipal citations, and release us, the sheriff made sure we would spend the night at the county's expense. If the courts would go bleeding heart, I'm sure he reckoned, at least law-and-order Sheriff Clarke would extract his pound of flesh—a night in the pokey for urban terrorists and anarchists. Sentence first; trial later.

The deputies who herded us into large holding cells had a laugh or two at my expense. It seems that along with me, my oldest son, my wife, and my ex-wife were all arrested and locked up in various cells a few yards from one another. My wife, Mary, and my ex-wife, Kathe, got to spend some quality time together in the same cell. Yes, my ears were buzzing. Most of the dozen or so men who shared a large cell with me were Black with maybe a third white. Most were older, but we had a few teens and twentysomethings. Everyone was agitated and watching what was happening on the floor, which held a half-dozen holding cells like ours. Most of my cellmates had never been in a jail before. They speculated to one another over why someone was pulled out of one cell and disappeared. Was he released? Why? Why did the guards move someone from one cell to another? Why were they talking to her? I sat down on the concrete floor and tried to rest. I told everyone that what was going on with the deputies' actions was beyond our understanding. Shift routines, possibly conflicting orders from superiors, and pure serendipity ruled. Don't try to figure it out, I told them, it doesn't matter. Just wait until they let us out.

But then one of the younger guys told us that he was afraid for his ailing grandmother, whom he lived with. She had a heart condition and would worry if he did not come home. So, we banged on the door to summon a guard. A middle-aged African American female deputy finally came over to the narrow slit in our door to see what the commotion was all about. She glared at us with squinted eyes as we explained our young cellmate's problem and his grandmother's ill health. Could he get his phone call so he could let her know he was alright? Her response was curt. "Don't start acting human on me now." She abruptly turned away and ignored our request. We were all a bit stunned, but it was our last interaction with guards that night. And the most telling. The next day, I was among the last released, twenty hours after getting busted.

People use dehumanization to justify treating people, as Smith says, as "less than human." They use it, especially, in occupations like police or jailers, as psychologist Philip Zimbardo (2007) classically showed. In a famous experiment (Haney et al. 1973), he gave students jobs acting as jailers and prisoners. The playacting jailers treated playacting prisoners brutally, just as they imagined a "real" jailer would do. Our Milwaukee jail deputies weren't acting and neither were we. For our deputy sheriff, human feelings among "criminals" were inconceivable. In jail, "them and us" comes down to who is on which side of the bars.

This story begins my argument of how we can fight stereotypes, dehumanization, and injustice in the courts. It is a daunting task, and, as you've already figured out, defeat is more likely than victory. I've also learned social change doesn't mainly take place in the courtroom. Our arrests took place within a broader movement affirming that Black lives matter. I think this is one of the most hopeful movements of our times, particularly since it "reframes" police killings and injustice as an issue of the basic human rights of African Americans.

During my 1960s activist days, I worked as a draft counselor and knew Selective Service law so well I wrote legal briefs for attorneys defending draft resisters. I was offered financial support to go to law school, but I declined, thinking the courts were poor places to bring change. I've seldom regretted not becoming a lawyer, but I have revised my view of how and where I can best fight for social change. The courts are not the most important venue but a significant one in the fight for social justice.

What I've learned is a variant of the trite old song, "All God's creatures got a place in the choir." You need sopranos, altos, and basses. As a white person, I've had to understand that I will play a different role than my non-white activist and research colleagues. As an academic, I spent more time in the classroom than on the streets. I also commuted to Chicago from Milwaukee, making sustained field research in either city difficult. In both cities, the press has often tried to make me the go-to "white gang expert," and I've tried to shy away from being too public, instead pushing to the fore voices from the community. But I also realized that my academic training and years of gang research gave me an opportunity to do something more than teach and write scholarly articles and books.

My work in court was my "place in the choir." My social science training, my decades of research, and—yes—my race gave me credibility to jurors and judges and even a prosecutor or two. I also realized that the "them and us" mentality influences both them and us. I've told how prosecutors called gang members "Followers of Our Lord King Satan" and how dehumanization justified the death penalty or long sentences. But "our side," the reformers or revolutionaries, is not immune to the "them and us" virus either. Raised in the sixties, I, too, mouthed the rhetoric of "police as pigs," and my own kids picked it up and repeated it to my later horror. It is easy to cross the line from seeing a police officer as an opponent to dehumanizing him or her. Treating police as all alike makes hatred easier and gives a boost to feelings of moral superiority. Writing this book also has taught me not to lump all prosecutors into a single category of demonizers, exemplified by Fred Bright in the Butts and Wilson trials. The movement for progressive prosecutors has a steep hill to climb, but some, like Chesa Boudin, Kim Foxx, and Larry Krasner, have taken up the challenge. It ain't gonna be easy for them. I hope this book helps.

The next two chapters conclude my tale with consideration of different tactics in the struggle for justice. In the next chapter, I examine the expert witness role as I have practiced it. I have some very harsh words for the notion of an expert witness as a "hired gun." I have not pleased every defense attorney, and I tell about the tensions in some of my cases. I explain the crucial lesson from my experience and studies in social psychology about reframing the stereotypes on gangs. I also reveal some mistakes I've made that others can avoid.

In the final chapter, I discuss the broader issue of why we demonize gangs and offer some suggestions on changes in law and policy. This book proposes an ethic of struggle regardless of success. While I support sweeping changes in our criminal justice system, the moral imperative depends not only on the success of systemic change but on personal action in the here and now. More bad things than good ones can happen in court but even the certainty of defeat is no reason to give up the fight. Sometimes what seems overall like a defeat might mean years less in prison for an individual. The struggle for a more humane sentencing policy will likely be won gradually, if at all. Still, I would relish a conversion or two among policy makers and I will not give up hope for substantial sentencing reforms. This book is my contribution to progressive change in our courts.

12

I Am Not a Hired Gun

Reframing and the Expert Witness Role

———

Field notes, September 23, 2019:
I snubbed him. Dr. Alphonso Valdez was sitting in a restaurant in Colorado Springs' Antlers Hotel late the night of the hearing. I walked in to see how long the bar was open and if I could buy a bottle of beer to help me unwind. He caught my eye and was clearly looking to have a conversation. I looked away and went back to my room. I immediately felt guilty. I was neither polite nor respectful.

On the other hand, I considered what he did as despicable. In a death penalty case, he took money—thousands of dollars—to write a report that was filled with scary stories of the Mexican Mafia that had nothing to do with this crime. He argued that a strong Sureño culture and the "coercive control" of the Mexican Mafia were responsible for two murders on the streets of Colorado Springs. Prosecutors commissioned his report to help frighten a jury to deliver a death sentence to Marco Garcia-Bravo.

I felt guilty walking away from him without talking. He and I had spent ten hours that day in court: first, he gave his report, then I tore it apart. He is a human being and a fellow expert on gangs. No, check that: he is a human being, but I don't feel like I'm a part of his gang expert fraternity. I was angered at his attempt to inflame the court about the Mexican Mafia with no foundation in the evidence. No prosecutor "seeking justice" would have used his report. I was asked to submit a critique of Valdez's report in support of the defense motion requesting an evidentiary hearing. What was at issue in the hearing was if "the probative value" of his report outweighed its "prejudicial impact." In other words, does his expert opinion enhance reason by the jury more than it raises fears? It certainly incited fear. The judge engaged with me throughout my testimony and at the end of the day the defense lawyers were delighted.

The issue for me was demonization and guilt by association. His report included all sorts of scary stories about Mexican Mafia–ordered murders and grisly California Sureño gang violence, none of it related to Colorado Springs or the crime at issue. My report cited the *Roark* decision by the U.S. Eighth Circuit. In that case, similar scary stories of the Hells Angels motorcycle gang were told to the jury. The judge ordered the jury to disregard them. Roark was convicted, but his conviction was overturned by the Eighth Circuit. "A bell once rung," they opined, "cannot easily be unrung." The subtext of my report was a warning to this judge that admitting Valdez's report might lead to a reversal of a conviction. In one of his many colloquies with me on the stand, the judge brought up Roark. He had read my report carefully, and the lawyers said it was my unflinching critique of Valdez's report that had persuaded the judge to grant an evidentiary hearing in the first place. The prosecutors were surprised and—it turned out—unprepared.

Valdez was an engaging witness, spewing war stories from California and his collaboration with Mexican Mafia turncoat leader Rene "Boxer" Enriquez, who he said "indoctrinated him" into the mysteries of La Eme, or the Mexican Mafia. He claimed "Sureño culture" was responsible for Garcia-Bravo carrying out the murders. His report was in stark contrast to the local police gang expert, Corporal Jeffrey Mitchell, who explained, matter-of-factly, that the Mexican Mafia had no presence in Colorado Springs and the murders were the result of local rivalries.

I asked in my report why an outside expert was needed when the state already had a knowledgeable police expert in local gangs? The answer I assume was that the state needed a substantial dose of scare tactics to get their death penalty, similar to Fred Bright's eliciting police expert testimony that FOLKS stands for "Followers of Our Lord King Satan." But more so, why did Dr. Valdez take thousands of dollars to make their case for them? I guess the answer lies in posing the question that way. But it also highlights why I do expert witness work and how my understanding of it differs from customary practice.

Expert witnesses are supposed to be qualified on narrow scientific grounds: is their testimony based on theories that are scientifically reliable and valid? Rule 702 of the Federal Code requires that "the expert's scientific, technical, or other specialized knowledge . . . help the trier of fact to understand the evidence or to determine a fact in issue." Valdez brazenly claimed that his knowledge of gangs through police investigation was vastly superior to academic gang research. I pointed out in my direct testimony that he had testified, earlier in the day, that when he went undercover he was amazed at what gang members told him. Hardly a vote of confidence in the quality of police gang knowledge.

Police "experts" are routinely qualified to testify about gangs. I recall Milledgeville's Ricky Horn admitting that what he knew about gangs came largely from "TV and the movies." Judges have nearly always allowed police experts to provide their law enforcement opinions in court. Carrie Thompson, Garcia-Bravo's attorney, laid out the legal arguments about the limits of police testimony. She undermined Valdez's credibility in a couple of hours of pitch-perfect cross-examination. In my direct and cross examination testimony, I basically argued that the prejudicial impact of his report outweighed any pro-bative value.

Valdez is not a local policeman. He is a professional witness, someone who makes a substantial part of his living as a "hired gun" for a prosecutor. His ethics can be summarized in his response to a question about how much money he billed for in this case, when he said, "I'm paid for my work like any other job." This is a stock answer.

Is this "my job," too, that I produce whatever is needed for the defense? No. I stated on the stand that "I am not a hired gun." I have only testified fif-teen times in my eighty-three cases. Most of the time, my written report or oral advice is sufficient. Most cases ended up not going to trial and that is often one of the hallmarks of successful work: getting the prosecutor to worry that their gang evidence might be exposed as stereotypes and conclude that a trial would be too much of a risk. But there are also many cases I've had where the defense doesn't like what I have to say. In several cases, the defense theory that their client was not a gang member fell apart after I interviewed them. Or the client confessed to me, and his attorneys thought my testimony could be dangerous.

For example, in a Texas case, the defendant explained to me the murder he was charged with was not gang related at all, as the prosecution had claimed. I discovered ample evidence to confirm this. He also told me he worked as an independent stickup man, not as a gang member but as a "ren-egade" robbing drug houses. He discovered he was given the wrong address of a drug house, and the family who lived there were just regular folks. When they tried to resist him, an intimidating large Black guy, he defended himself and shot and killed two of them. Wracked by guilt, he attempted "suicide by cop" when the police arrived. He was shot several times but not killed. The lawyers were unaware of the robbery motive of the murders, and, after I told them about it, they wouldn't allow me to testify. Their client being a renegade robbing drug houses sure enough disputed the gang angle but would hardly help with jurors. Since the prosecution's case was built on a "framing" of the murders as gang related, the defense lawyers settled on my previous written report that rebutted the gang motive from multiple sources but omitted a description of the actual murder scene.

My review of Valdez's report goes to the heart of why I do this work and how my work differs from the notion of an expert witness as a hired gun. My understanding of the power of stereotypes, along with their grisly adoption by prosecutors, is why I feel compelled to stand up to prejudice, racism, and demonization in a courtroom. That might sound a bit Weberian, my Protestant "will to duty." But I trace my motives to a different sociological concept of Max Weber's: the difference between instrumental and values rationality. In other words, I draw a distinction between just doing my job no matter what it is versus acting guided by some higher goal or value. My expert witness work lies within the latter tradition, exemplified in modern times by Alvin Gouldner (1968, 116), who argued that for sociologists "our allegiance is to values, not factions." Prosecutors and defense lawyers are both "factions" in my reading, one marshaling evidence to convict, the other to acquit. My motto, "research not stereotypes," is a variant of Gouldner's contrast of values to factional interests.

I've watched defense experts unethically tailor their testimony to fit the defense case. One academic expert blatantly denied that his client was a gang member, which he knew was a lie but a central component of defense strategy. I've been asked, and refused, to testify that the "gang made me do it" was a justification for homicide. While sometimes that is true, it usually is an excuse. That excuse didn't work in Auschwitz, and it shouldn't work on urban streets. And it doesn't work on me when my allies want me to place the "team" I find myself on ahead of the truth of the matter. I've been asked repeatedly to testify that a gang was not organized at all and is only a loose peer group. It often is, but sometimes it's not, and my book The In$ane Chicago Way (2015) looked at a highly organized attempt of certain Latino gangs to create a new Spanish mafia. Gangs do not fall into one of two groups: either a wild peer group or organized crime. They fall on a continuum. Evidence is needed to confirm the level of organization. The "Father of Gang Research," Fredric Thrasher's (1927, 5) dictum is still true: "No two gangs are alike." Much of my testimony in gang cases is to explain the uniqueness of a local gang and that it is not a clone of some gang in Chicago or Los Angeles.

I've come to agree with Susan Fiske that stereotyping is very difficult to overcome, if it can be at all. In court I feel like Sisyphus, rolling a boulder up a hill in Hades. With the summit in sight, it rolls back down again. In each trial, my debunking of stereotypes has to start over and over again from scratch. I challenge stereotypes not because I've been condemned to by the gods but because my values tell me it's right to keep pushing my research boulder up Hades's mountain of stereotypes. This is how I chose to use my academic training. It is not defense attorneys or their clients I most aim to please. It is my conscience and my sense of what is right and just.

Still, I regret I did not engage Dr. Valdez in a polite exchange. It's just that he and I have different values, and it was too hard to pretend civility.

––––––––

I learned to take field notes during my gang research days, and I extended that practice to my work in court. The above field note is an example of how I have written up my experiences immediately after a trial or event for over the past two decades. My field notes have served me well in recalling the facts of each case, how I made sense of them theoretically, and my own reactions and feelings. They also remind me of how frustrating this work is. King Sisyphus comes to mind often, since I typically can't see how my efforts make much of a difference. I feel the heavy boulder of my research hurtling down the damn hill of stereotypes and rolling right over both the defendant and me again and again. The judge in Marco's case decided Dr. Valdez's report could be admitted after all, allowing the specter of the Mexican Mafia and gruesome tales of California Sureño gang violence to frighten a Colorado Springs jury into handing down a sentence of death. My report gave grounds for appeal, his lawyer said. In the end, Marco was spared the death penalty and sentenced to life without parole.

Expert Witnesses, Gangs, and Stereotypes

Rather than a detailed technical analysis of the expert witness role, this chapter will discuss four examples of my courtroom work. I discuss what my expert witness work is not—acting as a hired gun—and what it is: reframing gang stereotypes. Typically, expert witnesses provide technical information, like ballistics of a bullet trajectory, cause of death, or geographically placing someone vis-à-vis a crime scene through cell phone tower triangulation. Expert witness testimony on gangs is similar but also different. Law enforcement testimony, as with Dr. Valdez's scare stories of La Eme or Ricky Horn claiming "Folks" stands for Followers of Our Lord King Satan, is crafted to reinforce stereotypes and play on jurors' emotions of fear and anger as well as their preexisting assumptions and cultural imaginings. As authoritative "experts," they dehumanize the defendant, often with a cartoonish stereotype of an unfeeling gang monster or an unthinking soldier carrying out orders. His or her life is reduced to a photograph at a crime scene. Such "experts" dispense with any "discrepant information" that might complicate their black-and-white picture of the Big Bad Wolf pouncing on Little Red Riding Hood. Trust them, police officers tell a jury. They know about gangs. They are the experts not some "ivory tower," "bleeding heart" academic.

My idea of expert witness testimony on gangs, on the other hand, is fundamentally aimed at debunking gang stereotypes. My testimony is not tailored to fit the defense frame, though I'm mindful of their strategy. Rather, I assert, sometimes to wary attorneys, the defense must adjust their frame, or story, to fit my expert testimony. The reason I've drawn so heavily in this book from the literature of social cognition is that this literature also gives some clues as to how stereotypes may be combated. As Gilbert and Fiske say (1998, 391):

> The good news is that people can sometimes control even apparently automatic biases, if appropriately motivated, given the right kind of information, and in the right mood. People therefore can make the hard choice.

The bad news is that a courtroom is not a suitable arena for making "the hard choice." Juries are motivated by prosecutors and even peers in the jury pool to make the easy, stereotype-congruent choices and do so again and again. The situation, a trial with the accused sitting in one corner and "the People," meaning the prosecutor, in another corner, is conducive to confirmation bias. Juries are inclined to believe the defendant is guilty because "the People" say he is and lean toward evidence that confirms guilt. Stereotypes are more easily accepted if proclaimed by a legitimate authority, like a DA speaking as the tribune of justice. Effective prosecutors know how to evoke emotion and confirmation bias in juries. Emotions of all types inhibit System 2 reasoning and encourage cognitive shortcuts, like gang stereotypes. Valdez's report would cue fear in a jury, and people hold closer to stereotypes when they are afraid.

Even so, the stories in this book have shown expert witness testimony on gangs can have a limited effect. I've given some examples of Rothbart's (1981) categories of stereotype change: the bookkeeping, subtyping, and conversion methods. Conversion of juries doesn't happen very much outside of John Grisham novels, though my Mahnomen challenge to prosecutors to indict the Looney Tunes "Folks" gang came close. Most often, a defense lawyer's case consists of compiling facts and arguments that add up to reasonable doubt of the prosecution's pile of facts. In sentencing, this bookkeeping method of defense combats the severity of the crime by weighing many aspects of a defendant's life against his fewer, if very serious, failings. Similarly, subtyping makes a jury use System 2 reasoning to consider the differences between gang members and not assume they are all alike. Still, the essence of the category "gang" in a jury's mind is violence, and it takes considerable forethought to figure out how to persuade a jury to question or complicate that stereotype. While I've applied what I've learned from social cognition theories, I'm afraid my experience tells me gang stereotypes are like zombies: they don't die easily and they keep coming back.

Defense Expectations

The Daubert test lists the factors with which a judge decides whether testimony can be considered expert. *Daubert v. Merrell Dow Pharmaceuticals* (1993) basically conceives an expert as a neutral scientist giving technical answers. For prosecutors and defense attorneys, an expert is someone who dresses up their case in academic or technical language. A John Grisham lawyer in his novel *Sycamore Row* gives the standard view of an expert: "Don't know where these experts are, but, hell, you can hire an expert to say anything."

Police "gang experts," like Valdez or Horn, predictably pile on one stereotype after another drawn from one-sided experiences of gangs and crime and driven by the need to convict, not to understand. They are paid to reinforce jury stereotypes of gangs with their police "insider" knowledge in order to pave the way to conviction and the harshest sentence. Rather than reframe, they reinforce the dominant media frame on gangs and dehumanize the offender. The defense, on the other hand, desperately needs to explain a crime in nonsensational terms and to humanize a gang member to get him off or to get a shorter sentence.

One point I make in all my gang homicide reports irritates some defense lawyers. I insist on expressing my condolences to the victim's family and loved ones in my written reports and, if possible, on the stand. Some defense attorneys have objected, based on fear that such words reinforce the horror of a murder. A murder *is* horrible, and we should never forget the victims. In the final analysis, the report is mine, and I insist on expressing empathetic feelings for the victim's family and loved ones.

———

One death penalty case I had in federal court in Missouri is an example of the need to reframe demonization but also exposes how the expert/defense attorney relationship can go wrong. Thomas D. Smith was a Blood accused of the murders of Paris Harbin and Chandy Plumb. He believed the victims stole crack cocaine and several thousand dollars of his drug money. There was no doubt Smith would be convicted, and I was hired to address the inevitable death penalty recommendation and assist one of the best mitigation specialists I've ever worked with, Cyndy Short. She and I went through Tulsa neighborhoods talking to neighbors and friends of Smith, who went by his middle name, Demetrius. Cyndy is extremely dedicated, driven to nail down all the details, and exhaustively searches for new witnesses and evidence to obtain mitigating testimony for the defense. We drove from place to place all day.

I had already met and interviewed Demetrius in Leavenworth federal prison and was struck by his feelings of guilt for the homicides and his very conventional attitudes. Cyndy and I talked the whole day and worked out a strategy on how to humanize him using my Homeboy typology. Homeboys are marked by conventional aspirations of settling down and feelings that criminal acts like selling drugs might be necessary but immoral. Similarly, they think violence sometimes is necessary but still wrong. New Jacks, on the other hand, a different category of gang member, see selling drugs as a way to make it big and violence as just part of the bargain. If I had to sum up New Jacks in a phrase, I'd say: "Frankly, they don't give a damn." Or, at least, they'd say they don't.

I intended to prepare a PowerPoint for trial and talked with Cyndy about how to present it in front of an all-white Missouri jury. But, when I flew in to testify, I was met by Demetrius's trial attorney, a timid man I had never met named Joyce, who would conduct my direct examination. Joyce spent less than an hour preparing me for trial. This ran counter to my experience preparing for trial with some of the best defense attorneys in the country. Brian Kammer and David Harth grilled me for hours getting ready to testify in Marion Wilson's case. We went through both direct and cross as they readied me for the prosecution's expected assault on my testimony. I had two JLWOP cases with Randolph Stone from the University of Chicago Law School. We prepped for hours with his colleague Herschella Conyers, and their law students, taking turns peppering questions at me that the prosecution might ask. We went over which approach worked best and what not to say. After their prep sessions, I was ready, and our cases went smoothly.

Demetrius's attorney didn't think we even needed to go through the questions he would ask. When I explained what Cyndy and I had agreed on, he disagreed. The defense had challenged the admission of Demetrius's gang membership in the trial, although the record was replete with references to his Blood membership, and the murders were both related to missing drug money and rivalry with the Crips. Joyce was not even on the same page as his mitigation specialist or cocounsel, Susan Hunt. While Demetrius and I connected in our interview, Joyce didn't like me and didn't want me to use the Homeboy typology. Since Cyndy and I had agreed this was the best approach, I insisted on going ahead. I was apprehensive, for good reason, it turned out.

In my interview with Demetrius, he admitted responsibility for the homicides but denied pulling the trigger. In fact, there was conflicting testimony on who did the shooting and the motives. Like most homicides or acts of violence, the circumstances are messy, not clear-cut nor clearly or consistently remembered. I was impressed by Demetrius's acceptance of responsibility, due to his anger over the stolen money and crack. He felt he was wronged, but also he had done wrong and felt he caused the two victim's deaths. I asked Demetrius about his aspirations if he got back on the streets. But more so we talked about how he would handle life in prison if the jury rejected the death penalty. I could see Demetrius had a volatile personality, but all he really ever wanted in life was to settle down and put the drama of the streets in the past. It wouldn't work out that way.

My testimony was a disaster. The assistant U.S. attorney, David Rush, interrupted me with objections after every phrase in my direct examination and pounced on each slide I presented. I couldn't get a complete thought out. Joyce, the appointed attorney, was silent and did not once come to my assistance. I explained how gangs came to Tulsa and the history of the Bloods, which derived from a local gang called the RIP Boys. Demetrius had moved his drug ring to Joplin, Missouri, in part, to avoid the violence in Tulsa. I explained how local gangs would affiliate around the branding of Chicago or Los Angeles gangs and remake their local beefs into rivalries between Crips and Bloods or Vice Lords and Gangster Disciples. I then explained that all gang members were not alike and went into my Homeboy typology. I listed reasons that Demetrius was clearly a Homeboy and backed it up with my interviews and biographical data. From the text beneath friendly images on my slides, I listed my talking points on why he was a Homeboy. Those I spoke with, both within the gang and outside it, spoke of Demetrius as a "decent" or "good" person. He was seen to have had promise in school. His family problems gave him almost "no chance" to escape Tulsa's wave of gangs. He cared about his family and friends and was loyal and protective of them. He was neither obsessed with money nor "cold" inside. By proceeding this way, rather than run from or combat the jury's deep-seated gang frame, I looked to use my research to add complexity within it, revealing subtleties of a person of which they hadn't been aware. This was intended to encourage them to use System 2 reasoning to consider that all gang members were not alike. It also carried the benefit of being true.

I told the court the crux of the matter was that Demetrius was not the heartless cold-blooded killer he was being made out to be. I cited, as examples, his taking the rap for his mother on a drug possession charge and his explanation of how his "business" in Joplin could help younger guys from Tulsa who were in a more violent environment. These were not the actions of a New Jack, who thinks only of himself. I reminded the jury that Demetrius's friends, his teachers, his relatives, and others had presented a picture of Demetrius that was very different from that painted by the prosecution. Katherine Flower-Hughes, one of his teachers, said, "He was just a very nice person." Even though most of his close cousins became members of the rival Crips, Demetrius treated them as family because family was stronger than the gang. One of his friends told me, killing people "is not who Thomas is." Bishop Smith, like every other adult I spoke with, said that "Thomas was always respectful around me." The bishop told me, "Thomas never even cursed in front of me."

The proper conclusion to draw, I told the jury, was not that our side says Thomas is a good boy and the prosecutor says he is an evil monster. What it meant was that he was morally conflicted, a "homeboy" that, like all of us, struggled with living up to his conventional morality. A decent person was in there, someone who wants to do right, and not a "cold-blooded" killer with no conscience.

Some people cheat on their spouses and get divorced. Does that mean they can't make their second marriage something that is worthwhile, and they won't ever be faithful or lead a respectable life? Had the jurors never done anything they were ashamed of?

The essence of the Homeboy is that he is someone who still holds on to conventional morality and the American Dream. *He is more like us inside than some hateful monster.* Demetrius Thomas was not a New Jack. He had strong conventional values and was aware of his moral responsibility for his actions. He told me that he accepted the verdict because, though he didn't pull the trigger, he accepts responsibility for setting up the chain of events that led to these killings.

Well, that is what I planned to say. I'm not sure how much I actually was able to get out: as mentioned above, Rush, the assistant U.S. attorney, interrupted me continually with objections and feigned injury to "common sense." My typology undercut his crudely drawn stereotype of Demetrius as no more than a killer gang member. He insisted on calling Demetrius "Mad Dog" Smith, a street name. The indictment and court documents, like the one below, all listed Thomas Smith but added "aka Mad Dog." (See Fig. 12.1.) All the newspaper articles I read on the trial reported Demetrius's name as Mad Dog, which they repeatedly featured in headlines, like this one from the January 30, 2007, *Joplin Globe*, "Witness: Mad Dog Knew Murder Victim Had His Drugs." The implication of using Demetrius's street name, the reader will recognize, is an unmistakable example of the function of dehumanization. What do you do with a mad dog? Of course, you have moral permission to put him down.

I watched the jury's eyes as assistant U.S. attorney Rush interrupted every sentence of my testimony. What I feared was that my research-based but emotional description of Demetrius as wanting the same things as you or me would be seen as the research findings of an ivory tower academic. For the typology to work, it has to be a sensible alternative to the stereotypes of both jurors' feelings and jurors' reasoning. When my attempts to fit Demetrius into the mold of one type of gang member and not another were continually interrupted, the typology lost salience. The jury stopped paying

```
                              IN THE
              UNITED STATES DISTRICT COURT FOR THE
                 WESTERN DISTRICT OF MISSOURI
                     SOUTHWESTERN DIVISION

UNITED STATES OF AMERICA,          )
                                   )
              Plaintiff,            )
                                   )
         v.                         )        No.02-05025-01-CR-SW-GAF
                                   )
THOMAS D. SMITH,                    )
aka "Mad Dog," aka "MD,"            )
                                   )
              Defendant.            )
```

Figure 12.1 Prosecutors succeeded in making sure Demetrius Smith wouldn't appear human, even in his case records. (*USA v. Thomas D. Smith.*)

attention to me. When stereotypes are challenged and they don't resonate, a "backfire effect" may set in. This means jurors strengthen their beliefs in stereotypes and reject an academic who, in turn, can be stereotyped as a "bleeding heart." Challenging stereotypes requires more than reciting research.

I was angrier with the defense attorney than with the assistant U.S. attorney. My main point, that Demetrius had some strong moral feelings, was drowned out in objections and in interruptions while Joyce sat silent. I was devastated. This young man's life was on the line, and I wasn't helping the jury see Demetrius from a more human angle, as someone with redeeming characteristics.

Fortunately, the cross-examination went much better. The assistant U.S. attorney couldn't interrupt his own questions as easily. I turned to the judge when he did interrupt me and asked to be allowed to answer. I was able to explain why I saw Demetrius as a "Homeboy" and why he wasn't the monster he was being depicted as. I repeated over and over that all gang members are not alike: really the most important point to get across. I got more of my points out in cross than I had in direct.

Demetrius's other attorney, Susan Hunt, who I had worked with earlier, said in her closing remarks at the sentencing phase: "Thomas Smith is a human being just like you and me. But the government wants to take all those human qualities away." Exactly. Fortunately, the jury rejected the death penalty. Demetrius, however, wasn't in a charitable mood. After the jury decided on life without parole he defiantly said to the judge, "So, Mr. Rush isn't going to kill the dog." I didn't blame his outburst. He understood the dehumanizing strategy being used against him.

I'm not sure I was ever so emotionally shaken in my life as when I flew back to Milwaukee before the jury returned with their verdict. I cannot over-emphasize how relieved I was when the jury came back with a sentence of life without parole, not death, though I felt I had failed. Perhaps the jury thought the assistant U.S. attorney was overdoing it, but more likely the sterling work Cyndy had done on Demetrius's troubled family background proved decisive. We'll never know. I conveyed my relief, my fears, and my frustrations with Joyce in a letter to Demetrius as soon as I heard the jury's verdict. The jury chose life. Far from a gun for hire, I felt like I'd delivered my message and succeeded in a small measure in spite of the lawyer who'd brought me in.

Emotions and Stereotypes

A murder trial is by definition a crucible of emotions, for both the victim's and the offender's families, the offender, the judge, the prosecutor, and the defense attorney as well as for the jury, and, I can tell you, for the expert witness. While evidence is supposed to determine guilt and often life or death in a capital murder trial, jurors can't help but feel a range of deep emotions. A murder primes thoughts of their own mortality, as terror management theory argues. I do not attempt to review the literature on jury deliberations. You can turn to Devine or other sources listed in the References. The main point of this chapter turns on my analysis of the role of the expert witness in gang cases. This book has given example after example of the power of stereotypes and how prosecutors take advantage of our implicit and explicit beliefs about gangs. I believe the principal role of the gang expert is to "reframe" the prosecution's stereotypes of a gang member into terms a jury can understand. Reframing, I've found, is not an unemotional process.

The expert is thought of as a neutral, cold, logical witness, more akin to Spock or Commander Data on the various *Star Trek* series, than the more emotional Captain Kirk, Janeway, or Picard. Sometimes that works as a performance, but the real emotions of a lost life need to be at the center of any testimony. What research on stereotypes teaches is that emotions of almost any type accelerate System 1 fast thinking, which overrides System 2 slow reasoning. If jurors are feeling emotions, especially anger or fear, they block out the difficult process of reasoning and tend to rely on stereotypes that are more available and take less cognitive effort. At the same time, to accept my frame, they need to recognize an emotional connection there, too, or it will come across as suspect academic jargon. The main reason I express sympathy for victims is that I feel it. But I also understand the depth of emotion involved and merely reciting research findings is unlikely to erode the natural antipathy of jurors toward the defendant. Such tactics often backfire, and jurors tune you out, leaving their stereotypes unchanged and their anger at a killer red hot.

Relying on the research of Kahneman and Fiske, I've put together this simple figure (see Fig. 12.2) categorizing the impact of emotion on jurors' stereotypes. The first set of three boxes deal with how emotions encourage stereotypes and the fourth with how emotions can prime attention to discrepant information and challenge stereotypes. You will note that in only one emotion, anxiety about making a mistake, will jurors tend to question stereotypes and use System 2 slow reasoning. Susan Fiske says when people are afraid of making invalid decisions, they stereotype less. That type of anxiety makes jurors more likely to consider "discrepant" information or things that don't fit in a simple "big bad wolf," or in Demetrius's case, a "mad dog," narrative.

In a death penalty case, where the verdict of guilty has already been decided, one way that anxiety about injustice or making a mistake takes root is by recognizing the humanity of the defendant. Had I been able to actually present my testimony coherently, I would have relayed my conver-

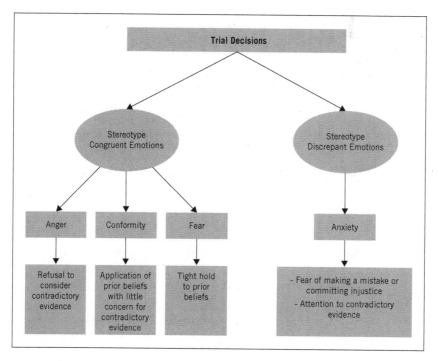

Figure 12.2 The effects of emotions on jurors' decision-making.

sations with Demetrius about his life in prison, his advice to his young son to avoid the streets, and his desire to read and grow as a person. You might kill a "mad dog," but killing Thomas Demetrius Smith, a real, living, breathing human being is more difficult. Fortunately, the jury was not convinced Demetrius was actually a mad dog. I'm sure their deliberations were not emotion-free but filled with anxiety about doing the right thing. I hoped their anxiety caused them to think twice about my typology, despite assistant U.S. attorney Rush's interruptions.

Demetrius himself was wracked with guilt about his role in the murders. I wasn't there, so I don't know if he did the shooting or not. What I have seen time and time again is that the act of murder not only takes a human life but shatters something human within everyone who participates in it. A killer trying to make sense of what happened produces narratives to himself of the murder that are much more complex than just evading or accepting responsibility. The reconstruction of a murder in a defendant's mind serves the function of neutralizing the overwhelming guilt he feels. It usually doesn't work. I don't think I need to remind you that mad dogs or monsters don't feel guilt or reconstruct events; only human beings need to.

Reframing

Recall Rothbart's three methods of how we can question stereotypes: book-keeping, conversion, and subtyping. All these methods are actually types of reframing, the central task of a gang expert witness for the defense. What the Homeboy subtyping intends to do is make the juror compare categories of gang members, to consider Demetrius as similar to someone who can settle down eventually, lead a decent life, and not always be a threat to the community. Just admitting that a gang member might want to have a life like them prompts a juror to think, to compare, to reason. Having to make a life-and-death decision causes anxiety, and, if the anxiety is related to fear of making a mistake, it encourages slow reasoning not automatic adherence to stereotypes.

Reframing is the central concept in Lakoff's work, especially his *Don't Think of an Elephant* (2004), his political advice to Democrats. Lakoff's study of neurological processes of the brain revealed to him that the facts aren't what is most important in the process of what Kahneman would call System 2 reasoning. The facts need to be interpreted by a frame. A frame in a trial is a story line that makes sense of the vast array of facts that can easily overwhelm a juror. The facts need to be there, but the decisive element is the frame, which is how the story organizes the evidence and makes sense out of it, leading to a verdict or sentencing decision. Thus, trials are frame contests: the prosecution's and defense's competing stories of the crime "frame" the evidence in familiar ways to a jury. The facts are usually relatively un-contested. For example, in a murder trial, there is always a dead body. A jury's verdict means they chose a frame that makes sense of how that person got dead and found the defendant "guilty" or "not guilty." The jury then sentences him to death or life without parole based in part on their consideration of the defendant's character.

Assistant U.S. attorney David Rush's interruptions were intended to obstruct my smooth telling of an alternative story, of reframing Demetrius's life into terms that might be understood by the jury and prompt some sympathy. I hope my attempts to reframe Demetrius's gang membership contributed a small bit toward the jury rejecting the death penalty.

JLWOP: Two Examples of Reframing Gangs

I can explain reframing better in two JLWOP cases in Chicago. To date, I have consulted or testified in ten JLWOP cases, including Jaime Ruiz whose story is told in Chapter 4 and Jacqueline Montañez who we met in Chapter 10. In these cases, juveniles were by law sentenced as adults to natural life in prison. The *Miller* decision said such sentences were cruel and unusual punishment since juveniles mature and nearly all have a capacity to change. Prosecutors use membership in a gang in prison as an example of what the *Miller* decision called "irreparable corruption" that would, therefore, justify a natural life sentence. "Don't you see," they imply or say directly, "he is still in a gang and therefore hasn't changed." Two JLWOP cases I had with Randolph Stone, University of Chicago law professor and former chief public defender in Chicago's Cook County, are examples of both how an expert witness can reframe gang issues and of the frustrations of even good work.

Randolph Stone and Herschella Conyers were associates of University of Chicago's Mandel Legal Clinic, which provided free representation for JLWOP offenders. Randolph is incredibly impressive, in total command of the facts and having a long history of human rights litigation. He had been a member of the Chicago mayor's Task Force on Police Accountability. Their report was the single best history of racism in the Chicago Police Department I ever read. Herschella was his associate, sharp, blunt, and effective.

Randolph retained me to testify about the gang membership in the re-sentencing of Michael Cooks and Kentrell Stoutmire. Michael Cooks was a Gangster Disciple but, like many younger gang members, he was most attached to his neighborhood, not the aging and fading 1990s Gangster Disciples hierarchy. He was a fourteen-year-old lookout at a drug house in 1992. When a dispute broke out, he panicked and shot and killed two people who were making a commotion that might call undue attention to the drug operation. In prison, he associated with people from his neighborhood and, eventually, left the Gangster Disciple organization that dominated prison life. The *Miller* decision meant his automatic life without parole sentence had to be reconsidered. My field notes once again are a better description than I could write now.

––––––––––

F ield notes, June 11, 2016:
The night before I testified, I had a dream. I almost never have dreams like this, but subconsciously I was aware of the stakes for my testimony on Michael Cooks's gang involvement. In my dreams, I was bare chested in a football game before an immense crowd. The game was almost over. We were behind. I came off the bench and either intercepted a pass or returned a kick—the details faded. But I took it to the house and scored, winning the game amid the cheers of an ecstatic, applauding crowd.

So much for my subconscious and back to real life: Cook County Courthouse, Room 308, Judge Michael McHale. McHale was the sentencing judge, back in 1992, for Michael Cooks, who at fourteen had killed two men while acting as a lookout for a Gangster Disciple drug spot. McHale would resentence a thirty-eight-year-old Cooks in light of the *Miller* decision. I had been ready to testify the week before, when the state announced that they were going to call eleven IDOC officers to testify. They actually called only one, who said he didn't remember Michael or the incident, and then said the others could not testify until the next week. I had traveled into Chicago to testify, but the ASA said her witnesses wouldn't be ready that day so maybe I should go first? I told Randolph Stone and Herschella Conyers that I would come back and testify after the guards. If this had been a prosecution ploy to get in the last word, I wouldn't let them. And I had plenty to say about Michael's IDOC record.

We met in the courthouse cafeteria, Herschella and Randolph, both African American, brilliant. They were surrounded by a plethora of mainly white law students, a Black/white dynamic that attested to the University of Chicago being able to bring in the best Black lawyers to teach elite mostly white students. Herschella told me I would be the last witness in the hearing. The state had failed to bring in the correctional officers, and their case seemed to be based on the assertion that Michael was a monster in 1992 and is still a monster today. My role as last witness, Randolph said, was to bat cleanup. I would close the case. It wasn't exactly my football dream but kept the sports metaphor.

Talking with Herschella, Michelle Geller, the case mitigation specialist, and students who had watched the hearing from the start, I asked about the prosecution's case. The ASA didn't appear to have much except for revisiting the crime in pictures and testimony from 1992. She characterized the

ASA as "passive-aggressive." The defense had put on James Garbarino, perhaps the nation's leading expert on the impact of violence on children. His affidavit was powerful, though I worried it would play into the prosecution's hands by stressing the damage of the abuse in Michael's childhood— in the effort to contextualize why Michael had committed his crime, I didn't want Michael to appear damaged to the point of subhuman. I decided that my testimony had to make change the underlying theme. Expert testimony on gangs can be effective, I've learned, if it can make variation understandable to a judge or jury, thus forcing consideration of a specific individual not a stereotype. This ideally means a judge decides on actual evidence and avoids the fundamental attribution error, attributing behavior to essential characteristics, not circumstances. It doesn't often work that way but that was going to be my play.

The ASA frames were "superpredator" and "gang member" and that said it all. It actually was all she said. Michael's Master File, his record including infractions in IDOC, had a few scattered tickets for gang activity, all but one from Pontiac prison more than twenty years before. A large courtroom audience looked on and the microphone was either off or on very low, so they strained to hear us. The ASA had a large sack on her desk labeled "IDOC Records," so I figured they were going to claim, as with Adolpho Davis who had been resentenced to life without parole, that Michael was an unrepentant Gangster Disciple who deserved "natural life." I was ready, having read the entire Master File and a more detailed intelligence report that gave handwritten explanations by correctional officers about a half dozen or so of Michael's prison tickets.

The first thing I noticed about the judge was that he appeared to be paying no attention to the two "character witnesses" about Michael: his brother and a childhood friend who was offering Michael a job once he was released. In this case, the judge was, well, judge and jury. He alone would decide Michael's fate. One small measure of success was just if I could get him to pay attention.

Herschella went through my qualifications and the ASA's only quibbling was to ask me whether I had ever trained police. My response that I trained them as students at the University of Illinois–Chicago was not what the ASA wanted, and she and I got testy for a minute. I caught myself, though, and the judge quickly lost patience with the ASA and qualified me as an expert in gangs. During Herschella's Daubert qualification, I stressed that my research was about change, and I studied gang members from adolescence to adulthood. I also was asked by the ASA, to my surprise and satisfaction, an almost snotty question, "Well, what DO you testify about?" She gave me a platform to explain I only take cases if they allow me to use research to contest stereotypes; that research tells us things about gangs that are not generally accepted. She wisely did not follow up. I would have had lots of examples.

Herschella had me go through my books, and I got a chance to explain *The In$ane Chicago Way* as a description of the 1990s gang wars. I said they exposed that the gang wars were caused by gang leaders out for power and money and cost thousands of lives. It gave the ASA no grounds to accuse me of being "soft on gangs," a trap I've learned to avoid in expert witness work. This was the first case where *In$ane* could be used profitably in my work. It won't be the last.

Herschella asked me about the history of the Gangster Disciples and the ASA objected, which was overruled by the judge who told me to make it brief. My pleasure. I stressed how the Gangster Disciples had changed and how the 1990s wars shattered the gang structure. This was important because it explains why rejoining the gang wasn't in the cards, even if Michael wanted to. "No one listens to Larry Hoover anymore," I said. Herschella's main point in her direct was to get me to detail the Homeboys, Dope Fiends, Legits, and New Jack typology. I had the judge's attention as he actually looked up from his notes and made eye contact. I framed the discussion that gang members were not all the same. I explained New Jacks as people with a long history of criminality and violence and an amoral perspective on life. Homeboys, I stressed, may have done horrible things but had conventional aspirations, came to a realization of the wrongs they have done, and wanted to settle down. Michael Cooks, I told Herschella and looking straight at the judge, was the definition of a Homeboy. Further, I was allowed to go on and talk about his "courage" for leaving the gang in prison, something that is rare and an example of how Michael has changed and matured. People who truly change, Sampson and Laub (1993) argue, can look back to a "turning point," and Michael consistently recalled his rejection of the Gangster Disciples while at Stateville prison.

On cross, the ASA had almost nothing to say. But she did set in motion some of the most effective exchanges of my testimony. I had referred to having been around the block as an interviewer for decades and was sensitive to being scammed and hustled. She asked me whether I understood Michael Cooks was aware that I was there to help him? That his answers would be tailored to putting himself in a favorable light, and whether I understood what he said was just "self report?"

Randolph came alive on the bench, and Herschella quickly followed with a redirect that pretty much punctured the "gang frame." She asked me why I believed Michael, and I repeated that his story of leaving the gang in 1988 was backed up by both the Master File and the -intelligence logs. I was aware of Michael's self-interest, but you never just take someone's word. I went back and looked at his record and noted that the Master File verified he hadn't had a fight in seventeen and a half years. And I quoted from the intelligence logs that one correctional officer mentioned in his notes in the

2000s that Michael had said he left the gang in 1988 and another reported Michael said he left the gang eight and a half years ago. Michael was telling the truth about having left the gang.

I was talking authoritatively but off the cuff, a style where I'm most effective. The judge was paying attention and, at one point, asked me what an "intelligence file" consisted of? Raw notes of correctional officers, I told him. It was painfully obvious that despite the large sack of IDOC records on the ASA's desk, she hadn't read them. No objections, no rebuttals, not a peep from her about the content of Michael's disciplinary record. She hadn't done her homework and was in defeated mode, wanting to get the hearing over after going back to her one "but he's a monster" point.

Seeing the ASA was ready to pack it in, I interrupted Herschella and said there was one more thing that convinced me Michael was telling the truth. The judge looked at me, and I made eye contact and said that Michael had not known why he shot Zaworski, the second guy. If he were trying to con me, he would have had a rap. Of course, I said to the judge, I understood what was going on in the second shooting and my mention of "forward panic" got the judge to slightly nod to me—he had read my report. I went on to make the point that the concept of forward panic was derived not from criminals but from studies of U.S. Army soldiers, who once they began a violent spree found it hard to stop. That is why Michael shot the second guy. He got carried away by emotion, by forward panic. I said I thought this was very important for the court to consider in resentencing. The judge held his gaze on me.

But the most important victory of the testimony came at the end of the ASA's cross. Exasperated by my distinctions between gang members, she said loudly, "This is not about gangs, it is about two murders." I had the distinct feeling of scoring the winning touchdown. She gave up the gang frame! I'd never seen that happen in court.

Theoretically, there are two broad ways of breaking a frame: subtyping—leave the stereotype untouched but say our guy doesn't fit it. Maybe he whistles Vivaldi. Or fits into another group, a process called "lateral inhibition." The second is to challenge the stereotype directly by stressing variation and getting the judge and jury to make distinctions, to individualize, and to avoid assigning behavior to an unchanging character of a monster/gang member.

Did it work? The judge is taking a two-week vacation—like me. He'll rule afterward. The ASA for her part didn't need to repeat "monster" over and over. The deed was monstrous, and the judge will properly take the seriousness of the crime into account. On the other hand, Michael Cooks is a clear case of what the Miller decision is about, a point both Garbarino and I made explicitly. The judge has said he has not decided if the sentencing range is forty years to natural life or twenty years to sixty years. If Michael gets sixty years, he'll be out by 2020 in his midforties. I guess that would be a victory.

What was scary about this case was that we were supremely prepared and made our case that *Miller* applies directly to Michael Cooks, who has reformed and sustained that change over more than a decade while incarcerated. Like the impressionable but flexible nature of youth described in *Miller*, Michael reflected on his "depravity," demonstrated remorse, and changed, illustrated by bravely leaving the gang while he was at Menard prison. Justice means he should be allowed to go on with his life. But while the ASA gave up the gang frame, the frame of the superpredator, the monster who did an act so horrible it can't be forgiven, may win out. In cases like this, facts are important but sometimes frames are even more important. We'll see how the judge rules.

––––––––

Michael's case is the definition of bittersweet. Randolph said that the judge cited my testimony in his comments on sentencing. He did choose the lesser twenty- to sixty-year sentencing range, but gave Michael the maximum within that range, sixty years. Michael was released on parole in 2019 after twenty-seven years in prison at age forty-one. Do you understand why I see my work metaphorically as pushing my research boulder up Sisyphus's stereotypical hill only to have it roll back down? Randolph's kind words that I "made a difference" didn't mean I had persuaded the judge to hand out a less than maximum sentence. Another way Randolph could have said it might have been that I didn't make a difference at all.

The most important aspect of my testimony was that the flummoxed ASA gave up on challenging me and admitted this case wasn't about gangs at all. This is what they paid me for: to get the gang frame out of the case. It was the only time in my eighty-three cases it ever happened, that a prosecutor would say "don't consider the gang in this crime." The judge's decision, though, suggests maybe I didn't succeed as much as I had hoped. Perhaps the superpredator frame just took over as the gang frame moved out. Maybe the game wasn't over.

Kentrell Stoutmire's case was much more difficult, the drama more intense, the lessons sharper, and the outcome surprisingly better.

Blood In Blood Out: Successfully Reframing a Stereotype

––––––––

K entrell was a challenging guy. I interviewed him in Cook County Jail in 2015 in August and September. The issue before the court was whether Kentrell, a lifelong Latin King, had "distanced himself from the gang." I had come up with that term in discussions with Randolph Stone and Herschella Conyers to describe how prisoners handled their gang membership. In Illinois prisons, being in a gang is almost mandatory for safety reasons. Illinois courts have recognized that gang membership is necessary for survival, especially for young inmates, and especially if you entered with an affiliation. You can't easily leave the gang, I argued. But you can "distance yourself" from it. I was dissatisfied with Kentrell's answers in our first interview. I felt he was evasive and not coming clean about his relationship to the gang. His case hinged on whether the judge thought he could escape from his lifelong attachment to the Latin Kings. I asked Randolph to get the jail to allow me to come back and interview him again. I planned to confront him and to figure it out for myself.

My second interview with him was emotionally turbulent. I told him I didn't believe his claims that he was no longer a King. It was too deep in him, I said. And his claims to me too convenient. Like I told the court with Michael Cooks, I'd been around the block and had a sense of being played. Kentrell exploded. He screamed loud enough for a guard to check on us, "What do I have to do to be believed!" As I continued to question him, I realized the answer was in his emotional distress. He was both a King and not a King. His Latin King identity gave him status and protected him in prison but was getting in the way of him being released. Cell bars weren't the only barrier keeping him from freedom. And now, he couldn't con the gang expert! He was an emotional mess.

So was I.

I met with Randolph, Herschella, and the law students a few days later. I argued that my statement and testimony should stress Kentrell's anguish, not claim he was free of his identity as a King and fully reformed. To argue that he was rehabilitated wouldn't be believable and would misrepresent Kentrell's mental state. Better to present him as a man struggling with his gang identity than someone who had gone beyond it. Randolph had some qualms about the testimony, but the decision was made to put me on the stand.

Court could not have got off on a worse foot. With me waiting outside in the hall, the ASA played a recording of a call Kentrell had made to fellow gang members in Chicago. In the call, he bragged of his gang status in prison and pride in the Latin Kings. He was performing for them, but this performance got no applause from his lawyers or me. My testimony would argue he was distancing himself from the gang, and the phone call directly contradicted my report. The witness before me, an IDOC gang intelligence officer, testified that Kentrell hadn't left the Latin Kings because the rule was "blood in, blood out." He would have been severely beaten—called "violated"—if he had left the gang, and prison doctors would have confirmed the beating.

I explained on the stand that abruptly quitting a gang in prison seldom happens. Michael Cooks was exceptional. I agreed quitting can be dangerous, especially for a veteran gang member like Kentrell who knows lots of gang secrets. Rather than formally quit, he chose to distance himself, I argued, and then gave examples—no confiscations of gang literature in his cell; no gang fights for many years; no tickets for gang activity. I repeated in my report what Kentrell had told me in our second interview:

> I made a decision in 2008, I can't keep doing the same thing over and over. I'm going to fall back, not hold rank. I'm going to get a job in the library. I felt I paid my dues. When I got back to Menard, that's what I did. I talked to (LK leaders there), asked can I get a job? Menard doesn't allow active gang members to hold a job. I stopped going to (gang) meetings and put in for the mental health program. I told some prison officials that I was going to walk.

But my testimony alone wasn't enough to knock away the media-reinforced myth of "blood in, blood out" so authoritatively applied to Kentrell by the testimony of the IDOC gang intelligence officer. I had thought long and hard about how to make leaving a gang comprehensible to this very austere white Chicago judge.

So, I confronted the gang intelligence testimony directly and reframed it. I said to the judge, "blood in, blood out is a myth, a stereotype. Leaving the gang in prison doesn't happen that way." Reframing means to explain a process or event in terms that are familiar to the audience. So, I pointed out that my wife, Mary Devitt, was in the court. She was descended from a long line of Irish Catholics but had left the church. She didn't just walk up to the priest one day and say, "I quit." Her parents would have strongly disapproved. Instead, she "distanced herself" from the church. She had been going to mass every Sunday, then she began to miss a few. Then it was only for Christmas and Easter. Finally, she stopped going altogether, and now she and I are Unitarians, but she will always have something of a Catholic inside her. That is how leaving the gang really works, I said, especially in prison. What is important is evidence that Kentrell is distancing himself and the lack of gang tickets and other points in my testimony confirm it. Exotic rituals of being violated happen mainly in the movies.

This reframing resonated with the judge. It undermined the gang intelligence stereotypes and made the process of leaving something as exotic as a street gang more prosaic and comprehensible to any churchgoing person. It also underscored what I had said was my rationale for expert testimony: my research questioning common beliefs. It gave me credibility.

One more test awaited me. I was not in the courtroom when they played Kentrell's damning phone call, but it had been referred to by the ASA in cross-examination. The judge didn't allow any questions about it to me since I hadn't heard it. But as I was leaving the stand, he asked me directly that if I had heard the call, would it have changed my testimony? I considered whether to go into a defense of my argument about distancing but decided a direct question deserved an equally direct answer. I looked at the judge and a nervous Kentrell and said, "I would have asked to interview him again."

I had remembered my last turbulent interview with Kentrell, and, if I had known about that call, I surely would have asked Randolph to let me go back. I would have confronted Kentrell with his bragging—and told him how stupid it was. All calls are recorded, and Kentrell wasn't the only case I've had where the defendant's phone calls are replayed in open court. The reality was Kentrell was afraid he would be branded a snitch and was trumpeting his credentials to his neighborhood homies. My third interview would likely have been as turbulent as the second. My job isn't to repeat whatever a defendant comes up with as justification for his actions or accept his recollection of events. It is to "reframe" his actions in human terms so a judge or jury can understand them and lets me explain how they are consistent with research. Humans are fallible and can be vain and selfish. I presented Kentrell as a flawed and conflicted man, incarcerated both by the prison he was in and by his gang identity.

My more down-to-earth description of Kentrell and reframing of his distancing from the gang apparently was effective. While Michael got sixty years, Kentrell got fifty-two and was no longer in maximum security. Fifty-two years was the shortest sentence of any of my JLWOP cases. Paradoxically, Kentrell was by far the most deeply involved with his gang identity of any of my cases. He is scheduled for release on parole in 2023.

Historical Reframing 1: Clarence Darrow

I didn't invent reframing in court. It has a long history in criminal trials. Clarence Darrow, in the murder trial in Detroit of Dr. Ossian Sweet, is an example of a particularly spectacular use of reframing. Dr. Sweet was an African American physician who had moved into an all-white neighborhood in Detroit in 1926. Of course, his new white neighbors greeted him with a race riot and surrounded the house. Sweet, with his family frightened inside with him, shot into the crowd and killed one of the rioters. Sweet was indicted for murder, and Darrow swooped into town to defend him.

Rather than dance around technicalities of the law, Darrow stated the contrasting frames in his opening remarks (Weinberg 1957, 233):

> I shall begin about where my friend Mr. Moll [Assistant Wayne County Prosecutor Lester Moll] began yesterday. He says lightly, gentlemen, that this isn't a race question. This is a murder case. We don't want any prejudice; we don't want the other side to have any. Race and color have nothing to do with this case. This is a case of murder.

Now, let's see; I am going to try to be as fair as I can with you gentlemen; still I don't mind being watched at that. I just want you to give such consideration to what I say as you think it is worth. I insist that there is nothing but prejudice in this case; that if it was reversed and eleven white men had shot and killed a Black while protecting their home and their lives against a mob of Blacks, no-body would have dreamed of having them indicted. I know what I am talking about, and so do you. They would have been given med-als instead.

This is one of the most famous trials in American jurisprudence. Darrow reframed an open-and-shut murder case. The case was about race prejudice, Darrow insisted, and he told the all-white jury they knew it, too. They did. Their verdict? Not guilty.

Historical Reframing 2: Rodney King

The Rodney King beating in 1991 shocked the nation since it was captured on video. What also shocked the nation was the acquittal of the officers in their first trial. What you might not know is that the officers' acquittal re-sulted from the defense attorneys reframing of the beating through the clever use of expert witness testimony. In a reversal of the tactics of Clarence Darrow, the defense took the context away from race and "reframed" it to a matter of police training.

The video, common sense would suggest, was damning evidence of po-lice brutality. But Sergeant Duke from the Los Angeles Police Department argued that each blow by Stacy Koon and the other officers was a propor-tionate response to an action by Rodney King. Yes, all forty-seven blows. He did this by slowing down the video and breaking down the blows as re-sponses to specific motions of Rodney King (1994, 17).

> Expert: There were, ten distinct (1.0) uses of force. rather than one
> single use of force. . . . In each of those uses of force there was an
> escalation and a de-escalation, (0.8) an assessment period, (1.5)
> and then an escalation and a de-escalation again. (0.7) And an-
> other assessment period.

What happened, according to a superb analysis by Charles Goodwin, was that the beating was played over and over again in slow motion, and each blow dissected according to LAPD training procedures. "The massive beating," Goodwin says (1994, 17), "is now transformed into ten separate events, each with its own sequence of stages." According to Goodwin (15), Koon gloated at the effect of "reframing" the video in slow motion:

> Sgt. Stacy Koon, spent much of his time between the two trials watching and rewatching the tape, seeing how it looked when projected on different walls of his house. Rather than wanting to minimize the events on the tape he told a reporter . . . that if we had our way, we'd go down to Dodger Stadium and rip off that big-screen Mitsubishi and bring it into the courtroom and say, "Hey, folks, you're in for the show of your life because when this tape gets blown up it's awesome."

Reframing is neither good nor bad, nor is it neutral. But when reframing coincided with some ingrained assumptions of the goodness of law enforcement and fears of angry Black men, the first jury came up with a verdict as remarkable as in Darrow's Ossian Sweet trial. King's trial swung its focus from the context of police brutality toward African Americans to an investigation of whether Stacy Koon and the others followed their police training. The first jury found that the officers legally followed their training and acquitted them. The second convicted two of the officers and acquitted two others. The Los Angeles African American community gave their verdict in the streets.

It is, perhaps, true that Koon and the other officers did follow their training as the expert witness Sergeant Duke argued. You can decide for yourself what that means about police training. The significance of the case was that the African American community in Los Angeles and substantial numbers of Americans saw through the "reframing" to the racism in operation, whether Koon followed his training or not. Unlike the first jury, many Americans believed what they saw with their eyes and fit the officer's actions into the context of a racist police environment in Los Angeles. Unlike Clarence Darrow, the attorneys for Koon and the others reframed the issues away from the context of race prejudice and gave jurors a "framing" in technical police manuals where they could justify a brutal beating.

In any regard, reframing is a powerful force in trials and is the central technique in my practice as an expert witness. I have had only limited success reframing gang issues, and, to conclude this book, my repeated references to Sisyphus need to be more thoroughly explored. Demonization long predates and will outlive the Trump era, and witch hunts and inquisitions are as much precedents of my gang cases as any court decision or Trumpian tirade. The final chapter examines the "them and us" mentality and how it sustains our mass incarceration society. I also tie up my argument that, while stereotyping and demonization won't easily be changed, that is no excuse to give up the fight.

CASE LAW

Daubert v. Merrell Dow Pharmaceuticals (92–102), 509 U.S. 579 (1993). Certiorari to the United States Court of Appeals for the Ninth Circuit No. 92–102. Argued March 30, 1993—Decided June 28, 1993.

U.S. District Court for the Western District of Missouri, Southwestern Division United States of America, Plaintiff, v. No. 02-05025-01-CR-SW-GAF, Thomas D. Smith, a.k.a. "Mad Dog," a.k.a. "MD," Defendant. Government's Response in Opposition to Defendant's Motion in Limine to Prohibit or in the Alternative Limit Testimony Regarding Defendant's Membership in a Gang.

13

Humanizing Justice

Francisco Martinez was a baby-faced fifteen-year-old. He was also a Maniac Latin Disciple in an exurban area just outside of Chicago and had just been convicted of murder. I was brought in at sentencing to explain how it could be "normal" for a kid like Francisco to have become a gang member at eleven years old. Francisco had parents who both had been gang members and the local Latin Disciple branch had been accessible and welcoming for a troubled, rebellious boy. Older gang leaders took advantage of him, like a child soldier, to do the dirty work, including "protection," meaning armed patrol of gang turf. When members of the Maniac Latin Disciple's mortal enemy, the Latin Kings, were thought to have been spotted nearby, an older gang leader told fifteen-year-old Francisco to "protect the hood" and gave him a handgun. He figured, better the kid risk his life or go to jail than he, the glorious leader. Francisco spotted the "enemy" on a hill several dozen yards away. He fired his handgun at them. He told me he thought his shots hit the ground. He was no marksman, but he was tragically unlucky. His wild shot, incredibly, hit and killed Jonathon Castillo, who he believed was an invading rival gang member. Francisco was reported as laughing as the enemy fell. It was like a video game. His victim wasn't a real person to him.

Francisco wasn't laughing when I met with him. He was facing a very long prison term. Things took a plunge for the worse when police told him that the person killed was not a Latin King. Francisco was disconsolate and cooperated with police in their investigation of the shooting. His cooperation meant that he would fear not only the rival Latin Kings when he went to prison but Latin Disciples as well, who might label him as a snitch. He was in serious trouble on all sides.

Francisco was a child who was caught up with a gang life that was exciting but had become coldly real. We went over his life from his family and school experiences through the events of the shooting. In my report, I explained that his laughter after the shooting was similar to Jackie Montañez or Keith Harbin's "neutralizing" the fact that they had violated a sacred moral prohibition against killing. One form Francisco's neutralization took was the dehumanization of his enemies, much like the psychology of those seeking the death penalty.

He asked me, at one point, if I had ever done something I knew was wrong. "Of course," I said, but I didn't need to add that I haven't killed anyone. Francisco was wracked with guilt, but, surprisingly, he told me that, if the victim had actually been a Latin King, he didn't think he would have any regrets. I'm not so sure.

We talked about his interests in life and what he did every day to survive in a county jail. I humanized him to the court in my report:

> But did you know Francisco loves to read? When I asked him if I could send him a book, he lighted up and said "Eclipse," by Stephanie Meyer. Looking over my shoulder he said "Meyer, with an 'e' not 'a.'" This isn't my idea of a great read but Meyer's books are intensely popular among teenagers of every race and class. As he described the plots of various books he liked, I thought sadly, "he's just a kid." That "kid" is there inside him alongside of the gangster, competing for his life.

My testimony engaged the suburban judge, who was incredulous that preteens might be involved with gangs. I made eye contact with the judge throughout my two hours on the stand and saw he was paying close attention. The prosecutor, aware that the judge was giving credence to my testimony, repeatedly interrupted my answers with objections on all sorts of minor points. His Honor, exhibiting the impatience that is the privilege of judges, at one point told the prosecutor to "stop interrupting the witness!" Here was a judge who actually wanted to understand the case better.

I had reached the judge and explained how Francisco could have been caught up in gang life. I had also dismissed the prosecutor's dehumanization of Francisco for laughing after the shooting. The judge promised his decision on the sentence soon after my testimony, so I waited in the courtroom with the public defender and Francisco's mother.

But my research-based, humanizing words didn't really matter. The judge sentenced the fifteen-year-old to thirty-three and a half years in state prison.

The judge said he was mandated by sentencing guidelines to give a term of thirty-two to forty years. Surprisingly, the defense attorney congratulated me. He said the public defenders' betting pool predicted thirty-eight or thirty-nine years. My testimony had shaved five years off. I commiserated with Francisco's mother. Neither of us got much satisfaction from a sentence that was more than twice as long as Francisco had been alive to that day. His mother had a teardrop tattoo next to her eyes, and the public defenders had not wanted her to come to the sentencing, fearing the judge would see the tattoo as a gang symbol. She snuck in anyway. I told her every time she sees the tattoo in the mirror to think of her son. We both cried.

The worst, though, came next. I was able to have a final meeting with Francisco after the sentencing, before he was whisked away to serve his sentence. We talked about how to survive in prison, how to maneuver his gang identity and minimize conflict. He was religious, and I told him that religion can sometimes be a "protective factor" from heavy gang involvement during long sentences. It was a really difficult conversation. He asked me, in his fifteen-year-old's voice, if maybe the judge would reconsider his sentence in ten years? He broke my heart. I wanted to give him hope, but he needed to hear the truth and brace for years and years of incarceration. I took a deep breath and told him conditions can always change, but the way the climate in this country is today, he would likely have to serve his entire sentence. Parole had been abolished, so he was looking at being in prison until he was almost fifty. I don't think there was any way for him to understand this. I cried again after he was taken back to his cell.

––––––––––

Francisco got thirty-three and a half years. The judge in Marco Garcia-Bravo's case decided that Dr. Valdez's demonizing report could be admitted after all, and Marco got life without parole. In many of my cases, when all is said and done, and even if I'm congratulated on doing my job well, I'm left wondering if I've had any impact at all. The public defender in Francisco's case said that the judge had no choice, and, in fact, the sentence he handed out was in the low end of the sentencing range. With the abolition of parole, Francisco will serve more than twice as long as the fifteen-year average sentence for murder in the United States, according to the Bureau of Justice Statistics. Sisyphus has come to my mind more than once. The damn boulder keeps rolling back down the hill, and I have felt it flattening both the defendant and me again and again. The pain is fresh every time. And it never goes away.

Long sentences and the abolition of parole give little reason for those convicted of serious crimes to "rehabilitate" during incarceration. What does it gain them to participate in treatment? Just surviving in a dog-eat-dog prison world consumes an inmate's consciousness. How the United States came to create a mass incarceration society is beyond the scope of this book. I refer you to the incisive works of David Garland (1990, 2001), Michael Tonry (2016), Jonathon Simon (2007), and Michelle Alexander (2010). But one thing is sure: the United States is *number one* in locking people up. (See Fig. 13.1.)

The length of sentences in the United States conditions the meaning of success in expert witness work. Remember, nearly all of the men and women in my cases were guilty and the only issue at stake in the hearing is the severity of their sentence. This is one reason why stereotypes and demonization matter: if the defendant is "less than human," a judge or jury can justify a harsh sentence, or, if available, the death penalty. Current law mandates some of the longest sentences in the world, and my work, at best, can cut only a few years off, as it did with Francisco.

Racism is the strongest component of dehumanization in the United States. Paul Butler (2017b, 18) explains the title concept of his book *Chokehold* thus: "Conjuring up a criminal is part of how many Americans process encountering a Black man. It's an instant reaction, a habit of mind, but one with tragic consequences." This is another way to explain implicit bias and the racial roots of demonization. As I write, the nation is transfixed by the on-camera murder of George Floyd by Minneapolis police officer Derek Chauvin. As a Black man, Floyd did not get the "benefit" of a trial for his crime of passing a bad $20 bill. He bore the full weight of the fury of Officer

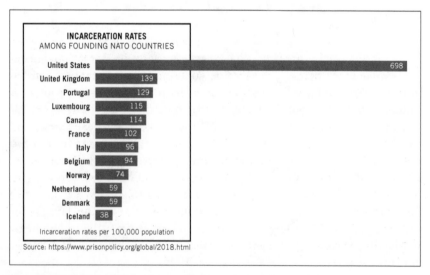

Figure 13.1 U.S. incarceration rates are off the charts. (Graph from Peter Wagner, "States of Incarceration: The Global Context, 2018." Prison Policy Initiative. Reprinted with permission from Prison Policy Initiative.)

Chauvin. How could Chauvin have considered Floyd as a fellow human being while kneeling on his windpipe for nine minutes and twenty-nine seconds as Floyd cried out that he could not breathe? Dehumanization means no restraint on how we punish, whether on the streets or in the courts.

At heart, the turn toward more severe punishments in the United States assumes that the vast majority of criminals who commit serious acts are either essentially evil or less than human. An inhuman subject means no "rehabilitation" is even possible: how do you redeem a Follower of Our Lord King Satan or a mad dog? The majority of people serving the equivalent of natural life sentences are African American. Black people are essentialized as animals or evil, too dangerous to ever allow out in our free society. Butler's research in *Chokehold* (2017a) reveals how, at the extreme, "criminals" like George Floyd can be executed even before trial.

My stereotype debunking and humanizing often falls on deaf ears in court since my frame and the prosecution's frame are polar opposites. If the defendant is thought to be evil, the prosecutor's frame is that evil people do evil things, end of story. If I try to explain context or variation in gang members or debunk any one of the numerous gang stereotypes lurking like a dark cloud over the trial, my arguments seldom can break through the prosecutor's dense frame of gangs as a "group of evil minds." None of my arguments matter if the judge or jury believes the defendant is no more than some kind of animal. Thus, the struggle is always uphill, to recall Sisyphus once again.

Daniel Hallin (1989) developed a useful concept in understanding press coverage of the Vietnam War, imagining a sphere of consensus within a sphere of legitimate controversy within a sphere of deviance. Hallin argued that, at the beginning of the war, dissent was dismissed as outside the sphere of legitimate controversy. Consensus at the beginning was that the Vietnam War was a life-and-death struggle against evil Communist dominoes, that unless stopped would one day knock down all of Western civilization. We can apply his notion of various spheres of public opinion to how juries and judges consider gangs. The notion that gangs might vary and have a history and be made up of human beings or different types of people is outside of Hallin's sphere of consensus and, in most cases, not even within his sphere of legitimate controversy. The stereotypical consensus is that gangs, and ergo, gang members are evil, and, in most cases, even a gang expert can't get the court to consider stereotypes of gangs as residing in the sphere of legitimate controversy. Rather, gangs, similar to Nazis, Communists, and terrorists, live in Hallin's sphere of deviance, or, for gangs, we might more accurately rename it the sphere of demonization. A prosecutor's demand for a maximum sentence is common sense, not just law-and-order ideology. A gang expert, like me, is the crazy one for questioning it.

In preparation for this book, I reviewed the history of the trial system. I read about the Inquisition, Salem and the U.S. witch hunts, the Russian show trials of the 1930s, and the 1950's U.S. red scare. There were certainly some common themes, like this one from historian Jonathan Kirsch's *The Grand Inquisitor's Manual* (2008, 12):

> As the inquisitors grasped, and as history has repeatedly proved, it is far easier for one human being to torture and kill another if he has convinced himself that the victim is not really human at all.

But as I read accounts of periods of history where moral panics swept societies for a time and then eased, I realized that the stereotyping and demonization of gangs is not exceptional, part of some embarrassing or outlandish moment in American history. The trials I have described in this book are not outliers, they are *normal*. Humanity's built-in preference for "us" and disgust for "them," racialized by American history, is embodied in gang trials. Aside from my testimony, no one blinked when Ricky Horn said FOLKS stood for Followers of Our Lord King Satan. It was "stereotype congruent" information. It was also absurd and had the obvious effect of making the death penalty for Robert Butts and Marion Wilson nothing more than common sense, really only a formality for juries. The trial was not, as it should have been, a dead serious consideration of whether to end the life of one more human being.

Psychologically, however, how do juries and judges come to accept such demonization in nonexceptional times? A substantial portion of the U.S. public is inclined toward a harsh view of human nature and the need for severe punishment. They need little persuasion. But how are such beliefs activated for entire juries composed of different kinds of people? We need to return to the concept of priming and link it to the role of the prosecutor.

Once More on Priming

The first chapters of this book spelled out the power of stereotypes and implicit bias. These folk explanations of gangs are fashioned into frames that fill in the blanks for us when information is missing. If gang members are violent at their core, if violence is the essence of the category "gang," surely, won't a jury agree any action by a gang member was motivated by his violent nature? Why have compassion for fifteen-year-old Francisco when he is no more than a violent gang thug? Hell, why even bother with the evidence? The justice system dismissed the counterframe of Francisco as "just a kid" as not stereotype congruent. Can't you imagine the prosecutor thinking, "Really, Dr. Hagedorn, isn't that beside the point?"

With Francisco watching, the judge was primed by the prosecutor to replace his fifteen-year-old baby-faced image with that of something less than human, the prototype of a gold-chain-wearing, gun-toting thug. I tried in vain to bring the focus back to the real Francisco. The function of priming in court is to take a judge or jury outside the evidence, in legal terms, and draw on existing stereotypes and story lines of the big bad wolf preying on little red riding hood. When life and death are on the line, and fear and anger are cued by conviction-focused prosecutors, juries and judges hold tightly to their stereotypes of gangs and are not easily able to even consider any discrepant information. In Francisco's case, the judge could hide behind sentencing guidelines, though it was well within his power to show compassion and discard them in this case. Few judges are so bold or courageous.

A number of court decisions and American Bar Association standards warn against "foul blows" and prosecutors' evoking emotions not reason. One decision chastised a prosecutor for referring to the defendant as a "hoodlum," mild language for the readers of this book. Babe Howell, in her review of prosecutorial misconduct in gang cases, states (2019, 706): "Inflammatory statements, even in pursuit of those charged with heinous offenses—especially in pursuit of those charged with heinous offenses—are inconsistent with the prosecutor's duty to do justice." I agree with Emily Bazelon (2019, 335) in her *Charged*, when she recommends that prosecutors "avoid dehumanizing language in court."

But my experience and studies deepen and particularize Bazelon's general recommendation. This book agrees with Howell that demonizing and reliance on common, harmful stereotypes are "common" in gang trials. I don't think calling the act of murder "evil" is out of bounds, though most are committed by damaged people caught up in emotions or situations they cannot easily control. What needs to be banned in courtrooms are prosecutors referencing the defendant, known to some of us as a human being, as evil, an animal, or anything less than human.

Allegations that a defendant is anything less than human render any judgment of a specific act as irrelevant because it is no longer the act that is on trial; the trial becomes only an opportunity for the juror to confirm the commonsense understanding that evil deeds are done by evil people. Under such a frame, no sentence can be too severe. Recall the deputy sheriff in my Introduction saying of Arthur Dent, if he wasn't guilty of this crime, he was guilty of something? This is another way of saying some people are evil and the evidence doesn't really matter. This is the definition of the fundamental attribution error. Such demonizing or dehumanizing of a defendant should be cause for a mistrial, since it makes a fair verdict or just sentence psychologically impossible. On what basis has the jury's decision been made? The evidence, or the imputed evil nature of the defendant? Any jury decision is fatally compromised if dehumanization of the defendant is allowed to intrude on the jury's deliberations.

Malcolm Gladwell (2004) in *Blink* has made a recommendation about curtailing stereotypes at criminal trials. He suggests that juries should be shielded from knowing anything about the defendant or his or her race or gender. Defendants should be kept in another room separate from the jury and even have their voices distorted. Rather than a practical matter, Gladwell's suggestion should be seen as his recognition of the awesome power of stereotypes and prejudice in court. Black defendants in capital cases "look deathworthy," to use Jennifer Eberhardt (2005) and her colleagues' shocking term. They look "deathworthy" because of our deep-seated racial stereotypes that are only magnified when the defendant is a gang member.

Someone like Patrick Stout, in Chapter 7, becomes seen as deathworthy by virtue of a triple threat of race, gender, and being a gang member. And the judge could not help but recall as a prototype the Tony Carruthers case, another Black gang member, whose trial he presided over, who buried his victims alive and threatened his judge and attorneys. Was Patrick Stout's death sentence determined solely by the evidence? With such frightening stereotypes of the murderous gang member primed by the prosecutor throughout the trial, how could any juror easily disentangle the prototype from Patrick Stout and the evidence?

If trials are to be determined by the evidence alone, dehumanizing language about the defendant needs to be forbidden. In the sentencing phase, similarly, prosecutors need to be restrained in their rhetoric of dehumanizing statements, such as calling a convicted defendant "unstoppable evil." This unsubtly hints to the jury that they can put a stop to his violence by sending him to his death. Doesn't the name "Mad Dog" Smith almost insist a jury should "put him down"? These are "foul blows," and prosecutors need to fear dehumanizing language will cost them a conviction and make them go through the trial all over again.

Paul Butler has provocatively asked the question in chapter 6 of his book *Let's Get Free* (2010), "Should good people become prosecutors?" The role of the prosecutor, studies like those by Zimbardo (2007) suggest, leads to Medwed's (2012) "prosecution complex" and tunnel vision that sees only the evidence that supports conviction. This can easily lead to a miscarriage of justice or justify overly harsh sentences. Prosecutors sometimes withhold evidence from discovery and commit other procedural errors. But I've found the most egregious practice of prosecutors, at least in gang cases, is their use of stereotypes and demonizing language. These inflammatory words and ideas flip the burden of proof: if the defendant is a gang member, and the gang member is by stereotype evil, then, of course, he is guilty unless some new Clarence Darrow can miraculously get a jury to acquit. If not this crime, after all, isn't he is guilty of something else? The evidence becomes no more than confirmation bias invoking what our stereotypes have already taught us about this monster before the trial even began.

I hasten, however, to remind you, unlike Bryan Stevenson's (2015) *Just Mercy*, this book is not about the actually innocent but the actually guilty. I have taken aim at the trials of gang members and demonstrated, in bookkeeping fashion, that it is *normal* for such trials to be marred by stereotypes and demonization. Since the defendant is evil incarnate, the reasoning goes, it doesn't matter *how* you end up putting him to death or locking him away forever as long as you get the monster out of sight and mind. I don't believe those sentiments represent the principles our system of justice was built on, and they offend my values. In my experience, gang members don't typically go to trial expecting justice. And, in most cases, prosecutors oblige their expectations, all too often by stereotyping, demonizing, and even outright lying.

I also believe our sentences are too long. Norway has a maximum sentence of twenty-one years for almost all crimes, including murder. Can you think of what has happened to you over the past twenty-one years and how painful it would have been for you to have missed that precious time? As I write, the coronavirus pandemic is causing many to rethink our overly long, unnecessarily punitive sentences and conditions in our prisons. Our tough-on-crime turn has all but abolished parole in most states. The rationale is that if people cannot change and there is no good in them anyway, they obviously need to be incapacitated for as long as possible.

Jackie Montañez got *sixty-three years* as a *resentencing* of her original life without parole term. A prosecutor commented that she was "lucky" she was a few weeks short of her sixteenth birthday at the time of the murders or he would have recommended the death penalty as the law allowed. No one, not the prosecutor, not the judge, nor her own defense attorneys, saw Jackie Montañez, a damaged, sexually abused teenager, as a human being desperately and destructively looking for a safe identity. How could there be any sympathy for a "cold blooded killer of whom Al Capone could be proud?" Alas, Jackie didn't find a safe identity in the gang either and has since spent nearly twice her years at the time of her offence in prison, struggling with her identity. She desperately wants to be free and live life like you and me. As I write this, she volunteered as an orderly in a Florida prison and has been exposed to coronavirus, which is running rampant in that facility. There doesn't seem to be a mechanism to allow her to be released before her mandatory 2023 date. Her lawyers, Aubri McDonald, I, and others keep trying to find a way.

Gang enhancement statutes are based on the idea that, if a prosecutor can call a crime "gang related," it deserves an even longer sentence since any gang member's character is irreparably corrupted. Gang enhancement statutes treat every gang member as the same, as stereotypes, like the big bad wolf. How can anyone in their right mind see a kid like fifteen-year-old Francisco as a big bad wolf? Here's how: stereotypes have an awesome power. They rely on a lifetime of exposure to media images and folk knowledge taught by parents, teachers, and peers. Stereotypes can make you see things that aren't there.

To shorten sentences or reestablish parole would require us to consider prison inmates as humans, not mad dogs or "unstoppable evil." I'm not particularly optimistic. The U.S. public is deeply divided on the death penalty and correctional policy, and the punitive turn in the 1980s will not be easily stemmed. What I'm arguing is that punitive policies are driven by fear and anger rooted in harmful, typically racialized stereotypes. Many prosecutions are based on the fundamental attribution error, that crime is not the result of circumstances or biography but the evil nature of criminals, who are actually monsters or some type of "other." To get the longest sentence prosecutors argue "they" are not like "us." So, we can be justified in not feeling any sympathy. It begins but doesn't end with race.

There is a poem by C. P. Cavafy (1975) that has always struck me as relevant to my experience of gangs in court. It is called "Waiting for the Barbarians" and is about Roman Empire soldiers patrolling the outskirts of the city on the lookout for the dread barbarian invasion. They can't find any invaders, and Cavafy's last two lines lament:

Now what's going to happen to us without barbarians?
Those people were a kind of solution.

Gangs are a kind of solution to the frustrations of the public, demands for more and more funding of police, and the occupational aspirations of prosecutors. The flip side to the unrestrained individualism that ignored the public good during the coronavirus pandemic is a deep hatred of the other. "They" are the real problem, as former President Trump reminded us daily. We need walls and scapegoats, so we are not hindered in any way from going about doing whatever we want to do, which we mistakenly call freedom. The problem, such thinking goes, is not our behavior but theirs. However, as much as the Trump era was filled with racism and xenophobia, the "us and them" mentality long preceded the current authoritarian turn and will remain. It is a persisting problem of human nature, primed today by demagogic political leaders. My studies in social psychology tell me we can never give up vigilance. Similarly, Derrick Bell (1980) taught us: racism is permanent.

In gang cases, prosecutors "prime" these innate feelings of "us and them" and the courtroom is the perfect arena for allowing our feelings of hostility to flow against a defendant who represents our worst fears of "them."

I've found that theories of violence in criminology can be applied in court, and not just to the gang members. For example, prosecutors learn tough on crime behavior from other members of the prosecutor's gang and lack meaningful social controls restraining them from demanding long sentences. French critic René Girard, in *Violence and the Sacred*, could be talking about prosecutors' appeals to juries when he said (1972, 2):

> When unappeased, violence always seeks and finds a surrogate victim. The creature that excited its fury is abruptly replaced by another, chosen only because it is vulnerable and close at hand.

Could there be a better description of the concept of the prototype replacing the real person, as we've seen with Patrick Stout or baby-faced Francisco? The fear of crime and anger at the victimizers are fanned by demonizing language. Psychologically, the defendant is convicted of all of what the court imagines are defects of his race or the sins of the stereotyped violent gang member. His or her conviction and terrible punishment is invoked to bind the community of "us" together. Shared hatred is a powerful adhesive. It is also like a tributary that flows into the Mississippi River of our dehumanization and racism, running down the center of our country's land and soul. In my ethics, it has no place in a courtroom.

Girard (15) goes on to explicitly examine the role of courts in cases of violence like those in this book.

> Our judicial system . . . does not suppress vengeance; rather it effectively limits it to a single act of reprisal, enacted by a sovereign authority specializing in this particular function.

Girard recognizes what much legal rhetoric ignores: our long sentences and the stubbornness of the death penalty represent unsatiated anger and frustration on the part of much of the public who are represented by the jury and encouraged by zealous prosecutors. Criminological theories of frustration leading to aggression can be applied to prosecutors and judges in the courtroom just as easily as to gang members on the streets. It is the prosecutor who stirs up those generalized feelings of frustration in the jury and turns them into rage against a particular defendant. It is the judge who executes justice on a defendant who represents evil. Girard adds a phrase (24) that could have been written for this book. He says court officials need to, at long last, "realize that there is no real difference between their principle of justice and the concept of revenge."

There is a relationship between the horrifying acts of street violence in my cases and the nearly unrestrained violence of our punitive society. Girard argues provocatively (31) that "Violence is like a raging fire that feeds on its very objects intended to smother its flames." In our justice system, those objects are our courts, and the instruments of violence are those prosecutors who use stereotypes and demonizing language that undermines the very fabric of justice. I end this part on a final word from Girard. A trial, in his terms, is a ritual of justice and (37), "Ritual is nothing more than the regular exercise of 'good' violence."

Can Prosecutors Be Good People?

The use of stereotypes by prosecutors leads us away from a consideration of the real gang member, the human being, like Francisco, the kid who likes to read. Once stereotypes rule, dehumanization can seamlessly slip in since we are no longer in any realm of reality but have passed over into the realm of demonization. In this realm or sphere, Thomas Smith can be dehumanized as a "mad dog," or Jacqueline Montañez turned into a cartoon character and called without judicial rebuke "the teen queen of criminals." I fight stereotyping in court because it does violence to both the evidence and the defendant. Law does not rule; trials turn into a volcano of pent-up frustrations that allow implicit and explicit bias to erupt at the defendant and smother him or her in a lava flow of stereotypes and demonization. I offer the cases in this book as evidence that I am not exaggerating.

As noted earlier, Paul Butler asked, controversially, "Can good people be prosecutors?" He is in a unique position to ask that since he was a prominent African American prosecutor and understood his behavior as reacting to both his profession and the frustrations in his own life. In *Chokehold* (2017a, 32), he explains:

> That's some of the work I did as a prosecutor, and I freakin' loved it. Maybe I saw my work as vindication against the Black boys who had bullied me when I was a kid. Maybe I liked holding myself out to the world as one of the good Black guys. Every time I stepped into court and sat at the prosecutor's table I sent the message that not every African American man was like the bad dude I was prosecuting. My work was the lawyer's version of Chris Rock's old joke about "Black people versus n----s."

Then he got accidentally arrested and realized as a defendant he was stereotyped as a "n----," not treated as a Black person. To his arresting officer, there was only one kind of African American—not two. The arresting officer "testi-lied" on the stand, and only Butler's hiring of a top-notch defense attorney got him acquitted. This experience "converted" him, in this book's parlance of how psychological change takes place. The corollary question, which Butler also considers, whether a good person should become a prosecutor, recalled to me my own teaching experience with students who wanted to become Chicago police. Since my Gangs and the Media course discussed the history of Chicago police corruption and brutality, students regularly came up to me and confidentially asked my opinion on whether they should become Chicago police officers.

I nearly always said yes, absolutely. Students who had taken my classes on the power of the media stereotype and had heard the gang members I brought into class to talk had experiences and learning that would serve them well as police officers. However, I told each of them, "Realize, being a Chicago Police officer is fraught with moral danger." The job itself relies on shorthand, System 1 fast thinking. Stereotypes are useful to the police officer and gang members are crudely dehumanized so it becomes easy to justify brutal behavior. "You may not like the person you'll become," I told them.

Stereotypes are useful for prosecutors as well, and, as we've seen, dehumanization is necessary to justify the long sentences they advocate. If you've ever been to a maximum security prison, like Stateville Correctional Center outside Chicago, you know you would not want your dog locked up in such a place and surely not for dozens of years. Would those years likely transform an offending canine into a civilized, tamed cuddly pooch? Or being caged, would the dog run a greater risk of becoming snarling mad at his treatment, holding it in until provoked to lash out? Why do we think human beings would respond politely to the trauma of decades of being locked up in small cages? We apparently don't care; if we understand defendants as animals to begin with, then in our minds nothing will change their vicious nature and the longer they are locked up the better. The purpose of punishment is punishment. Their pain brings us relief.

The movement toward electing progressive prosecutors is a hopeful sign, but sentencing guidelines need to change, as seen with Francisco's case. For prosecutors, getting a conviction, as with nearly all the cases in this book, is easy. However, it is necessary to cross over into the realm of stereotypes and the language of dehumanization to justify the harshest sentences. Current sentencing guidelines are concerned with incapacitating irredeemable animals, not rehabilitating human beings. Getting convictions and the longest sentence, not doing justice, is what gets a DA promoted or reelected in most contexts. A prosecutor neutralizes any reservations about "winning" a death or life without parole sentence by dehumanizing the defendant in their minds, too—their dehumanization is not just for the juror but for their own peace of mind. That objective motivated the infamous contest between Chicago's Cook County prosecutors to see who would be the first to convict four thousand pounds of defendants. Those prosecutors delighted in their refusal to recognize the defendants not as human beings but just pounds of flesh.

I agree with Haney that the fundamental attribution error is at the root of the punitive turn in the 1980s. It also drives the xenophobia and authoritarianism of the Trump era. Since the slavery of African Americans and genocide of native peoples, "them and us" thinking has been the warp and woof of American culture. It won't go away with an election, and it haunts not only those with power but those of us who protest and seek fundamental change. Police still are called "pigs" and the targets of our protests dehumanized. One slogan in the George Floyd marches I attended was ACAB: "All Cops Are Bastards." Such hatred can build temporary unity, but it threatens our capacity to secure lasting change.

Sadly, the End Returns to the Beginning

If you expected an uplifting end to this book, you haven't been paying attention. This book has "reframed" the trials of gang members by vividly describing the reliance of prosecutors on stereotypes and demonization to get convictions and the longest possible sentences. They do it because it works. It works because it is based on our own psychological reliance on stereotypes and "us" and "them" thinking. It works because deep inside us there is a view of the "just society" where evildoers are nonhuman wolves, and since we were children, we rooted for the wolves to be plopped into a boiling kettle of water and scalded to death. That is our primordial belief in justice, and it is primed by prosecutors in every gang case when the defendant is said to be an animal, a monster, or, in any way, "less than human."

I'm not an expert on reforming criminal justice policy. The George Floyd murder has caused the nation to question the basic fairness of policing and exposed its dehumanizing violence. The coronavirus pandemic overall can hopefully spark a debate on the inhumanity of our prisons that might go beyond palliative measures for geriatric inmates. Perhaps we are at a "conversion" point on criminal justice, where new institutions can be imagined and brought into being. Perhaps the pendulum is turning away from the most punitive sentencing policies, but the current xenophobia and our politicians' daily recourse to "them and us" rhetoric does not buttress such hope.

Unlike Emily Bazelon, Bryan Stevenson, or the Innocence Project, I've chosen for my subject for this book the least sympathetic population: gang members who kill. I've used my own expert witness work to demonstrate that even the trials of the actually and obviously guilty are not decided solely on the evidence. Some prosecutors seem to delight in rolling in the mud of demonization to perform a dirty dance of overkill. The purpose of prosecutors' ritual is to transform the individual on trial into something else, something disgusting and barbaric. Evidence and reason can be left behind when you are sentencing to death a Follower of Our Lord King Satan.

Like the early sociologist Emile Durkheim (1897), who chose a supremely individual act, suicide, as his example of the importance of broader variables like religion, I've chosen guilty gang members as my example of the injustice of American courts. Rather than demonstrate the power of sociology to explain injustice, I've examined the social psychology, not of gangs, but of us all. How we treat the obviously guilty exposes fundamental problems in the routine prosecution of justice.

I've taken you on a journey through the power of stereotypes and frames, to how and why demonization works, to my own seldom successful attempts to reframe gang stereotypes in court. In a break from my old social science style of writing, I've told you stories from the courtroom that I hope will prime in you a sense of injustice and move you to support an agenda of reform. I could put forth a progressive list of reforms I support, but the real message of this book is the never-ending need to confront our all-too-human behavior of stereotyping and demonizing. That has been my goal as an expert witness, and this book is my testament to the awesome power of stereotypes. My image of Camus's Sisyphus is meant to stubbornly hang in your mind's eye. Like Dr. King, we will never make it to the mountaintop, but we find purpose in the fact that we don't stop trying.

Effective stories end with the success of the good guys and justice prevailing. Think of Bryan Stevenson's exoneration of Walter McMillian or of John Grisham's novels. My stories do not end well. But my point is not that good always prevails but rather that evil always needs to be fought. And I've come to believe that we fight for what is just not because we always realistically expect to win but because it is just and right to do so. In our society, the tears of Francisco's mother are more likely than the cheers at Walter McMillian's exoneration. This book began with the story of Robert Butts's execution. I end with my field notes on Marion Wilson's death by lethal injection, which took place just as I was beginning to write this book.

Field notes, March 28, 1996–June 20, 2019:
Twenty-three years, two months; 8,510 days between the deaths of Donovan Parks and Marion Wilson. Marion would live a total of forty-two years, and no more, and spent most of his life inside a prison cell. With his last words, he said he "never took a life." In this he was as resolute as his co-offender, Robert Butts. Each claimed the other was the triggerman. Both sets of attorneys asserted in their decades-long appeal process that the other defendant pulled the trigger.

I stayed away from that argument in my work on each case. Both Marion and Robert had explained to me, convincingly, how the other one had done the shooting. Legally, it didn't matter: the shooting was done in the course of a robbery, making the crime "malice murder." Morally, I didn't think it mattered either. Both men stole Parks's car with the intention of selling it to a chop shop. But, after the unexpected murder, they thought better of it and torched the car, trying to cover their tracks. After they were arrested, both men told police the other one had done the shooting, seeking to escape a feared sentence of death.

I consulted on both cases. When Robert's attorneys hired me after I had testified for Marion, they wanted to know my views of who was culpable? I told them at the time that my testimony was not about who pulled the trigger, but the stereotypes of the gang testimony by law enforcement and lies and sensationalism of the ethically challenged prosecutor, Fred Bright. I didn't need to believe either of the defendants about who actually blew Mr. Parks's brains out with a shotgun that night. I've learned in my forty years of research that gang members lie as much as . . . policemen. Both Robert and Marion were encouraged by their lawyers to believe that their chances of escaping the death penalty lay to a large degree on blaming their codefendant for being the triggerman. For both the defense and the prosecution, the truth didn't matter, and I wonder if over time both men came to believe their own conflicting accounts? Both went to their deaths proclaiming they had not killed anyone.

Donovan Parks's family was a major force throughout the appeal process for both Robert and Marion, arguing for execution as a way to allow them to get on with their lives. They didn't care which one of the two young men pulled the trigger; they wanted justice, which was their name for vengeance. I understand the Parks family's anger. An eye for an eye lies deep in our fundamental moral sense of reciprocity. Marion's and Robert's deaths may give them closure. But probably not. Donovan's life was not brought back as the body count grew to three. Marion's twenty-three-year-old daughter, Tykecia, yelled out as her father was led to the death chamber, "I want my daddy. I want my daddy back!" Are those the cries of justice? These heart-piercing screams erupt from a cycle of violence, what Girard calls a raging fire. This is what fuels violence on the streets of Chicago today, attempts to salve the collective wounds when a "brother" is killed by "enemies." One violent act leads to another . . . and they both comprise a culture of death.

The modern justice system was founded on a belief that justice needed to be taken away from the open wounds of kinship revenge and the obligation to retaliate. But, in today's punishment society, the state has become the main cheerleader for vengeance. The trials of both Robert and Marion were marred by sensationalist lies and stereotypes of gangs in order to get a death penalty sentence. Both Robert and Marion were culpable, but how do you understand the mendacity and vindictiveness of the prosecutor, Fred Bright, who told both juries that the defendant in each of the separate trials was the one who pulled the trigger? Jury interviews revealed that Bright's false claims that Milledgeville was in the midst of a wave of gang violence had both surprised jurors and scared them. Bright was effective: two for two. Both men were executed. I'm sure he was proud.

In their clemency petitions to the Georgia Pardon Board (Widder et al. 2019, 1), Marion's lawyers pointed out:

> District Attorney Fred Bright, who obtained the death penalties for two men despite the existence of only one bullet, had the dubious distinction of being the most zealous death-penalty prosecutor in Georgia, obtaining more death sentences than any other Georgia prosecutor from 1995 to 2004, having sought the death penalty in twenty-one of thirty-one eligible murders.

A special place in human rights hell is reserved for Howard Sills, who had embarrassingly claimed that "F shot" stood for "Folks" in trying to make the crime appear gang related. In a letter to the pardon board, who was considering a last-day appeal for clemency twenty-three years later, Sills continued to call for blood. He wrote about Marion:

> His greatest legacy besides the crimes he perpetrated (against Parks) . . . was that he will be remembered as the father of gang activity in Milledgeville, . . . an insidious tumor brought by him to that community which has metastasized to a point where random drive-by shootings are almost a routine daily occurrence.

Let me count the lies. Marion returned from youth prison and hung out with an already existing peer group in the Manor, an out-of-the-way housing project on the outskirts of Milledgeville. Delinquent peer groups hung out for many years in Milledgeville, first being labeled "gangs" in the 1980s and 1990s as a national gang scare turned into a moral panic. Sills's incredible claim that drive-by shootings "are almost a routine daily occurrence" has no basis in police statistics nor in any reality outside of Sills's narrow mind and inflammatory, vengeful rhetoric.

Sills's vindictive letter to the pardon board, calling for Marion's death, went on to cement the "gang-related" nature of the murder by claiming:

> He also explained the workings of the "Folk," its language, it's "sets," and how a person got in the gang and achieved rank within the orga-

nization. We inquired about how one's status in the gang might increase by committing various crimes, especially violent crimes. Wilson's response to the question of his rank may have been the most
disturbing thing revealed in the entire investigation. We asked does
his robbery and murder increase your rank or status in the "Folk?" His
almost boastful reply was, "Nah, man, I can't get no higher. I'm the
Goddamn enforcer!" I don't think I will ever forget those words.

I read the transcript of Marion's interrogation and interviewed Marion as
well. He told them nothing about how to get into the Folks gang nor how
"rank" is attained. Sills's comments about how the gang operated were
taken solely from sensationalist documents of the GGIA, reinforcing and cel-
ebrating stereotypes. Marion did say "he was the goddam chief enforcer"
but he also told them it was a title he got in youth prison, and he was not part
of the set of teenage delinquents in a Milledgeville housing project called the
Manor. He denied being any kind of leader. Sills omits in his letter that Marion
was putting him on when he said he had only one guy under him, "Kunta
Kinte." Sills and Massee didn't seem to get it. Maybe they thought Kunta
Kinte was real, too?

Sills's hateful letter was the last chapter in Fred Bright's successful effort to brand the murder as gang related in order to get a death penalty.
Marion's clemency petition, written by Brian Kammer (Widder 2019), painfully pointed out:

Fred Bright, in particular, is notorious for bad faith attempts to inject
gang elements into criminal cases. In two cases contemporaneous with
Marion's, Bright was found by the Georgia Supreme Court to have
acted in bad faith in arguing to the jury that a murder was gang-related
but offering no meaningful evidence to prove it. See Alexander v. State,
270 Ga. 346 (1998); Hartry v. State, 270 Ga. 596 (1999). Bright, in both
cases, attempted to argue that the defendants and their cohorts were,
specifically, members of the Folks gang. See Alexander, 270 Ga. at 348;
Hartry, 270 Ga. at 598. And in both cases, where Bright failed to offer
evidence of gang activity, the Supreme Court of Georgia held that such
statements were not made in good faith. See Alexander, 270 Ga. at
350; Hartry, 270 Ga. at 599.

I reached out to Brian shortly before Marion's execution. There was nothing more to do, he said. Legally, the exposure of lies, stereotypes, and "bad
faith" inflammatory rhetoric didn't matter.
On the main issue over which the death penalty was contested, who
pulled the trigger, I agreed with the law: it didn't really matter, they both col-

luded in the murder of an innocent man. But it is also the law, or the U.S. Supreme Court's interpretation of the law, that allows prosecutors and law enforcement to lie and emotionally manipulate juries to kill a human being. An eye for an eye. Especially if they are Black. And young men. And you can call them gang members.

———

Why should I write this book when so often the attempt to break these stereotypes really doesn't matter? Or does it? Albert Einstein apocryphally said that the definition of insanity is doing the same thing over and over again and expecting a different result. I guess I must be insane. But like Sisyphus who was condemned by the gods to keep rolling that boulder up the hill, I am condemned by my values to fight, even if defeat is certain. My work is begging for a criminal justice system that is based on evidence and an understanding of the flaws of humanity. I admit some people may be so emotionally damaged they can't help themselves from doing others harm. But I am also in sympathy with Bryan Stevenson's question: why do we want to kill the broken people? Why do we want to take our anger and frustration out on people who live lives in such constant emotional pain? The reality of murder, in the cases I've discussed here, is that violence is complicated and messy. What is simplistically claimed by prosecutors to be gang related often boils down to immature, emotional, or misguided loyalties, like those of young Francisco or a confused Johnnie Norman in Chapter 2, or a sexually abused Jacqueline Montañez. Such messy and complicated reasons for a homicide do not excuse it, of course, but make it a human act. Jurors can realize they too have such emotions and might even dare to think: "There but for the Grace of God go I."

Does that happen? Not very often. The stories in this book depict an unforgiving criminal justice system. Even when judges show an ounce of compassion, like with Francisco, guidelines seldom allow compassion to be expressed in reasonable sentences. In court, I often feel like I want to cry out at demonizing prosecutors like Fred Bright using the words of the Army's Chief Counsel Joseph Welch in 1954 at the red-baiting Senator Joseph McCarthy: "Have you no sense of decency sir?" I grew up in Wisconsin when McCarthy was a popular senator. Some called him Saint Joe, and any criticism of him was suspect. The Army-McCarthy hearings finally brought him down. I'm under no illusion that prosecutors' reliance on stereotypes and demonization will fade quickly, discredited like Senator McCarthy, into the past. Fortunately, not all prosecutors are like Fred Bright. However, the yellow brick road of stereotypes and demonization lies in front of prosecutors, leading them to Oz, where they might discover that justice is only revenge.

But dim prospects of victory do not mean injustice should not be confronted. I do not believe change will come only through court decisions. As I write, Black Lives Matters protests in the streets are questioning the basic institutions of our society. Judges too are taking notice. *Brown v. Board of Education* was decided with the international condemnation of American racial practices firmly in the U.S. Supreme Court's mind as the civil rights movement began to shake America. A change in white America's racial attitudes is taking place. I told you the story of 1967 when I marched for open housing into a hostile crowd of thousands of rioting white people on Milwaukee's south side. As I write this chapter in 2020, I marched again to the south side, fifty-three years later to protest the killing of George Floyd. This time, we were greeted by hundreds of white people, coming out of their homes and businesses, not to riot, but to give us snacks and cold water on a hot day, display signs of "Black Lives Matter," and cheer our march.

I think the most hope for change comes not from smart lawyers or expert witnesses but from the demands in the streets of Black and other people of color to be treated as human beings. I think these protests can encourage and drive forward the movement for progressive prosecutors. They offer hope that stereotypes can be exposed, demonization curtailed, and people can change.

The End of the Story

As I wrote this book, I felt an uncomfortable affinity for men facing the death penalty. I am at the end of both my career and my life, to my surprise having made it into my seventies. In the past few years, I've been hit by a car and enjoyed my first Flight for Life helicopter ride and emergency surgery. I've suffered a silent heart attack and stroke. I have diabetes. I'm facing my own death sentence, which will take place in the not-so-distant future. My court cases, in a way, are like facing my own date with death. I know I'm going to lose, but what do I do as the fatal hour approaches?

Camus's version of the Sisyphus tale ends with Camus deciding Sisyphus must be happy. I won't go that far. But if I did not roll that boulder back up the hill again and again, I would be disappointed in myself. I would have collaborated in allowing my research and knowledge to go unused in the struggle for justice and the battle against prejudice and racism. This book offers my expert witness technical skill and reframing tactics but also argues for a set of values. These values are exemplified by my motto, "research not stereotypes." I testify because stereotyping allows decisions of the court to be based on factors outside the evidence. Demonization means the defendant who the judge or jury sees is not the real human being sitting at the defense table but what I've called a prototype; a psychological phantasm of fears and anger that looks like unstoppable evil, a mad dog, or the teen queen of criminals. Prosecutors prime that scary prototype, which consciously and subconsciously turns jurors' and judges' fears and frustrations into the violence of harsh sentences.

Prosecutors have a mandate to carry out the law but also "do justice." Following the notion of subtyping, prosecutors surely fall into more categories than "progressive" and "demonizing." Like gang members, they are a diverse set. We should not fall into the trap of stereotyping or dehumanizing prosecutors, but we need to see them as individuals as well as representatives of their profession. To answer Paul Butler, of course they can be good people. But, as I told my students about becoming police officers, the profession of public prosecutor is fraught with moral danger. I've shown prosecutors can do harm, lots of harm. They also can do good, though that is more difficult and requires struggle.

I'm not sure I'll do more expert witness cases, given my age and health. But I did march in protest of the killing of George Floyd and will do so again. There are many places in the choir for us to sing the song of justice. Like millions of Americans today, my values say I cannot be silent. Sadly, Sisyphus's hill, a metaphor for the way we naturally think in categories, is there every morning when the sun comes up and will still be there as it sets. I'm tired now and may need to rest more often than before. But this book is written to encourage others to find their place in the choir and sing the song of justice as loudly, as melodiously, and for as long as they can.

CASE LAW

Berger v. United States, supra, 295 U.S. at 88, 55 S. Ct. at 633.

Hall v. United States, supra, 419 F.2d at 587.

United States v. Hayward, supra, 420 F.2d at 146.

United States v. Modica, 663 F.2d 1173 (2d Cir. 1981).

United States v. Murphy, 374 F.2d 651, 655 (2d Cir.), cert. denied, 389 U.S. 836, 88 S. Ct. 47, 19 L.Ed.2d 98 (1967).

Epilogue to the Stories

Narseal Batiste was sentenced to 162 months in federal prison followed by thirty-five years of supervised parole. He was incarcerated in San Antonio, Texas. He was released March 25, 2018. He was represented in his third trial by Ana Jhones of Miami.

Robert Butts's life came to an end on May 4, 2018, by lethal injection in the Georgia Diagnostic and Classification Prison. His federal defender, Bo King, fought for him to the bitter end and witnessed the execution. Bo King and Victoria Calvert, a pro bono attorney from the corporate powerhouse law firm King and Spaulding who later joined the Federal Defenders, were Robert's staunchest allies. Susan Lehmann, their mitigation specialist, built a deep relationship with Robert and his family.

Michael Cooks was released on parole in 2019 after twenty-seven years in prison at age forty-one. His attorneys, Randolph Stone and Herschella Conyers of the University of Chicago's Edwin Mandel Legal Aid Clinic represented him in a JLWOP resentencing.

Arthur Dent's life without parole sentence means he will likely die in prison. He is currently incarcerated at Illinois's maximum security Stateville Correctional Facility and was represented by Andrea Lyon, called the "Angel of Death Row."

Ike Easley is ineligible for parole and is currently in maximum security in Stateville Correctional Center. He will likely die behind bars. His trusted civil rights attorney, Aviva Futorian, fought for his life and advised me in my defense of Ike at Governor Ryan's clemency hearing.

Marco Garcia-Bravo was spared the death penalty when Colorado abolished it during his trial. Before the trial began, Marco's attorney, Carrie Thompson, waged a determined defense against the state's expert, Alphonso Valdez, who falsely framed Marco as a Mexican Mafia operative and attempted to get him sentenced to death.

Keith Harbin will also likely die behind bars. He is currently serving his life sentence in Earnest C. Brooks Correctional Facility near Muskegon, Michigan. His local attorney, David Zessin, reached out to me in order to counter the fabrications and demonization by the state's "expert," George Knox.

Francisco Martinez is currently incarcerated at maximum security Pontiac Correctional Center in central Illinois. He is not scheduled to be paroled until August 1, 2042. His public defender at the time of his trial, Marty Shaffer, is now in private practice.

Jacqueline Montañez is in the Florida prison system after being transferred from Illinois for her safety. She was sentenced to life without parole as a juvenile, which was converted to sixty-three years in a resentencing. Persistent efforts by her Northwestern University Bluhm Legal Clinic attorney, Alison Flaum, to get her early release have failed. Jackie will likely not be free until her mandatory release date of July 7, 2023. She has been behind bars since 1992 when she was fifteen years old.

Chester Niven's maximum release date is not until 2037, twenty years from his conviction. He is currently eligible for parole and, according to his lawyer, Lee Sexton, he will almost certainly be released well before his mandatory release date.

Johnnie Norman is set for release June 1, 2023, from the Alabama Department of Corrections. He is a "minimal out" prisoner and, according to his strong advocate, mitigation specialist Susan Lehman, could be released at any time.

Jaime Ruiz has a projected parole date of February 4, 2036. He is incarcerated at Lawrence Correctional Center, a medium security prison in southern Illinois. He continues to have strong family backing. He was ably represented pro bono by Kristine Schanbacher and other attorneys from Dentons, who bill themselves as the world's largest law firm.

Timothy Shanks had charges dismissed at trial and left Mahnomen, Minnesota, immediately. His local attorney, Peter Cannon, defied all odds in contesting the state's gang-related narrative.

Thomas D. Smith is sentenced to spend his entire life behind bars. He is currently incarcerated at the super max federal penitentiary in Florence, Colorado. His mitigation team, led by attorney Cyndy Short, successfully persuaded the jury not to sentence him to death.

James Patrick Stout will likely die in a Tennessee prison. An official from the Turner Center where Patrick is incarcerated wrote me that Patrick was working as a mentor in Pathfinders, a program for young gang members in prison. Brad MacClean of the Tennessee Office of the Post-Conviction Defender devised a legal strategy that for the first time made use of the power of stereotypes and reversed Patrick's death sentence.

Kentrell Stoutmire was also represented by Stone and Conyers. He is scheduled to be released from the IDOC in 2023. His original JLWOP sentence was reduced to fifty-two years.

Tadarius Williams was released March 19, 2011, and sentenced to time served, according to his attorney, Leigh Ann Webster. His release took place after the Georgia Supreme Court overturned Judge Reuben Green and ordered a new trial. The order for a new trial was based in part on what I called the "far-fetched" testimony of police "gang expert," Cobb County Investigator Charles Lyda.

Marion Wilson was executed in the same prison where Robert Butts's life ended, the Georgia Diagnostic and Classification Prison, on June 20, 2019, despite heroic efforts by Brian Kammer and the nonprofit Georgia Resource Center.

References

Alexander, Michelle. 2010. *The New Jim Crow: Mass Incarceration in the Age of Color-blindness*. New York: New Press.

Alinsky, Saul D. 1971. *Rules for Radicals: A Practical Primer for Realistic Radicals*. New York: Random House.

Allport, Gordon W. 1954. *The Nature of Prejudice*. Reading, MA: Addison-Wesley.

Anderson, John, Sergeant Mark Nye, Ron Freitas, and Jarrett Wolf. 2009. "Gang Prosecution Manual." Washington, DC: National Youth Gang Center, U.S. Department of Justice.

Araiza, William D. 2017. *Animus: A Short Introduction to Bias in the Law*. New York: New York University Press.

Atwood, Margaret. 1986. *The Handmaid's Tale*. Boston: Houghton Mifflin Harcourt. Kindle.

Baldwin County Sheriff's Department. 1996. Transcript of First Statement of Marion Wilson. Case No. 9604512. Undated, unpaginated.

Banaji, Mahzarin R., and Anthony G. Greewald. 2013. *Blindspot: Hidden Biases of Good People*. New York: Delacorte.

Barber, William J., with Jonathan Wilson-Hartgrove. 2016. *The Third Reconstruction: Moral Mondays, Fusion Politics, and the Rise of a New Justice Movement*. Boston: Beacon.

Bazelon, Emily. 2019. *Charged: The New Movement to Transform American Prosecution and End Mass Incarceration*. New York: Random House.

Bell, Derrick, ed. 1980. *Shades of Brown: New Perspectives on School Desegregation*. New York: Teachers College Press.

———. 1992. *Faces at the Bottom of the Well: The Permanence of Racism*. New York: Basic Books.

Benferado, Adam. 2015. *Unfair: The New Science of Criminal Injustice*. New York: Crown.

Benford, Robert D. 1997. "An Insider's Critique of the Social Movement Framing Perspective." *Sociological Inquiry* 67 (4): 409–30.

Berkowitz, Leonard. 1993. *Aggression: Its Causes, Consequences, and Control.* New York: McGraw-Hill.

Berreby, David. 2005. *Us and Them: The Science of Identity.* Chicago: University of Chicago Press.

Block, Melissa. 2013. "The Low-Tech Way Guns Get Traced." National Public Radio, May 20, 2013.

Bloom, Paul. 2016. *Against Empathy: The Case for Rational Compassion.* New York: HarperCollins. EPUB.

Bloom, Robert. 2002. *Ratting: The Use and Abuse of Informants in the American Justice System.* Westport, CT: Praeger.

———. 2019. "What Jurors Should Know about Informants: The Need for Expert Testimony." Boston: Boston College Law School.

Buonomano, Dean. 2011. *Brain Bugs: How the Brain's Flaws Shape Our Lives.* New York: W. W. Norton.

Butler, Paul. 2010. *Let's Get Free: A Hip-Hop Theory of Justice.* New York: New Press.

———. 2017a. *Chokehold: Policing Black Men.* New York: New Press.

———. 2017b. *Chokehold: Policing Black Men.* New York: New Press. Kindle.

———. 2020. "Policing in the US Is Not about Enforcing Law. It's about Enforcing White Supremacy." *The Guardian*, Op-Ed, May 30, 2020. Available at https://www.theguardian.com/commentisfree/2020/may/30/policing-in-the-us-is-not-about-enforcing-law-its-about-enforcing-white-supremacy.

Butts, Robert. 2013. *A Portrait of My Journey: Memoirs from Death Row.* Lexington, KY.

Cappella, Joseph N., and Kathleen Hall Jamieson. 1996. "News Frames, Political Cynicism, and Media Cynicism." *Annals of the American Academy of Political and Social Science* 546 (1996): 71–84.

Castells, Manuel. 2009. *Communication Power.* Oxford: Oxford University Press.

———. 2012. *Networks of Outrage and Hope.* Cambridge, UK: Polity.

Cavafy, C. P. (1975) 1992. "Waiting for the Barbarians." In *Collected Poems*, edited by George Savidis, translated by Edmund Keeley and Philip Sherrard. Princeton, NJ: Princeton University Press.

Child, Lee. 2012. *Killing Floor.* New York: Jove.

Cloward, Richard, and Lloyd Ohlin. 1960. *Delinquency and Opportunity.* Glencoe, IL: Free Press.

Cohen, Stanley. 1972. *Moral Panics and Folk Devils.* London: MacGibbon and Kee.

Collins, Randall. 2008. *Violence: A Micro-sociological Theory.* Princeton, NJ: Princeton University Press.

Conrad, Joseph. 1899. *Heart of Darkness.* London: Blackwood's Magazine.

Damasio, Antonio. 1994. *Descartes' Error.* New York: Vintage.

Davis, Angela J. 2001. "The American Prosecutor: Independence, Power, and the Threat of Tyranny." *Iowa Law Review* 86:393–465.

———. 2007. *Arbitrary Justice: The Power of the American Prosecutor.* New York: Oxford University Press.

Davis, Kevin. 2007. *Defending the Damned: Inside a Dark Corner of the Criminal Justice System.* New York: Atria Books.

Devine, Dennis J. 2012. *Jury Decision Making: The State of the Science.* New York: New York University Press.

DiSalvo, David. 2013. *Brain Changer: How Harnessing Your Brain's Power to Adapt Can Change Your Life*. Dallas, TX: Bembella Books.

Dolovich, Sharon, and Alexandra Natapoff, eds. 2017. *The New Criminal Justice Thinking*. New York: New York University Press.

Du Bois, W.E.B. (1902) 1989. *The Souls of Black Folk*. Reprint, New York: Penguin Books.

Durkheim, Emile. (1897) 1951. *Suicide: A Study in Sociology*. New York: Free Press.

Eberhardt, Jennifer L. 2019. *Biased: Uncovering the Hidden Prejudice That Shapes What We See, Think, and Do*. New York: Viking. Kindle.

Eberhardt, Jennifer L., Paul G. Davies, Valerie J. Purdie-Vaughns, and Sheri Lynn Johnson. 2005. "Looking Deathworthy: Perceived Stereotypicality of Black Defendants Predicts Capital-Sentencing Outcomes." *Psychological Science* 17 (5): 383–86.

Edsall, Thomas. 2019. "No Hate Left Behind. Lethal Partisanship Is Taking Us into Dangerous Territory." *New York Times*, March 13, 2019. Accessed March 21, 2019. Available at https://www.nytimes.com/2019/03/13/opinion/hate-politics.html.

Eisen, Mitchell L., Brenna Dotson, and Gregory Dohi. 2014. "Probative or Prejudicial: Can Gang Evidence Trump Reasonable Doubt?" *UCLA Law Review* 62 (Disc 2).

Eisen, Mitchell L., Brenna Dotson, and Alma Olaguez. 2014. "Practitioner: Exploring the Prejudicial Effect of Gang Evidence: Under What Conditions Will Jurors Ignore Reasonable Doubt." *California State Law Review* 11 *Criminal Law Brief* 41 (Fall).

Eisen, Mitchell L., David Drachman, Cheryl Groskopf, Robert Enoch, and Amanda Clement. 2009. "The Biasing Effect of Gang Evidence on Juror Verdicts." Los Angeles: California State University.

Elbaum, Max. (2002) 2018. *Revolution in the Air: Sixties Radicals Turn to Lenin, Mao, and Che*. Reprint, London: Verso.

Ellul, Jacques. 1967. *The Technological Society*. New York: Vintage.

"The El Rukn Embarrassment." 1993. *Chicago Tribune*, June 11, 1993. Accessed October 13, 2019. Available at https://www.chicagotribune.com/news/ct-xpm-1993-06-11 -9306110002-story.html.

Fields, Barbara Jeanne. 1990. "Slavery, Race and Ideology in the United States of America." *New Left Review* 181 (May–June): 95–118.

Fiske, Susan T. (1954) 1978. "Stereotyping, Prejudice, and Discrimination." In *The Handbook of Social Psychology*, edited by D. T. Gilbert, Susan T. Fiske, and Gardner Lindzey, 357–411. Reprint, Boston: McGraw-Hill.

———. 1994. "Preface." In *Stereotypes and Social Cognition*, by Jacques-Philippe Leyens, Vincent Yzerbyt, and Georges Schadron. Thousand Oaks, CA: Sage.

Fiske, Susan T., and Shelley E. Taylor. 1991. *Social Cognition*. New York: McGraw-Hill.

Fleury-Steiner, Benjamin. 2004. *Jurors' Stories of Death: How America's Death Penalty Invests in Inequality*. Ann Arbor: University of Michigan Press.

Gamson, William A., Bruce Fireman, and Steven Rytina. 1982. *Encounters with Unjust Authority*. Homewood, IL: Dorsey.

Gamson, W. A., and A. Modigliani. 1994. "The Changing Culture of Affirmative Action." In *Equal Employment Opportunity: Labor Market Discrimination and Public Policy*, edited by P. Burstein, 373–94. New York: Aldine de Gruyter.

Garland, David. 1990. *Punishment and Modern Society: A Study in Social Theory*. Oxford: Oxford University Press.

———. 2001. *The Culture of Control: Crime and Social Order in Contemporary Society*. Chicago: University of Chicago Press.

Gilovich, Thomas. 1991. *How We Know It Isn't So: The Fallibility of Reason in Everyday Life*. New York: Free Press.

Girard, René. 1972. *Violence and the Sacred*. Baltimore, MD: University of John Hopkins.

Gladwell, Malcolm. 2004. *Blink: The Power of Thinking without Thinking*. New York: Back Bay Books.

Goffman, Erving. 1974. *Frame Analysis: An Essay on the Organization of Experience*. Cambridge, MA: Harvard University Press.

Goodwin, Charles. 1994. "Professional Vision." *American Anthropologist* 96 (3): 606–33.

Gould, Stephen Jay. 1983. "What, If Anything, Is a Zebra?" In *Hen's Teeth and Horses Toes*. New York: Norton.

Gouldner, Alvin. 1968. "The Sociologist as Partisan: Sociology and the Welfare State." *American Sociologist* (May): 103–16.

Green, Bruce A. 1999. "Why Should Prosecutors 'Seek Justice'?" *Fordham Urban Law Journal* 26 (3): 607–43.

Greenberg, Jeff, Sheldon Solomon, Mitchell Veeder, Tom Pyszczynski, Abram Rosenblatt, Shari Kirkland, and Deborah Lyon. 1990. "Evidence for Terror Management Theory II: The Effects of Mortality Salience on Reactions to Those Who Threaten or Bolster the Cultural Worldview." *Journal of Personality and Social Psychology* 58 (2): 308–18.

Gross, Samuel R., Maurice Possley, and Klara Stephens. 2017. "Race and Wrongful Convictions in the United States." Irvine, CA: National Registry of Wrongful Convictions.

Grossman, Dave. 2009. *On Killing: The Psychological Cost of Learning to Kill in War and Society*. New York: Back Bay Books.

Guetersioh, M. K. 2002. "Witnesses' Portrayals of Easley Vary Widely." *Pantagraph*, October 25, 2002.

Hagedorn, John M. 1994. "Homeboys, Dope Fiends, Legits, and New Jacks: Adult Gang Members, Drugs, and Work." *Criminology* 32 (2): 197–219.

———. 1998. *People and Folks: Gangs, Crime, and the Underclass in a Rustbelt City*. 2nd ed. Chicago: Lakeview. First published 1988.

———. 2008. *A World of Gangs: Armed Young Men and Gangsta Culture*. Minneapolis: University of Minnesota Press.

———. 2015. *The In$ane Chicago Way: The Daring Plan by Chicago Gangs to Create a Spanish Mafia*. Chicago: University of Chicago Press.

Hagedorn, John, Teresa Córdova, Roberto Aspholm, Andrew Papachristos, and Lance Williams. 2019. "The Fracturing of Gangs and Violence in Chicago: A Research Based Reorientation of Violence Prevention and Intervention Policy." Chicago: Great Cities Institute.

Hallin, David. 1989. *The Uncensored War: The Media and Vietnam*. Oakland: University of California Press.

Handley, Ian M., and Brett M. Runnion. 2011. "Evidence That Unconscious Thinking Influences Persuasion Based on Argument Quality." *Social Cognition* 29 (6): 666–82.

Haney, Craig. 1995. "The Social Context of Capital Murder: Social Histories and the Logic of Mitigation." *Santa Clara Law Review* 35:547–90.

———. 2004. "Condemning the Other in Death Penalty Trials: Biographical Racism, Structural Mitigation, and the Empathic Divide." *De Paul Law Review* 53 (Summer): 1557–89.

———. 2006. *Reforming Punishment: Psychological Limits to the Pains of Imprisonment*. Washington, DC: American Psychological Association.

Haney, C., W. C. Banks, and P. G. Zimbardo. 1973. "A Study of Prisoners and Guards in a Simulated Prison." *Naval Research Review* 30:4–17.

Hannah-Jones, Nikole. 2020. "What Is Owed?" *New York Times Magazine*, June 30, 2020.

Hobbes, Thomas. (1651) 2017. *Leviathan*. New York: Penguin.

Horkheimer, Max, and Theodor W. Adorno. (1944) 1998. *Dialectic of Enlightenment*. Reprint, New York: Continuum.

House Committee on Internal Security, United States Congress. 1974. "Hearings, Reports and Prints of the House Committee on Internal Security." Washington, DC: U.S. House of Representatives.

Howell, K. Babe. 2019. "Prosecutorial Misconduct: Mass Gang Indictments and Inflammatory Statements." *Dickinson Law Review* 123:691–712.

Innocence Project Staff. "Informing Injustice: The Disturbing Use of Jailhouse Informants." 2019. Innocence Project. New Haven, CT. March 6, 2019. Accessed October 11, 2019. Available at https://www.innocenceproject.org/informing-injustice/.

Ionesco, Eugène. 1960. *Rhinoceros and Other Plays*. New York: Grove. Kindle.

Jackson, Alan. 2004. "Prosecuting Gang Cases: What Local Prosecutors Need to Know." Alexandria, VA: American Prosecutors Research Institute.

Jones, Ann. 1996. *Women Who Kill*. Boston: Beacon.

Kadri, Sadakat. 2005. *The Trial: A History from Socrates to O.J. Simpson*. London: Harper Perennial.

Kahneman, Daniel. 2011. *Thinking, Fast and Slow*. New York: Farrar, Straus and Giroux.

King Center. "The King Philosophy." Accessed September 11, 2019. Available at https://thekingcenter.org/king-philosophy/.

Kipling, Rudyard. 1926. *Debits and Credits*. New York: Doubleday.

Kirsch, Jonathon. 2008. *The Grand Inquisitor's Manual*. New York: HarperCollins. EPUB.

Lakoff, George. 1987. *Women, Fire, and Dangerous Things: What Categories Reveal about the Mind*. Chicago: University of Chicago Press.

———. 2002. *Moral Politics: How Liberals and Conservatives Think*. Chicago: University of Chicago Press.

———. 2004. *Don't Think of an Elephant! Know Your Values and Frame the Debate—The Essential Guide for Progressives*. White River Junction, VT: Chelsea Green.

———. 2008. *The Political Mind: Why You Can't Understand 21st-Century Politics with an 18th-Century Brain*. New York: Viking.

Lakoff, George, and Mark Johnson. 2003. *Metaphors We Live By*. Chicago: University of Chicago Press.

LaRocque, Lynnette. 1995. "Baldwin Co. Sheriff Dept. Training Manual on Gangs." Milledgeville, GA.

Lerner, Michael J. 1980. *The Belief in a Just World*. New York: Plenum.

Lewis, Sinclair. 1935. *It Can't Happen Here*. New York: Signet.

Leyens, Jacques-Philippe, Vincent Yzerbyt, and Georges Schadron. 1994. *Stereotypes and Social Cognition*. Thousand Oaks, CA: Sage.

Lindqvist, Sven, and Joan Tate. 1996. *Exterminate All the Brutes*. New York: New Press. Distributed by W. W. Norton.

Lippmann, Walter. (1922) 1991. *Public Opinion*. Transaction Publishers. New Brunswick and London.

Lyon, Andrea D. 2010. *Angel of Death Row: My Life as a Death Penalty Defense Lawyer*. New York: Kaplan Publishing.

MacCoun, Robert J. 1989. "Experimental Research on Jury Decision-Making." *Science* 244 (4908): 1046–50.

Mankell, Henning. 2000. *The Fifth Woman (Kurt Wallander Mystery Book 6)*. New York: New Press. Kindle.

Manning, Peter, and Keith Hawkins. 1990. "Legal Decisions: A Frame Analytic Perspective." In *Beyond Goffman: Studies on Communication, Institution, and Social Interaction*, edited by Stephen H. Riggins, 203–33. Berlin: Mouton De Gruyter.

Manvell, Roger, and Heinrich Fraenkel. 2010. *Doctor Goebbels: His Life and Death*. Skyhorse. First published 1960.

Maruna, Shadd. 2001. *Making Good: How Ex-Convicts Reform and Rebuild Their Lives*. Washington, DC: American Psychological Association.

Matza, David. 1964. *Delinquency and Drift*. New York: John Wiley and Sons.

Maxson, Cheryl. 1996. "Street Gang Members on the Move: The Role of Migration in the Proliferation of Street Gangs in the U.S." Center for the Study of Crime and Social Control, Social Science Research Institute, University of Southern California.

Maynard, Douglas W., and John F. Manzo. 1993. "On the Sociology of Justice: Theoretical Notes from an Actual Jury Deliberation." *Sociological Theory* 11 (2): 171–93.

McAdam, Doug. 1999. *Political Process and the Development of Black Insurgency, 1930–1970*. Chicago: University of Chicago Press.

McDonald, Aubri F. 2016. "Framing in Criminal Trials: The Murder Case of Jacqueline Montanez." PhD thesis. University of Illinois Chicago.

Medwed, David S. 2012. *Prosecution Complex: America's Race to Convict and Its Impact on the Innocent*. New York: New York University Press. Kindle.

Mills, C. Wright. 1959. *The Sociological Imagination*. Oxford: Oxford University Press.

Minsky, Marvin. 1975. "A Framework for Representing Knowledge." In *A Psychology of Computer Visions*, edited by P. H. Winston. New York: McGraw-Hill.

Moore, Joan W. 1985. "Isolation and Stigmatization in the Development of an Underclass: The Case of Chicano Gangs in East Los Angeles." *Social Problems* 33 (1): 1–10.

Moore, Natalie, Lance Williams. 2010. *The Almighty Black P. Stone Nation*. Chicago: Lawrence Hill Books.

Moore, Sarah G., David T. Neal, Gavan J. Fitzsimons, and Baba Shiv. 2012. "Wolves in Sheep's Clothing: How and When Hypothetical Questions Influence Behavior." *Organizational Behavior and Human Decision Processes* 117:168–78.

Muhammad, Khalil Gibran. 2010. *The Condemnation of Blackness: Race, Crime, and the Making of Modern Urban America*. Cambridge, MA: Harvard University Press.

Muir, William Ker. 1977. *Police: Street Corner Politicians*. Chicago: University of Chicago Press.

Murphy, Senator Chris. 2020. *New York Times*, Op-Ed, February 1, 2020. Accessed April 1, 2020. Available at https://www.nytimes.com/2020/02/01/opinion/sunday/trump-impeachment-trial-witnesses.html.

Natapoff, Alexandra. 2011. *Snitching: Criminal Informants and the Erosion of American Justice*. New York: New York University Press.

Nellis, Ashley. 2017. "Still Life: America's Increasing Use of Life and Long-Term Sentences." May. Washington, DC: Sentencing Project.

New York Times, September 26, 2018. Accessed July11, 2021. Available at https://www.nytimes.com/2018/09/26/us/politics/read-brett-kavanaughs-complete-opening-statement.html.

Nyhan, Brendan, and Jason Reifler. 2011. "When Corrections Fail: The Persistence of Political Misperceptions." *Political Behavior* 32 (2): 303–30.

Office of the Inspector General. 2005. *The Federal Bureau of Investigation's Compliance with the Attorney General's Investigative Guidelines*, Special Report, chap. 3: "The Attorney General's Guidelines regarding the Use of Confidential Informants." September 2005. Available at https://oig.justice.gov/special/0509/chapter3.htm. Cited in Bloom, 2018.

Official Code of Georgia (OCGA). 2005. Atlanta, Georgia.

Pagels, Elaine. 1995. *The Origin of Satan*. New York: Random House.

People v. Lupparello. 1986. 231 Cal.Rptr. 832. 187 Cal.App.3d 410. Court of Appeal, Fourth District, Division 1, California. Nov. 25, 1986. Review denied Feb. 11, 1987. m[187 Cal.App.3d 417].

Prejean, Sister Helen. 1993. *Dead Man Walking: An Eyewitness Account of the Death Penalty in the United States*. New York: Vintage.

Roget's Thesaurus. 1995. "Gang Member." Microsoft Bookshelf Edition.

Rothbart, Mary K. 1981. "Memory Process and Social Beliefs." In *Cognitive Processes in Stereotyping and Intergroup Behavior*, edited by D. L. Hamilton, 145–81. Hillsdale, NJ: Erlbaum.

Ryan, George. 2003. "I Must Act." Address at Northwestern University. January 11, 2003. Available at https://deathpenaltyinfo.org/stories/in-ryans-words-i-must-act.

Sampson, Robert J., and John H. Laub. 1993. *Crime in the Making: Pathways and Turning Points through Life*. Cambridge, MA: Harvard University Press.

Schacter, Daniel L. 2001. *The Seven Sins of Memory: How the Mind Forgets and Remembers*. Boston: Houghton Mifflin.

Schwartz, Raft. "Trump Leads Supporters in Racist 'Animals' Chant at Nashville Rally." *Splinter News*, June 6, 2018. Accessed January 26, 2019. Available at https://splinter news.com/trump-leads-supporters-in-racist-animals-chant-at-nashv-18264158 32?utm_source=splinter_newsletter&utm_medium=email&utm_campaign=2018 -06-03.

The Sentencing Project. 2019. *Women and Girls Serving Life Sentences*. Washington, DC. June 2019. Available at https://www.sentencingproject.org/wp-content/uploads/2019 /07/Women-and-Girls-Serving-Life-Sentences.pdf.

Sills, Howard. 2019. Letter to Georgia Board of Pardons and Parole.

Simon, Herbert. 1956. *Models of Man*. New York: John Wiley and Sons.

Simon, Jonathon. 2007. *Governing through Crime: How the War on Crime Transformed American Democracy and Created a Culture of Fear*. New York: Oxford University Press.

Smith, David Livingstone. 2012. *Less Than Human: Why We Demean, Enslave, and Exterminate Others*. New York: St. Martin's Griffin.

Smith, Wes, and Ray Gibson. 1988. "Pontiac State Prison Still a Battleground." *Chicago Tribune*, July 17, 1988.

Snow, David A., E. Burke Rochford Jr., Steven K. Worden, and Robert F. Benford. 1997. "Frame Alignment, Processes, Micromobilization, and Movement Participation." In *Social Movements: Perspectives and Issues*, edited by S. M. Buechler and F. Kurt Cylke Jr., 211–28. Mountain View, CA: Mayfield.

Spence, Gerry. 2005. *Win Your Case: How to Present, Persuade, Prevail—Every Place Every Time*. New York: St. Martin's.

Stanley, Jason. 2018. *How Fascism Works: The Politics of Us and Them*. New York: Random House.

Staples, Brent. 2018. "The Racist Trope That Won't Die." *New York Times*, Op-Ed, August 6, 2018. Available at https://www.nytimes.com/2018/06/17/opinion/roseanne-racism-blacks -apes.html?action=click&pgtype=Homepage&clickSource=story-heading&module

=opinion-c-col-right-region&region=opinion-c-col-right-region&WT.nav=opinion-c
-col-right-region.

Stevenson, Bryan. 2015. *Just Mercy: A Story of Justice and Redemption.* New York: Spiegel and Grau.

Steele, Claude. 2010. *Whistling Vivaldi: And Other Clues to How Stereotypes Affect Us.* New York: W. W. Norton & Company.

Stewart, Robert W., and Staff Writers. 1989. "Jailhouse Snitches: Trading Lies for Freedom." *Los Angeles Times,* April 16, 1989.

Superior Court of Butts County. 2005. State of Georgia, Marion Wilson, Petitioner v. Habeas Corpus Derrick Schofield, Warden, Georgia Diagnostic Prison, Respondent. Evidentiary Hearing Transcript Summary.

Superior Court of Cobb County, Georgia. 2014. State of Georgia v. Tadarius Williams. Case Number 14-9-2291-51. Jury Trial Volume III of V.

Svendson, Lars. 2001. *A Philosophy of Evil.* Oslo, Norway: Dalkey Archive.

Tannenbaum, Frank. 1939. *Crime and the Community.* New York: Columbia University.

Thrasher, Frederic. 1927. *The Gang: A Study of 1313 Gangs in Chicago.* Chicago: University of Chicago.

Tonry, Michael. 2016. *Sentencing Fragments: Penal Reform in America, 1975–2025.* New York: Oxford University Press.

Tonry, Michael, and Mark H. Moore, eds. 1998. *Youth Violence,* Vol. 24. Edited by Michael Tonry. Chicago: University of Chicago Press.

Tyler, Tom R. 2007. "Procedural Justice and the Courts." *Court Review: Journal of the American Judges Association* 44 (1–2): 26–31.

Van Cleve, Nicole Gonzalez. 2016. *Crook County: Racism and Injustice in America's Largest Criminal Court.* Stanford, CA: Stanford University Press.

Voltaire (Francois-Marie Arout). 2020. *Candide.* Scotts Valley, CA: Create Space Independent Publishing Platform.

Warden, Rob. 2004. *The Snitch System.* Northwestern University Center on Wrongful Convictions. Available at https://files.deathpenaltyinfo.org/legacy/documents/SnitchSystemBooklet.pdf.

Weinberg, Arthur, ed. 1957. *Attorney for the Damned: Clarence Darrow in the Courtroom.* Chicago: University of Chicago Press.

Wilson, James Q. 1968. *Varieties of Police Behavior: The Management of Law and Order in Eight Communities.* Cambridge, MA: Harvard University Press.

Winter, Nicolas J. G. 2008. *Dangerous Frames: How Ideas about Race and Gender Shape Public Opinion.* Chicago: University of Chicago Press.

Winter, Steven A. 2001. *A Clearing in the Forest: Law, Life, and Mind.* Chicago: University of Chicago Press.

Wynter, Sylvia. 1994. "'No Humans Involved': An Open Letter to My Colleagues." *Institute NHI* 1 (1): 42–73.

Yellin, Emily. 2018. "She Speaks for All of Us." *New York Times,* Op-Ed, September 27, 2018. Accessed September 28, 2018. Available at https://www.nytimes.com/2018/09/27/opinion/blasey-ford-sexual-assault-survivors.html?action=click&module=Opinion&pgtype=Homepage.

Zimbardo, Philip G. 2007. *The Lucifer Effect: Understanding How Good People Turn Evil.* New York: Random House.

Index

71; in Timothy Shanks case, 54; in
Demetrius Smith case, 171; in Kentrell
Stoutmire case, 178–179; in Ike Easley
case, 111, 118
Reframing police violence, 144, 154; in
Rodney King case, 180–181
Rehabilitation and reform, 12, 128, 138,
140, 143, 187
Research not stereotypes motto, 3, 160, 202
Rhinoceros, 3, 26
RIP Boys gang, 165
Rodgers, Cornelius, 50
Rothbart, Mary K., categories of stereotype
change, 162, 170. *See* Stereotype Change
Ruiz, Jamie, 59–64
Rules for Radicals, 67
Rush, Benjamin, 138
Rush, David, 165–166, 171
Ryan, George, 109, 111, 118–119, 128

Satisficing, 35
Schacter, Daniel, 63
Schanbacher, Kristine, 206
Seay, Aaron, 7, 9
Sentencing, approach and testimony, 65,
71, 91, 111, 118, 126, 162, 170, 183–186;
punitive trend, 137–140, 156, 185–186,
189–192, 195–196
Sentencing Project, 45, 120, 130
Sexton, Lee, 29, 32–33, 206
Shaffer, Marty, 206
Shanks, Timothy, 50–54, 206
Shelby County jail, 92
Short, Cyndy, 163, 206
Sills, Howard, 19–21, 24–25, 199–200
Simon, Herbert, 35
Sims, William, 30, 33
Sisyphus, myth of, 7, 160, 161, 176, 185, 187,
197, 202–203
Slow thinking, 34–35, 37, 41, 96–97, 162,
165, 168–170. *See also* Kahneman
Smith, Bud, 38, 40–41
Smith, David Livingstone, 120–121, 124,
137, 139, 141
Smith, Thomas D., 163–168, 170, 194; court
record, 167f; epilogue, 206
Snitches/snitching, 60, 74–76, 79–81
Social movements: outrage as motivation,
67; use of framing by, 66–68
Somatic markers, 35
Sotomayor, Sonia, 63

Soung, Patricia, 129, 133
Spergel, Irving, 50
Sphere of consensus, 187
Staples, Brent, 95
Stateville, Illinois prison, 10, 116, 174, 195;
epilogue, 205
Steele, Claude, 95–96
Stereotype change, Gilbert and Fiske, 162;
Rothbart's categories: bookkeeping,
45–48, 64–65, 162, 191; conversion, 42,
46, 49, 102, 156, 162; subtyping, 32, 45,
70–71, 162, 175, 203
Stereotypes: in place of evidence, 11,
94; cognition and, 25–27; congruent
information, 188; curtailing for juries,
190; in defiance of all evidence,
54, 190; fast thinking and, 34–36;
gang stereotypes, 3–6, 27–28;
gang stereotypes, origins, 20–22;
internalization of, 24; open mindedness
and, 26–27; persistence of, 28, 33, 160,
162; priming, 27, 93, 95–99; rethinking,
45; useful for prosecutors, 22–23, 33, 195
*Stereotyping, Prejudice, and
Discrimination*, 25
Stevenson, Bryan, 2, 6, 17–18, 45, 94, 201
Stigmatization of groups, 67
Stone, Randolph, 164, 171–172, 174, 176–
177, 179, 205, 207
Stout, James Patrick, 4, 89–94, 190;
epilogue, 206–207
Stoutmire, Kentrell, 176–179; epilogue, 207
Stromberg, Scott, 69
Sweet, Ossian, 179, 181
Sympathy for offenders, 110, 171, 191–192,
201; for victims, 163, 169
System I thinking. *See* Fast thinking
System II thinking. *See* Slow thinking

Tannenbaum, Frank, 128
Tattoos, 4, 90, 91–93; and priming, 4,
93–95; teardrop tattoos, 89, 90, 92, 185;
six pointed star, 52, 89
Taylor, Robert, 110, 116, 126
Terror management theory, 97, 117, 168
Thinking Fast and Slow, 34–36
Thompson, Carrie, 159, 206
Thrasher, Fredric, 160
Trials, as ceremonies of the victory of "us"
over "them," 123; and confirmation bias,
96; and dehumanizing language, 190;

John M. Hagedorn is Professor Emeritus of Criminology, Law, and Justice and James J. Stukel Faculty Fellow, Great Cities Institute, at the University of Illinois–Chicago. He is the author or editor of seven books, including *The In$ane Chicago Way: The Daring Plan by Chicago Gangs to Create a Spanish Mafia, A World of Gangs: Armed Young Men and Gangsta Culture,* and *People and Folks: Gangs, Crime, and the Underclass in a Rustbelt City.* He has served as expert witness in seventy-three gang-related court cases, including sixty for homicide, in seventeen of which the accused faced the death penalty.